Teacher education in transition

Developing Teacher Education

Series Editors: Hazel Hagger and Donald McIntyre

The focus of this series is on teacher education, with particular reference to the problems that research has revealed in established approaches to teacher education, to solutions that have been offered to these problems, and to elucidation of the underlying processes of teachers' learning on which effective solutions must depend. While different countries have inherited different systems of teacher education, and are therefore faced with different problems, all countries are faced with the same dilemmas of helping beginning and serving teachers to teach as well as possible within their existing schools while at the same time mobilizing their critical and creative thinking so they can contribute to the development of better schools for the future. Authors in this series explore such opportunities and challenges and seek to understand and explain how the processes of professional learning and of facilitating that learning can best be understood.

Published and forthcoming titles:

John Furlong, Len Barton, Sheila Miles, Caroline Whiting and Geoff Whitty:
  Teacher Education in Transition
Hazel Hagger and Donald McIntyre: *Learning about Teaching from Teachers*
Donald McIntyre: *Learning to Teach*
Les Tickle: *Teacher Induction: The Way Ahead*

Teacher education in transition

Re-forming professionalism?

John Furlong, Len Barton, Sheila Miles, Caroline Whiting and Geoff Whitty

Open University Press
Buckingham · Philadelphia

Open University Press
Celtic Court
22 Ballmoor
Buckingham
MK18 1XW

email: enquiries@openup.co.uk
world wide web: www.openup.co.uk

and
325 Chestnut Street
Philadelphia, PA 19106, USA

First Published 2000

A catalogue record of this book is available from the British Library

ISBN   0 335 20039 7 (pb)   0 335 20040 0 (hb)

Library of Congress Cataloging-in-Publication Data
Teacher education in transition: re-forming professionalism? / John Furlong . . .
[*et al.*].
    p. cm. – (Developing teacher education)
    Includes bibliographical references and index.
    ISBN 0-335-20039-7 (pbk.) – ISBN 0-335-20040-0 (hbk.)
    1. Teachers–Training of–Great Britain–Case studies.   2. Education and state–Great
Britain–Case studies.   3. Educational change–Great Britain–Case studies.   I. Furlong,
John.   II. Series.
LB1725.G6 T382 2000
370'.71'1–dc21   99-056964

Typeset by Graphicraft Limited, Hong Kong
Printed in Great Britain by St Edmundsbury Press Ltd, Bury St Edmunds, Suffolk

Contents

Series editors' preface

During the last decade, initial teacher education in England has been the subject of massive change. At one level, this change can be seen as a long overdue recognition of the capacity of schools, and especially of the teachers who work in them, to make a major contribution to the professional education of those entering the profession. How this can best be done, against a background of almost a century in which teachers have had very little such involvement, but in which both what is sought from schooling and our understanding of schooling have expanded greatly, is a highly exciting question. What problems, and especially what opportunities, it will involve we are only beginning to discover. One of the aims of this series is to contribute to the exploration of the opportunities and to the solution of the problems.

The shift to a largely school-based system has however been far from the only change in initial teacher education during the last decade; and indeed it can properly be seen as merely one part of a broader and quite systematic change. The enhanced role of schools in initial teacher education, and the correspondingly reduced role of higher education, was achieved neither through consensus nor through gradual development: it was achieved through unilateral government intervention of a quite unprecedented kind. It is this degree of government direction which characterises the broader change. As the authors of this book themselves describe this change, 'the system has been moved from one of diversity and autonomy to one of unanimity and central control. What the government, and particularly the TTA, had wanted, was a common system with common standards and procedures no matter who was providing the training or where: this was how the TTA defined quality. By the end of the 1990s this had been largely achieved.' This book offers an excellent account of that change.

As series editors, we especially welcome this book, for several reasons, as one of the first of the series. As was to be expected from such a distinguished group of authors, among England's leading sociologists of education, it is a highly scholarly account of this crucial last decade, providing a carefully documented history of government initiatives interwoven with thoroughly researched evidence about the consequences of those initiatives for the organization and practice of teacher education in England. It provides too a national picture of the ways in which different groups in schools and higher education have found the changes as empowering or constraining, and the benefits and disadvantages they have experienced. Furthermore, it cautiously considers how best these initiatives and changes can best be understood in relation to other developments, in England and internationally. This will surely be regarded in future years as the authoritative text on what happened in English teacher education in the 1990s.

This is however a book of more than academic importance. It is a book which definitively takes stock, telling us where we have got to nationally in initial teacher education, showing us a broad but perceptive and reliable picture of the strengths and limitations of the system at work. It tells us about the reality to which we have to attend, here and now. Whatever our individual enthusiasms, interests, fears and agendas, it describes the national context in which we are working and to which we must address our efforts if we want them to have more than local significance. It tells us both that the last decade has seen some significant achievements in initial teacher education, which we would be very foolish to ignore, and also that the immense potential of real partnership between schools and higher education is generally very far from being realized. The picture it offers is not a simple one, but rather one which challenges us to think deeply.

Finally, this book is valuable because the challenge it offers is quite explicit. As the title makes clear, it is a book which asks questions, and these questions are about the nature of teacher professionalism. Although the main text is one which describes and explains, there is a sustained sub-text which asks important questions, rooted in a contrast between teachers', and especially teacher educators', traditional aspiration to a professionalism of collective and even individual autonomy and, on the other hand, government's wish to promote a new teacher professionalism, rooted in disciplined conformity to high common (and if necessary imposed) standards. The central question is: do teachers and teacher educators have a credible alternative conception of teacher professionalism which they can offer to politicians for the twenty-first century?

Hazel Hagger
Donald McIntyre

Acknowledgements

We are grateful to the Economic and Social Research Council for their support of the two MOTE projects whose findings are reported in this book. These were: 'Modes of Teacher Education: Towards a Basis for Comparison' (Project no. R000232810), which ran from 1991–92, and 'Changing Modes of Professionalism? A Case Study of Teacher Education in Transition' (Project no. R000234185), which ran from 1993–96.

We wish to record our thanks to Elizabeth Barrett and Conor Galvin for their important contributions to the success of these projects. Their contribution is particularly evident in Chapters 3 and 4. We would also like to thank: Sir William Taylor for comments on earlier drafts of several of the chapters in this book; members of the RATE research team in the USA and the SITE team in Australia; and other contributors to an invitational conference held at the University of Sheffield in September 1996, designed to help us to formulate the argument contained in Chapter 10. However, the present authors take full responsibility for the particular way in which the findings of the projects are presented here.

Most of all, we are indebted to the many lecturers, teachers and students who collaborated with us on these projects at a time of intense pressure on the education service in general and on initial teacher education in particular.

Abbreviations

AT	articled teacher
ATL	Association of Teachers and Lecturers
BA/BSc	Bachelor of Arts/Bachelor of Science degree
BEd	Bachelor of Education degree
CATE	Council for the Accreditation of Teacher Education
CHE	college of higher education
CNAA	Council for National Academic Awards
DES	Department of Education and Science
DfE	Department for Education
DfEE	Department for Education and Employment
EPS	educational and professional studies
ESRC	Economic and Social Research Council
FE	further education
GCSE	General Certificate of Secondary Education
GTC	General Teaching Council
HEFCE	Higher Education Funding Council (England)
HEI	higher education institution
HNC	Higher National Certificate
HND	Higher National Diploma
HMCI	Her Majesty's Chief Inspector of Schools
HMI	Her Majesty's Inspectorate of Schools
ICT	information and communication technology
ITE	initial teacher education
ITT	initial teacher training
LEA	local education authority
LT	licensed teacher
MOTE	Modes of Teacher Education Project

NAS/UWT	National Association of Schoolmasters and Union of Women Teachers
NATFHE	National Association of Teachers in Further and Higher Education
NCATE	National Council for the Accreditation of Teacher Education (USA)
NQT	newly qualified teacher
NVQ	national vocational qualification
OECD	Organization for Economic Cooperation and Development
Ofsted	Office for Standards in Education
QTS	qualified teacher status
PCET	Polytechnics Council for the Education of Teachers
PE	physical education
PGCE	Postgraduate Certificate in Education
RAE	Research Assessment Exercise
RATE	Research About Teacher Education Project (USA)
RE	religious education
SCETT	Standing Committee on the Education and Training of Teachers
SCITT	school-centred initial teacher training
SCOP	Standing Conference of Principals
SITE	Survey of Initial Teacher Education (Australia)
SSR	staff–student ratio
TES	Times Educational Supplement
TP	teaching practice
TTA	Teacher Training Agency
UCET	Universities Council for the Education of Teachers

Tables and figures

1 Teacher education, policy and professionalism

People are always wanting teachers to change. Rarely has this been more true than in recent years. These times of global competitiveness, like all moments of economic crisis, are producing immense moral panics about how we are preparing the generations of the future in our respective nations . . . Few people want to do much about the economy, but everyone – politicians, the media and the public alike – wants to do something about education.

(A. Hargreaves 1994: 5)

Introduction

Hargreaves is right. Today, people, and especially governments, do want teachers to change. In England, one of the central areas that contemporary governments have looked at in their attempt to change teachers has been the system of initial teacher training. It may be a false assumption, but it has nevertheless been assumed that one significant way of influencing the skills, knowledge and values of teachers – in other words, their professionalism – is to change the form and content of their initial training. As we will demonstrate in this opening chapter, this has meant that initial teacher education has increasingly become a major site for political debate and struggle in recent years.

It was not always so. At the beginning of the 1980s, and indeed throughout most of this century (Gardner 1993; 1996), the content and structure of teacher education and training courses in England and Wales was principally a matter for universities and colleges themselves (Wilkin 1996); as a policy area, teacher education was something of a backwater. But, by the end of that decade, it had become a key issue in government educational policy. Central control had increased dramatically and, once established, the speed of change imposed on the system became progressively more intense. The changes of the 1980s included the establishment of the Council for the Accreditation of Teacher Education (CATE) (DES 1984) and its subsequent modification (DES 1989a); the revision of conventional training courses – the one year PGCE and the four year BEd – including government specification of course content (DES 1989a); and the introduction of shortened BEd courses, part-time PGCEs and conversion courses for graduates wishing to convert their first degree to enable them to teach shortage subjects. Other more radical innovations launched at the end of the decade included the development of the largely school-based 'articled teacher' and 'licensed teacher' (DES 1989b) routes to qualified teacher status (QTS).[1]

In this ferment of policy change those in higher education who were traditionally responsible for initial teacher education lost a significant proportion of their professional autonomy – their ability to employ whom they wished and to define the form and content of training courses. As a result, initial teacher education, during the 1980s, increasingly became a major site for ideological struggle between the government and others, especially those in higher education, with an interest in the professional formation of teachers.

It was against this background of policy change and political struggle that, in 1990, four of the present authors, then based in different universities and colleges in England and Wales, applied to the Economic and Social Research Council (ESRC) to mount a national research project to monitor the changes being introduced. The result was the establishment of the first Modes of Teacher Education (MOTE) project, which ran from 1991 to 1992.[2]

What became apparent during the life of this first project was that the 1990s were not to be a period where the system would be allowed to settle down to accommodate all of the changes introduced; rather it was to be a period of further radical reform. The same research team therefore applied to the ESRC to fund a second project to extend and develop findings from the earlier MOTE study and explore the implications of the next round of reforms. The second project ran from 1993 to 1996.[3]

As we had predicted, the second period of our research saw the policy process intensify. In 1992 and 1993 the government issued two new circulars for primary and secondary initial teacher education (DfE 1992, 1993a) which radically altered the relationships between schools and higher education institutions (HEIs) and sharpened the emphasis on practical training. What we had not anticipated was the breadth and depth of subsequent reforms. During the life of the project, these included the abolition of CATE and the establishment of the Teacher Training Agency (TTA), which took over most of the functions of CATE as well as the funding of all initial teacher education in England (though not Wales, Scotland or Northern Ireland); the development of a new inspection framework for initial teacher education from the Office for Standards in Education (Ofsted); the ending of the articled teacher scheme, and the establishment of school-centred teacher training

(SCITT) schemes, which did not necessarily entail any higher education involvement; and the launching of The Open University's own teacher training courses by distance learning.[4]

The empirical parts of the MOTE projects were therefore undertaken against a background of rapidly changing policy and since their completion the pace of reform has not slackened.[5] As we discuss in more detail in Chapter 9, in the late 1990s the TTA and Ofsted extended and sharpened their roles and there were ever more detailed interventions into the curriculum with new 'standards' for training and the development of a national curriculum for trainee teachers in English, mathematics, science and information and communications technology (ICT) (DfEE 1998a).

It is important to recognize at the outset that changes in the field of higher education were by no means confined to initial teacher education during the 1990s. As Bridges (1996) highlights, the curriculum changes thrust upon universities' and colleges' schools of education were certainly not unique; they were mirrored, perhaps indirectly, in many sections of higher education. If one looks further afield, the vast majority of public service professionals in the United Kingdom and in many other parts of the world were experiencing changing and more challenging relationships with the state during the same period (see for example Dunleavy and Hood 1994; Pollitt 1994; Bottery 1998; Carter 1998; Clarke and Newman 1998).

Nevertheless we would suggest that, perhaps because of the historically tenuous hold that teacher education has had within higher education (Gardner 1996), the scope and depth of the reforms were particularly strong in our own field. Certainly the scope of the reforms we witnessed more than justified our initial interest in the implications of what was happening to the professional formation of teachers in England and Wales. We would suggest that the vast majority of these policy initiatives on initial teacher education during the period we studied were indeed framed with the explicit aspiration of changing the nature of teacher professionalism. As we will demonstrate below, throughout the 1980s and 1990s, the New Right and other critics were increasingly successful in establishing the issue of teacher professionalism as a legitimate topic for government policy; and it is a concern that has now been taken on by the new Labour government (DfEE 1998b). Moreover, as we will also argue in Chapter 10, such a concern was not an entirely domestic affair in that our evidence would suggest that, in other parts of the English-speaking world, similar issues were coming onto the agenda.

We would also suggest that an explicit attempt to change teacher professionalism through initial teacher education had at times to be pursued alongside two other policy concerns that were also significant in influencing the policies actually produced. These were first, the imperative of maintaining an adequate supply of well-qualified applicants for initial teacher education; and second, the aspiration on the part of the state to establish greater accountability for the content and quality of initial teacher education. These three policy concerns – teacher professionalism, maintaining supply, and creating greater accountability within a national framework for training –

have all been influential on the policy initiatives that have been produced in recent years. However, we would maintain that it has been concerns about the nature of teacher professionalism itself that have remained the most enduring focus of national policy in this area and that they have influenced policy in the other two areas.

Teacher education and teacher professionalism

> We trust our health to the physician; our fortune and sometimes our life and reputation to the lawyer and attorney. Such confidence could not safely be reposed in people of a very mean or low condition. Their reward must be such, therefore, as may give them that rank in society which so important a trust requires. The long time and great expense which must be laid out in their education when combined with this circumstance, necessarily enhances still further the price of their labour.
>
> (Adam Smith, *Wealth of Nations*, quoted in MacDonald 1995)

Despite the widespread use of the term, the concept of a 'professional' remains deeply contested in our society. As Hoyle and John (1995) have suggested, debates around the notion of what it means to be a professional focus on three central issues – knowledge, autonomy and responsibility. Moreover, they suggest that, despite many recent challenges in relation to teachers' professionalism, these three issues remain important to consider. Their significance can be illustrated by examining a traditional conception of professionalism.

The idea that an occupational group such as lawyers, doctors or teachers have a specialized body of knowledge is central to any traditional definition of professionalism. Professionals are seen to base their practice on a body of technical or specialist knowledge that is beyond the reach of lay people. Hoyle and John (1995) argue that traditionally this knowledge is seen as having two component parts: first it has been tested by scientific method, thereby acquiring validity; second it is supported by a variety of theoretical models and case descriptions which allow it to be applied in specific cases. It is because professionals need to develop this body of 'knowledge-based skills' that they need long periods of training, significant parts of which need to go on within higher education.

> Professionals, through specialist and usually long periods of training, are taught to understand this research validated knowledge and to apply it constructively and intelligently according to the technical rules governing the conduct of the profession.
>
> (Hoyle and John 1995: 46)

Closely related to the idea that professionals utilize a specialist body of knowledge is the argument for autonomy. This, Hoyle and John (1995: 77) suggest, is because professionals are seen as working in complex and unpredictable situations:

As professionals work in uncertain situations in which judgement is more important than routine, it is essential to effective practice that they should be sufficiently free from bureaucratic and political constraint to act on judgements made in the best interests (as they see them) of the clients.

Of critical importance here is the suggestion that professionals make judgements on behalf of clients *as they see them*. It is for the professional to interpret those interests. To draw a distinction utilized by Hoyle and John, they do not act as an 'agent' of someone else (for example the government); they act as a 'principal' making their own judgements.

This brings us to the final dimension in the classical conception of professionalism – that is, responsibility. Exercising judgement in relation to clients' interests does not simply demand the application of specialist knowledge, it also entails values. Professionals need to balance their own and their clients' interests through 'a voluntaristic commitment to a set of principles governing good practice and the realisation of these through day-to-day professional activities' (Hoyle and John 1995: 104). Significantly, although the capacity for making sound judgements is a vital quality for professionals to have, it is not one, Hoyle and John argue, for which there are any obvious forms of training.

The three concepts of knowledge, autonomy and responsibility, central to a traditional notion of professionalism, are often seen as closely interrelated. It is because professionals face complex and unpredictable situations that they need a specialized body of knowledge; if they are to apply that knowledge, it is argued that they need the autonomy to make their own judgements. Given that they have that autonomy, it is essential that they act with responsibility – collectively they need to develop appropriate professional values.

This view of what it means to be a professional, which still has wide currency within our society, has been challenged on many counts. For example in teaching, as elsewhere, there are profound debates surrounding the nature of professional knowledge. The suggestion that professional knowledge can be based on 'scientific principles' and that it can be 'applied' in a straightforward way has been deeply contested (for example Schön 1983, 1987; Hirst 1996). The demands that teachers should be granted autonomy and that they should define what it means to act responsibly has also been challenged. New Right critics, for example O'Hear 1998a, 1998b; Lawlor 1990, have argued that claims for autonomy have more to do with professionals protecting their own interests and avoiding accountability than with the unpredictability of situations. Rather than acting with responsibility, the 'educational establishment' have been concerned 'to organise the system for their convenience rather than to respond to the demands of its consumers' (Ranson 1990: 8) – parents, employers and children. As a result, from the 1980s onwards, there has been an increasing shift from what is sometimes called 'licensed' autonomy to 'regulated' autonomy (Dale 1989).

However, it is not our aim at this point to provide an overview of the debates concerning the nature of teacher professionalism. Rather it is to highlight the point that changes in the nature of knowledge, autonomy and responsibility can alter the nature of teacher professionalism itself. It is for this reason we would argue that the policy initiatives in initial teacher education of the 1990s are so significant. As we will see below, many of the changes introduced in the 1990s have been concerned to influence the nature of professional knowledge, skills and values that student teachers are expected to have and are given the opportunity to develop. Debates around the form and content of initial teacher education are therefore debates about the very nature of teacher professionalism itself.

Of course a great many other factors affect teacher professionalism too. During the past decade, initiatives such as the introduction of the National Curriculum, league tables, and teacher appraisal (to mention only a few) have served to challenge traditional conceptions of autonomy within the teaching profession. However, we would suggest that the aspiration to change teacher professionalism by influencing the nature of the knowledge, skills and values to which *new* teachers are exposed is at least as significant. The assumption behind policy within this area has been that changes in the form and content of initial teacher education will, in the long run, serve to construct a new generation of teachers with different forms of knowledge, different skills and different professional values.

But how and why did the initial preparation of our teachers become such a political issue and what have the implications of the changes actually been? The aim of this book is precisely to explore these questions, drawing on the two MOTE projects to document the changes in initial teacher education that we have witnessed and to contribute to a discussion about their causes and implications.

The empirical work in our two MOTE studies had a number of different elements. They both included a questionnaire survey of all initial teacher education providers in England and Wales. These two national surveys, carried out in 1991 and 1996, covered all forms of initial teacher education – the Licensed Teacher and SCITT schemes as well as those led by higher education. In addition, case studies were undertaken of 50 individual courses. In the first project the case studies included five Licensed Teacher schemes; in the second project they included three SCITT schemes and two distance learning courses.[6] Most of the case studies comprised two principal elements: site visits to interview and observe lecturers, school 'mentors' and students during their training; and follow-up questionnaires to students at the completion of their course and during the first year of their teaching.[7]

Contexts for policy analysis

In some ways, our research on initial teacher education reported here may be considered to be part of what in recent years has come to be known as 'policy scholarship'. Unlike 'policy science', which excludes wider contextual considerations 'by its sharply focused concern with the specifics of a particular set of policy initiatives', policy scholarship is concerned with 'internal contradictions within policy formulations, and the wider structuring and constraining effects of the social and economic relations within which policy making is taking place' (Grace 1991: 26). In exploring the origins and implications of policy change, we therefore need to begin by recognizing the complexity of the policy process and its various facets. Furthermore, teacher education policies, like any other, necessarily go through many stages and phases between the time they are originally conceived and when they come to have an effect on what students actually learn during their training. In order to develop a fuller conception of the policy process, we will draw on Ball's suggestion (Bowe and Ball 1992; Ball 1994) that we need to distinguish between a range of different 'contexts' in policy analysis.

Bowe and Ball (1992) usefully distinguish between three key policy 'contexts', each of which they argue may have their own complexities and contradictions in the policy process. They are 'loosely coupled' and, according to Ball (1994), there is no one simple direction of flow between them. First there is the 'context of influence' where groups close to the government use their networks to try to initiate particular policies. They help create a 'policy discourse' which, as we will argue in Chapter 10, may itself be influenced by debates taking place in relation to other areas of government policy, and even in other countries. In this policy discourse, there will necessarily be competing voices that change over time and have different degrees of influence over those in power. However, as Bowe and Ball also point out, those involved in the 'context of influence' do not themselves directly determine policy. As pressure groups frequently find, there is often a gap between their concerns and specific policies themselves. There is, Bowe and Ball suggest, an 'uneasy relationship' between the 'context of influence' and the 'context of text production' where 'texts' include both the official documents that 'represent' the policy and the 'spin' that is put upon them for the benefit of the contexts of influence and practice.

There are complexities within individual policy texts that need to be recognized as well. As representations of ideas, policy texts such as acts of parliament and government circulars are themselves the product of struggle and compromise. As a result they are not necessarily internally coherent; they cannot always be read as a direct expression of a particular ideological perspective. Different parts of them may therefore directly or indirectly give rise to contradictory interpretations and outcomes.

The third context that needs to be recognized, and the one that is most central to this book, is the 'context of practice', of which there may often be more than one. If texts are to be influential, they have to be what conventional policy analysts would call 'implemented'. But implementation allows, indeed demands, interpretation and the policies themselves in a real sense are changed in this process. As Bowe and Ball (1992: 22) say:

Practitioners do not confront policy texts as naive readers, they come with histories, with experience, with values and purposes of their own. They have vested interests in the meaning of policy. Policies will be interpreted differently as the histories, experience, values, purposes and interests which make up any area differ. The simple point is that policy writers cannot control the meanings of their texts.

We therefore need to ask how particular policy texts are responded to – accepted, challenged, bypassed and in some cases transformed by those outside government who are responsible for implementing them. However, this is not to say that texts can be interpreted in any way the reader wishes. Rather, texts, as Fiske (1987: 26) suggests, need to be seen as a 'potential of meanings' that can be achieved in a number of ways.

> Of course this potential is proscribed and not infinite; the text does not determine its meaning so much as delimit the arena of struggle for that meaning by marking out the terrain within which its variety of readings can be negotiated.

Yet, as Bowe and Ball (1992) point out, in some cases the 'potential of meanings' is more loosely defined than in others. Drawing on the distinction between *writerly* and *readerly* texts, they describe those policies where there is a broad terrain of interpretation as writerly – meaning that those responsible for implementation have at least some freedom to rewrite the policy for themselves. Other policies are much more readerly, being more precisely written and often more thoroughly policed. As a consequence they have to be read more directly as they were intended by those who wrote them. As we will see later in this chapter, successive policy initiative texts within the field of initial teacher education have been deliberately designed progressively to delimit the degree of interpretation available to those responsible for implementing them. There has been a concerted attempt to make policies more and more readerly. Nevertheless, it is essential to recognize that, however tightly written and policed they may be, policies still have to be interpreted if they are to be realized within a particular context of practice.

Much of our MOTE research concerns 'contexts of practice'. In Chapters 2 to 7 we examine, on a national scale, the way in which the various policies that have been introduced have in reality influenced the content and structure of initial teacher education in universities, colleges and schools. We investigate how they have been accepted, challenged, bypassed, transformed and what their consequences have been for course design. We also examine the outcomes of these changed policies by looking at what we might call the context of student experience. It is one thing for course leaders to design new courses in response to particular policy texts; how those new courses are actually experienced by students could well be a different matter. In Chapter 8 we therefore draw on our two MOTE projects to describe the changing context of student experience.

Substantively, therefore, our research focused on contexts of practice, including the context of student experience. However, if we are to understand the background and implications of our findings, it is important to set out the context of influence and the context of text production as well. In the remainder of this opening chapter we look at the first of these – the context of influence. We identify the range of different voices within the contemporary policy debate on teacher education that have attempted to shape and influence the texts actually produced.[8]

Voices in the context of influence

In understanding the context of influence of policy change since the early 1980s, it is helpful to identify four different voices in the policy debate on initial teacher education. The first two are part of the New Right (neo-liberals and neo-conservatives) and the third came from within the teacher education profession. All of these three groups have been directly concerned with the nature of teacher professionalism. As we will see, over the last 20 years the degree to which these different voices have influenced substantive policies has varied as the political fortunes of the different constituencies have risen and fallen. A fourth, technocratic or managerial voice, from administrators within central state bureaucracies (Salter and Tapper 1981) has sometimes given priority to different policy concerns, such as the need to ensure the supply of teachers and a desire to introduce more accountability into the system. More recently, this last voice has sometimes seemed to lend support to the political project of the New Right, though under the new Labour government, it may now be moving in a somewhat different direction – what O'Brien (1998) calls 'centralist progressivism'.

Neo-liberal perspectives

Throughout the 1980s and early 1990s, successive Conservative governments were concerned to challenge the social democratic consensus of earlier years and to restructure the Welfare State (Dunleavy and Hood 1994; Pollitt 1994; Clarke and Newman 1998). Their policies and motivations were shaped and nurtured by what have come to be known as New Right ideologies, though one of the difficulties in using this term is the danger of implying a coherence and homogeneity of ideas that does not in reality exist. There are two major strands of thought within the New Right position, those of the neo-liberal market advocates and the neo-conservative defenders of the traditional forms of authority and national culture. Political analysts have delineated the differences between these two traditions but also some points of commonality (Gamble 1983, 1988). Both neo-conservatives and neo-liberals are critical of egalitarianism and collectivism, which they allege have encouraged an anti-enterprise and permissive culture.

Central to the neo-liberal position is the claim that market forces are both an efficient and a fair means for allocating resources and more responsive to the felt needs of individuals becoming self-reliant and independent of the state. As Henig (1994: 5) notes:

> In a strange twist, the shift away from democratic processes and institutions is defended by reference to values we associate with democracy. Markets, it has been argued, can become more democratic than democracy itself.

Market forces are alleged to be an efficient means of creating the conditions and relationships necessary for freedom of consumers, for allocating scarce resources, generating diversity and providing the form of flexibility the changing world order requires. As a result, Conservative governments attempted to extend free market principles into whole new areas of social activity, including the provision of welfare services. In the field of education, the establishment of open access to schools, league tables, local financial management and the introduction of new types of school (grant maintained schools, city technology colleges) are obvious examples of attempts to introduce a competitive 'quasi-market' (Whitty *et al.* 1998).

In the field of initial teacher education, there has been a recurrent assertion amongst neo-liberals that initial training is unnecessary, even harmful – the product of 'producer capture' by the educational establishment. As a leader article in the *Daily Telegraph* put it in 1996:

> We have argued for years that the twin causes of the disastrously low standards in schools are teacher training institutions that fill their students' heads with rubbish and inspectors who have enforced adherence to a defunct ideology.

Often the implication is that teacher training courses actually diminish the effectiveness of teachers. From a neo-liberal point of view, if the quality of training itself is to be improved, the government needs to insist that it is opened up as much as possible to the 'market' of schools so that practical work takes precedence over higher education-based training. Market realities are the best 'educator'. Ideally, there would be a free market in training itself, where schools would be allowed to recruit whomsoever they wanted – trained or untrained. If this were the case then it is assumed that headteachers would favour straightforward graduates over those who had 'suffered' from professional training.

Neo-conservative perspectives

Neo-conservative ideas are rather different for they emphasize traditional authority and national identity. They have particular force in the field of education. From the neo-conservative perspective, the central aim of education is the preservation of a refined cultural heritage. In the words of the Hillgate Group (1989: 1), education 'depends on . . . the preservation of knowledge, skills, culture and moral values and their transmission to the young'. As a view of education, neo-conservatism found its first contemporary vocal expression in the Black Papers issued in 1969 (Cox and Dyson 1969). One can also see the influence of this line of thinking in the establishment of the broad structure of the National Curriculum with its emphasis on traditional subjects.

The views of neo-conservatives on teacher education in the 1980s were trenchant. For example, the Hillgate Group (1989) accused most courses of being intellectually 'feeble and biased' and being overly concerned with topics such as race, sex, class and even 'anti-imperialist' education. According to the Hillgate Group, these 'preoccupations' appeared 'designed to stir up disaffection, to preach a spurious gospel of "equality" and to subvert the entire traditional curriculum' (Hillgate 1989: 5). If our cultural heritage was to be passed on to our children then teachers themselves had to be thoroughly educated in the disciplines they taught. The primary task for initial teacher education, from this perspective, is therefore to develop professionals who are themselves experts in their own subject area. Such preparation should take precedence over training in pedagogy; indeed according to Lawlor (1990) the chief weakness of current approaches to initial training is that they are dominated by preparing students on *how* to teach rather than *what* to teach.

On the development of practical teaching competence, neo-conservative commentators, like the neo-liberals, have argued for a school-based, apprenticeship model. For example, O'Hear (1988a, b) argued that teaching was an essentially practical skill that could not be learned from the kind of theoretical study of teaching that he suggested dominated current courses. In similar vein, the Hillgate Group argued that there was a long tradition going back to Aristotle of regarding some skills, including many that are difficult, complex and of high moral and cultural value, as best learned by the emulation of experienced practitioners and by supervised practice under guidance. 'In the case of such skills, apprenticeship should take precedence over instruction and even when formal instruction is necessary it can never substitute for real practical training' (Hillgate Group 1989: 9).

For both neo-liberals and neo-conservatives, therefore, higher education-based training is at best of secondary importance; at worst it is positively harmful. As teaching is an essentially practical activity, the most important 'trainer' beyond being deeply immersed in your own 'subject' is experience itself. Students need a thorough grounding in what they are to teach and then to actually do the job of teaching; there is no other way of learning. Lawlor (1990: 38) made the point most forcibly by arguing for the entire abolition of formal training, which she believes often 'undermines' the subject specialism of graduates who enter teaching. Instead, 'graduates [should] be sent to school to train on the job, designated to an experienced mentor – a senior teacher in the subject'.

It is hard to underestimate the influence of the New Right critique of initial teacher education during the 1980s and early 1990s. As we will see below, their views progressively had more and more influence on policy texts produced during that period.

The views of the profession

But what of the profession's own views? One of the problems in answering that question is that it depends on what we mean by the profession. The interests of the teaching profession in schools (itself represented by competing trade unions) have not always been the same as those of teacher educators in higher education. For example, they might agree about the threat to professional status from the Licensed Teacher Scheme but be rather more enthusiastic about school-based training within properly accredited courses, provided resources flowed from higher education into schools. Often, however, the different professional groups have worked together. Their different representative bodies had a common forum in SCETT (Standing Committee for the Education and Training of Teachers) and, despite the growing centralisation of government policy, in the early part of the 1980s at least, professional groups continued to have a voice in the contexts of influence.

School teaching unions had other priorities in their conflicts with the Thatcher government by the late 1980s and, for the most part, the professional voice in relation to teacher education increasingly became mainly that of higher education-based teacher educators.[9] Throughout the 1970s and 1980s, a number of training institutions had already begun to redesign their courses to place greater emphasis on practical training. As Wilkin (1996) argues, the developments were particular noticeable within CNAA validated courses.[10] Although not directly responsible for curriculum design, the CNAA provided a 'generally supportive but critical environment in which the college leadership could introduce innovative courses which gave greater priority to the practical aspects of training' (Wilkin 1996: 114).

The initial reason for redesigning courses in this way was to respond to continued demands from students and from teachers that the theory taught in training institutions should be more directly relevant to schools than it had been in the past. From these redesigned courses, as well as from the Articled Teacher scheme (see Chapter 3), developed a body of research and writing (Furlong *et al.* 1988; Benton 1990; Wilkin 1992; McIntyre *et al.* 1993; Furlong and Maynard 1995) that provided clearer professional and intellectual justification for a restructuring of initial teacher education that involved a growing role for schools in the process.

Some of the best known work in this field at the time came from research and development conducted at Cambridge and Oxford universities. The Cambridge research, undertaken by Furlong *et al.* (1988), involved an evaluation of two primary and two secondary 'school-based' PGCE courses where teachers had a far greater role in the design and day-to-day practice of the training. The courses selected for study included both CNAA and university validated ones. The research project was funded by the Department of Education and Science; presumably it was intended to point the direction for future course development. However, it was a different course – that developed at Oxford University – that in 1987 succeeded in drawing public and professional attention to the value of school-based training (Benton 1990). Although they were developed separately, and although there were important differences between them (McIntyre 1991), the Oxford and Cambridge visions of training and the role they assigned to school teachers were very similar.

Both the Oxford and Cambridge schemes insisted that no satisfactory initial teacher education course would be possible without much closer and more effective integration of school-based and university-based elements of the course than has been common. Both schemes also recognized the importance of the different contributions that practising school teachers and university lecturers can make. The conditions of university lecturers' work, McIntyre (1991: 114) suggests,

> enable and oblige them, much more than is generally possible for practising teachers, to know about alternative teaching approaches being used elsewhere, to study relevant research and theoretical literature and to explicate and critically examine the principles which should or could inform the practice of teaching.

However, it was only practising school teachers who could directly introduce students to the practice of teaching (McIntyre 1991: 141) and

> especially to the use of the contextualised knowledge (of individual pupils, of established relationships with classes, of resources and their availability and of schools, customs and procedures) which is such a crucial element of professional teaching.

The vision of professionalism promoted by the Oxford course was one of strong practical skills personally understood and justified through an intellectually rigorous process.

The 1980s were therefore a period of very lively debate within the field of initial teacher education in England and Wales, much of it focusing on the need for a new, more practically focused vision of professionalism. While there was some common ground between the different protagonists, there were very important and real differences between them.

The concerns of the state

It is also important to recognize that throughout the 1980s and 1990s, the ministry responsible for the production of policies – now called the Department for Education and Employment – was not simply responsive to the views put forward by those outside government;[11] it had its own concerns and priorities that themselves served to influence and or modify the texts actually produced. As we have already indicated, two policy concerns have been particularly important for those at the centre – first, the need to ensure an adequate supply of teachers and second, the concern to re-establish a national framework as a means of enhancing quality.

The Department has for many years been responsible for managing the supply of teachers, which means modelling demand for teachers as well as the output of courses (DfEE 1997a). To predict demand, their model takes account of the movements of teachers into and out of maintained schools, projects these movements in each future year and derives totals of teachers needed by phase, sex and age. To predict supply, the model makes assumptions about in-course wastage and the balance between courses of different lengths. From these different calculations, the numbers of newly qualified teachers who need to complete courses in order to balance supply and demand in maintained nursery, primary and secondary schools are calculated and assigned to particular training institutions.

The modelling of supply is therefore a complex but relatively straightforward technical process. Ensuring that there is an adequate supply of appropriately qualified applicants for courses is, at times, more problematic. In particular, the economic booms of the late 1980s and middle to late 1990s meant that, at those times, the issue of ensuring adequate supply became increasingly difficult and therefore a major priority for policy. As we will see below, this concern with supply in part stimulated the search for new routes into the profession; it probably also helped to maintain the existence of the BEd as the major route for the training of primary school teachers despite serious criticisms made of the degree by New Right and other critics (D. Hargreaves 1994; Lawlor 1990).

A second concern of the state has been and remains that of establishing a national framework of accountability. This concern was stimulated throughout the 1980s by extensive DES and HMI evidence which questioned the quality of existing approaches to initial teacher education. During the 1980s these two bodies issued a vast array of research findings (HMI 1982, 1988a), inspection reports and documents (DES 1983, 1988a; HMI 1983, 1987, 1988b) and directives (DES 1984, 1989a; DfE 1992), many of them implicitly and explicitly critical of existing approaches to teacher education. In almost every case, the focus of those criticisms was on the development of students' practical teaching competence.

Two stand out as of particular political importance – they were the two national surveys of newly qualified teachers in schools conducted by HMI in 1981 and 1987 (HMI 1982, 1988a). As we will see in more detail in Chapter 8, these surveys, each of which looked at approximately 300 new teachers working in England and Wales, were highly influential in the growing demands for reform, not least because their findings readily led to alarmist headlines in the press. The first survey found that, while the majority of newly qualified teachers were well trained, appointed to appropriate posts and given appropriate support in their new schools, a significant minority were not. In the judgement of HMI, nearly one in four were in some respects poorly equipped with the skills needed for teaching. This view was corroborated by the new teachers themselves. On a range of key practical teaching skills, between one-fifth and three-fifths of teachers rated themselves as having been inadequately prepared. The 1987 survey revealed that things had improved somewhat, though there was still considerable cause for concern. In the view of HMI, 20 per cent of primary and 11 per cent of secondary teachers lacked some or many basic skills. Two-thirds of new teachers themselves were well or reasonably well satisfied with the training they had received; one-third were not.

Despite the improvement by 1987, newly qualified teachers in both surveys complained that in their courses too much emphasis had been placed on academic study in general and on education studies in particular and that there was too little emphasis on teaching method and teaching practice. Clearly something had to be done to increase the quality of training and particularly the quality of practical training in schools. From the state's point of view, that demanded re-establishing central control. As we will see, this linking of quality and control has become an increasingly important policy objective of the state throughout the last two decades.

However, it has also become more directly aligned with the other policy objective of reconstructing teacher professionalism. To this extent, the distinctive voice of Salter and Tapper's (1981) state bureaucrats has been rather less in evidence in recent years, as it has become increasingly politicized. Apple (1998) has suggested that the so-called 'conservative restoration' in education has been fuelled by four groups, the neo-liberals, the neo-conservatives, authoritarian populists and some members of the new middle classes. These might include key officials in new state agencies. Certainly, as we indicate in Chapter 10, a shift from the traditional bureaucratic state to what is sometimes termed the evaluative state has led to a growth in non-elected intermediary bodies – trusts, agencies and quangos – between government and service providers. These are often headed by a new breed of government appointees, who tend to have a higher public profile than conventional state bureaucrats and tend to be more directly involved in setting broader political agendas through close contacts with politicians (and not just ministers) and with the media. In relation to teacher education, both Chris Woodhead at Ofsted and Anthea Millett at the TTA have often seemed to relish this role. Significantly, Chris Woodhead openly joined a group of New Right critics of teacher education in a meeting with UCET in 1997 and even agreed to sum up their case (UCET 1997).

Conclusion

During the 1980s and 1990s there have therefore been a range of different voices within the policy debate on initial teacher education, but increasingly the teacher education profession and especially those in universities and colleges have felt themselves under siege from the other groups involved. However, as we indicated above, there is seldom a straightforward relationship between particular voices in the context of influence and the actual policy texts that are produced. At different times in the 1980s and 1990s, the views of these groups had an influence on substantive policies. Some policy texts have prioritized neo-conservative ideas, some neo-liberal views and others those of the profession itself. Often those views have been influenced by and had to be achieved through the concerns of state-appointed officials.

As Bowe and Ball (1992) suggest, however, practitioners do not interpret policy texts naively – they have their own histories and values, they also work within their own particular institutional constraints. There is therefore potentially a gap between what is actually implemented and what is intended by those responsible for framing particular policy texts. There is perhaps an even bigger gap between what is practised and the aspirations of those in the 'context of influence' who argued for particular policies in the first place. Documenting and analysing the way in which practice actually changes is therefore a vitally important part of the policy analysis process. It is certainly as important as analysing the public pronouncements of policy makers themselves and we make no apologies for devoting a significant part of our empirical work to this end.

In our empirical work we had two aims. Our first, and most important aim was to document the 'context of practice' in initial teacher education, plotting the ways in which those responsible for designing and teaching courses actually responded to the range of rapid policy changes that were introduced between the late 1980s and mid-1990s. In the next three chapters we focus on the first period of our research – the early 1990s. We begin by examining the policy texts that were influential at the time and then draw on our research to describe the changing context of practice that emerged in response to these texts; in Chapters 5, 6 and 7 we do the same in relation to the period covered by our second study – the middle 1990s. Our second, and within the limited resources of our project, necessarily subsidiary aim, was to document the implications of the changes that were introduced for student experience itself. In Chapter 8 we report our findings on the changing context of student experience. In Chapter 9 we bring our study up to date by looking at policy initiatives in the late 1990s and in Chapter 10 we consider some of the broader implications of our research by exploring the global context of the changing face of teacher professionalism.

Notes

1 The nature of these new routes is discussed in more detail in Chapter 4.
2 'Modes of Teacher Education: Towards a Basis for Comparison' (ESRC project no. R000232810).
3 'Changing Modes of Professionalism? A Case Study of Teacher Education in Transition' (ESRC project no. R000234185).

4 These developments are discussed in more detail in Chapter 5.

5 The generic title of MOTE was used informally for both projects.

6 Limitations of access made it impossible to include all aspects in a small number of the case studies.

7 Full details of the methodology are provided in the Appendix.

8 In our final chapter, we comment on the relevance of two further 'contexts', introduced by Ball (1994: 26).

9 In the early 1990s, though, an 'alternative' school voice emerged from some of the early exponents of School-Centred Initial Teacher Education. See, for example, Berrill (1994).

10 The CNAA (Council for National Academic Awards) was the statutory body established to validate degrees in the newly expanded 'non-university' sector of higher education, that is, polytechnics and colleges of higher education.

11 In 1992 it changed its name from the Department of Education and Science (DES) to the Department for Education (DfE). In 1995 it was amalgamated with the Department of Employment to become the DfEE.

2 The policy context of MOTE 1 – the early 1990s

Introduction

One of the challenges of undertaking policy research in the field of teacher education is that there is always a necessary time lag between particular policy initiatives and changes in practice. Even in the PGCE, changes take at least one year to implement; in the BEd they may take up to four years. In the early 1990s, when our first MOTE project began, different cohorts of students within the same institution were often undertaking their courses under different regulations. This was because new policy texts often appeared before the previous ones had been fully implemented. At the time of our fieldwork, most institutions were in the process of responding to policy texts introduced in 1989, though some students on longer courses, particularly the four-year BEd, were still working under 1984 regulations. As we will see in Chapter 5, however, even before the earlier implementation process was complete, radically different regulations were being introduced.[1]

In this and the next two chapters we set out some of the findings from our first MOTE study. In this chapter, following a brief historical introduction, we set the policy context for our research, looking in detail at the key policy texts that influenced the practice we saw. In Chapter 3, we draw on our empirical findings to examine how 'mainstream' initial teacher education provision had been restructured at the time, particularly in response to Circular 24/89 (DES 1989a). In Chapter 4 we look at a number of innovative 'new routes' into teaching introduced by the government. We conclude Chapter 4 by reflecting on what our findings from the first MOTE study suggest about changing models of teacher education and professionalism at that time.

The historical legacy

Before describing the policy texts influential in the early 1990s, it is valuable briefly to outline the earlier period of postwar teacher educational policy. This is important not merely for the sake of historical interest but because we can only understand the response of contemporary practitioners to the context of practice if we have some insight into the histories, experiences and values of teacher educators themselves, many of whom (like the authors) were professionally formed in periods prior to that under study. Wilkin (1996) in her study of teacher education in the 1960s, 1970s and 1980s provides a good starting point.

The 1960s – teacher education and social democracy

According to Wilkin (1996) the 'context of influence' in the postwar period was clear and coherent. Both of the main political parties of the time subscribed to the ideology of social democracy – an ideology that, in the field of higher education, found its expression in the Robbins Report of 1963. The Robbins Report argued that, 'The good society desires equality of opportunity for its citizens to become not merely good producers but also good men and women'. In the specific context of higher education that meant that 'courses of higher education should be available for all those who are qualified by ability and attainment to pursue them and who wish to do so' (Robbins 1963: para. 31).

This social democratic ideal had an influence on the Committee's conception of teacher education too. The Committee's vision of a professional teacher was of someone who had had a strong personal education; they therefore believed that such personal education should take priority over practical training. Teacher training colleges were to be rapidly expanded to respond to the growing demand for teachers and were to be brought into the higher education system (they were, significantly, to change their name to become 'colleges of education'); courses were to be made 'degree worthy'. Wilkin suggests that the main vehicle for ensuring the 'degree worthiness' of the newly born BEd degree was to be subject studies and 'education' – reinterpreted as the study of the four 'ologies' – sociology, history, psychology and philosophy. University validated syllabuses were in effect the 'texts' of this new approach to professional training in colleges. In line with the social democratic ideal, the academic study of the disciplines was conceived of as 'part of the education of the scholar who happened to want to be a teacher' (Bell 1981:13) but the disciplines were also justified in terms of their content. Because psychology, and to a lesser extent sociology and the other 'ologies', contributed to the study of progressivism, they too supported the social democratic ideal.

Wilkin suggests that the Robbins Report's conception of professional education was not, in reality, successful. There were significant unresolved epistemological difficulties concerning the relationship between theory and practice and in the context of practice the majority of lecturers and students remained sceptical about the value of an overly academic approach to professional preparation. Once the 'degree worthiness' of the new BEd had been accepted, the Robbins Report's conception of a liberally educated professional was challenged and the search for a professionally oriented degree rapidly gained momentum.

The 1970s – fragmentation and autonomy

In contrast to the 1960s, Wilkin suggests that the 1970s was a period of ideological confusion. In education in general, including teacher education, there was no consistent ideological context of influence inside or outside the government and no coherent presentation of principles and priorities. The decade opened promisingly enough with the new Conservative government establishing a series of 'expert' committees to tackle the major problems of the day. The James Committee (James 1972), established to examine teacher education, was the first of these. Its proposals were radical with its vision of 'three cycles' of linked education and training (personal, initial training and in-service) and statutory rights for teachers to have one term's study leave every seven years. However, the report of 1972 was not followed up in any significant way by the governments of the mid-1970s; it remained one voice amongst many. As Porter (1996: 45), one of the members of the original committee, has written:

> The proposals of the James Committee were accepted because politically correct rhetoric required acceptance. They were not implemented because of political, economic and demographic factors. They were also rejected because they argued for the development of a well informed professional group that would have the confidence to change schools in the light of experience and research and the independence to sustain the changes in the face of political and economic pressures. In the light of the contemporary Realpolitik that was one bridge too far.

In the event, during the 1970s, central government's involvement in teacher education policy was largely limited to managing provision in line with changes in demography; the result was a severe reduction in student numbers and the closure of many colleges of education in the wake of the unfortunately-named 1972 White Paper, *Education: A Framework for Expansion* (DES 1972).

The ideological vacuum that developed around educational policy allowed the professions themselves – professional teacher educators, the CNAA, philosophers of education, the teaching unions and Her Majesty's Inspectorate (HMI) – to take a lead in shaping the practice of teacher education. The result was one of increasingly fragmented provision. 'Throughout the decade there was considerable variation in courses of initial training on almost every dimension; the weighting of theory and practice, integration of the elements, time spent in school, relationships with teachers and so on' (Wilkin 1996: 121). On the one hand there were the fiercely autonomous 'old' universities where, with some important exceptions, a strong emphasis on theory continued to hold sway (Patrick *et al.* 1982). By contrast, amongst CNAA validated institutions, there was a slow trend towards a curriculum in which the disciplines of education became less prominent, where the status of professionally oriented courses (e.g. curriculum studies, language and education) rose and students spent more time in school. Overall, Wilkin suggests that the professionals involved in leading the debate on teacher education were slowly changing their vision of professionalism from an emphasis on the need for personal intellectual development to one of professional competence. However, even in CNAA validated courses, the system was still managed and run by those in higher education. Although the language of partnership with schools started to emerge in some institutions, the practice of partnership was largely illusory and many students and practising teachers remained critical of what they felt still to be an overacademic approach to professional education.

When the Thatcher government came to power in 1979, it inherited a system of initial teacher education that had in recent years rapidly expanded and then contracted as projections of teacher supply had changed. The need to maintain a flexible system of supply therefore remained a high priority for successive Conservative Secretaries of State. Substantively the system of the late 1970s had a number of distinctive features about it. First, despite some general trends, it was highly diverse. There were three different types of institutional providers – universities, polytechnics and colleges – each with their own histories, commitments and professional associations;[2] course content and structure varied widely too. Second, despite the slow trend towards professional relevance, courses remained distant from schools and as a result student and teacher criticism of the system remained strong. Third, as a professional group, teacher educators were divided amongst themselves. Even within the same institution they were often heterogeneous, having been recruited at different historical periods. Some were highly academic in their commitments; others were much more professionally oriented (a trend that was reinforced after the introduction of the requirement for all teacher educators responsible for pedagogy to have 'recent, relevant and successful' school experience (DES 1984)). Finally, what those lecturers as a group did have in common was that they were used to being largely autonomous in their management of what they considered to be their own system.

Key policy texts of the 1980s

Interestingly, the incoming Conservative government of 1979 was at first slow to develop any significant policies in initial teacher education – in fact not until its second term of office did it make any significant moves. During the early 1980s, neo-liberal ideas started to be influential. In 1982, the then Secretary of State Sir Keith Joseph commissioned the Cambridge research into school-based teacher education described in Chapter 1 (Furlong *et al.* 1988). The project was given a high national profile and was explicitly mentioned in the White Paper of the time, *Teaching Quality* (DES 1983); clearly it was intended to indicate the preferred direction of government policy. Opening up training courses to the 'realities' of schooling was seen as a good thing; it would in itself, it was assumed, improve the quality of training. The need to use a high profile research project to influence national policy is indicative of the lack of direct power the Secretary of State had in the early 1980s over the detail of course structure and content. If change was to be achieved, then the largely autonomous teacher education profession itself had to be persuaded of its value and the use of a well-publicized research project was an established strategy for encouraging change. However, if this was the initial strategy, Sir Keith Joseph was clearly unconvinced about its efficacy, for within two years (well before the project was completed) he had dramatically increased the power of his office for more direct intervention.

Specific intervention first began in 1984 with the issuing of DES Circular 3/84 (DES 1984). It was this circular that established the Council for the Accreditation of Teacher Education (CATE) which was charged with the responsibility of overseeing initial teacher education in England and Wales on behalf of the Secretary of State. In retrospect, the substantive changes focusing on professionalism introduced by Circular 3/84 do not seem particularly radical, though they do indicate the influence of neo-liberal thinking: college and university lecturers responsible for pedagogy in teacher education courses had to return periodically to schools to undertake 'recent and relevant' school experience; teachers had to be involved in the process of interviewing students; the time that students had to spend in schools during their training was defined for the first time. Such proposals now seem relatively modest, though the government's interest in opening up professional training to the realities of the market was clearly signalled. However, constitutionally, the circular was revolutionary (Wilkin 1991, 1996). For the first time it established the right of the Secretary of State to have a say in the detailed content and structure of initial teacher education in England, thereby marking the end of higher education's (and even the old universities') autonomy. In establishing the mechanism of increased central control, the circular was of fundamental and lasting significance for the rebuilding of a national system of initial teacher education.

As indicated above, by the time we came to undertake the first MOTE project in the early 1990s, most institutions were in the process of responding to a second round of Conservative government initiatives issued in 1989. The first, and for most institutions the most significant, was Circular 24/89 (DES 1989a) which was issued in November 1989 following a consultation document in May of the same year. The new circular took a number of steps to strengthen central control of training courses and challenge the autonomy of higher education institutions. In the first instance the circular revised and extended the powers of the Council for the Accreditation of Teacher Education and added a new layer of bureaucracy to the accreditation system. Local CATE committees were set up to oversee all teacher training courses, reviewing 'in detail' new or amended courses and ensuring that courses 'continue to satisfy the new criteria'. The committees were to include a range of representatives, including those from business and industry; representatives from higher education institutions involved in initial teacher education had to be in the minority and the chair had to be 'independent' of higher education.

The new circular also confirmed the government's interest in the development of a more practically focused form of professional preparation. The regulations, introduced in 1984, that lecturers responsible for 'pedagogy' should return to the classroom for 'recent and relevant' school experience, were more clearly defined; they must go back to school for the equivalent of one term in every five years. The amount of time students had to spend in school was increased too – to 75 days for one-, two- and three-year courses and 100 days for four-year courses. PGCE courses were lengthened from 34 to 36 weeks.

The twin concerns of limiting the autonomy of higher education and developing a more practical form of training were both signalled in the thrust towards closer collaboration with schools. As the first criterion of the new circular put it:

> Institutions should establish links with local authorities and a number and variety of schools, and should develop and run the professional and educational aspects of courses in initial teacher training in close working relationship with those schools.
>
> (DES 1989a: para. 1.1)

Specifically that meant that institutions had to ensure that experienced teachers from their schools were involved in course planning and evaluation, student selection and the assessment of practical work. Teachers also had to be invited to make contributions to appropriate lectures, seminars and other activities. However, despite these very stringent constraints on higher education, in one sense their ultimate power was not challenged, for it was they who were to be responsible for leading and managing the new 'partnerships'. For example, '*Institutions* should satisfy themselves that teachers are appropriately prepared before they undertake such activities' (DES 1989a: para. 1.3, emphasis added). As we argue in more detail in Chapter 7, those in higher education remained 'the experts' and the guardians of the quality of contributions made by schools. However, they were now to be overseen and their 'expertise' was to be directed towards areas defined centrally.

In relation to the content of training, the circular broke new ground by defining a range of topics that had to be addressed within courses. Importantly, parts of this emerging curriculum for initial teacher education, notably those concerned with information technology, were expressed in terms of 'outputs' or 'exit criteria' – 'statements of what students should be able to show they know, understand and can do by the end of their training' (DES 1989a: para. 16). In the next circular (DfE 1992) these were to be further developed into 'competences'.

In looking at this new 'curriculum', it is important to emphasize that all four elements of the traditional curriculum within initial teacher education were still there – subject studies, subject application (and curriculum studies for primary courses), educational and professional studies and then finally school experience. The new circular had things to say about each of these.

On subject studies, perhaps influenced by the neo-conservative lobby, there was a strengthening of the links between what students studied within their degree and what they were expected to teach. In both primary and secondary courses, subject studies, whether as part of a BEd or other first degree, were now required to be related closely to the National Curriculum. The interpretation of this requirement in some institutions meant that many people with 'inappropriate' degrees (including many of the 'dangerous' social sciences such as sociology and media studies) were effectively excluded from the teaching profession. There were real difficulties for some applicants with joint degrees as well.

On primary 'curriculum courses', the circular extended control even further by requiring courses to devote 100 hours to maths and English, although, at that stage, it stopped short from defining the content of those courses. For educational and professional studies, however, it did define a content with an eclectic range of issues drawn from the traditional teacher education curriculum mixed with the government of the day's current concerns. So for example there were references to the Kingman Report on the teaching of English (DES 1988c) and the Elton Report (DES 1989d) on discipline in schools. Surprisingly (and probably much to the irritation of some neo-conservatives) there were also a number of references to more traditional issues such as those concerned with equal opportunities:

> Courses should prepare students for teaching the full range of pupils and for the diversity of ability, behaviour, social background and ethnic and cultural origin they are likely to encounter among pupils in ordinary schools . . . students should learn to guard against preconceptions based on race, gender, religion or other attributes of pupils and understand the need to promote equal opportunities.
>
> (DfE 1992: Annex A, para. 6.3)

Finally, on school experience, as we have already noted, the circular extended students' time in schools. Significantly, however, the circular maintained a rather traditional vision of the aims of such experience and how it should be integrated with higher education-based courses: 'Institutions should ensure that school experience is used as far as possible to *illuminate* students' educational, professional and curriculum studies and their applications work' (DfE 1992: Annex B, para. 2.4, emphasis added).

Nevertheless, as discussed in more detail in Chapter 4, the government was, at the same time, also experimenting with more fully school-based approaches to training through the Articled and Licensed Teacher schemes.

Conclusion

The two key government circulars on teacher education in the 1980s (DES 1984, 1989a) therefore served two interrelated purposes – they aimed to re-establish a national system of accountability in initial teacher education and progressively to introduce a more practically focused professionalism by opening up training courses to the realities of the 'market' of school. As a result, the academic study of education was intended to be increasingly marginalized. What they were not designed to do, despite the demands of the neo-liberals, was to create a 'free market' where students could choose for themselves whether or not to train – to have done so would have undermined the government's centralist aspirations. Nor, despite the criticisms of other influential figures such as D. Hargreaves (1994) did they lead to the abolition of the BEd – this would have fundamentally compromised supply into primary teaching. In these texts therefore we can see the careful balancing of the three policy objectives that we outlined in Chapter 1.

How then did higher education institutions respond to these policy changes and what were the implications for changing models of professionalism? These were the key questions of our first MOTE project and in the next two chapters we set out some of our key findings from this project. At the end of Chapter 4 we reflect on the implications of what we found for changing models of teacher education.

Notes

1 In more recent times, the speed of change has increased dramatically with the DfEE now expecting courses to change in response to new regulations within less than a year.
2 The universities were represented by the Universities Council for the Education of Teachers (UCET); the Polytechnics by the Polytechnics Council for the Education of Teachers (PCET) and the colleges by the Teacher Education Committee of the Standing Conference of Principals (SCOP).

3 Continuity and change in course provision

Introduction

As we indicated in Chapter 1, our first research project comprised two elements: a national survey of all initial teacher education provision in England and Wales conducted in 1991 and case studies of 50 individual courses including five Licensed Teacher Schemes carried out in 1992. It is today perhaps hard to imagine, but it is symptomatic of the fragmentation of teacher education provision in England and Wales at the beginning of the 1990s that, when we began our research, there was no overall description of the system available. The Department of Education and Science themselves had no reliable list of courses in the country or the numbers of students on them.[1] A preliminary aim of our first national survey was therefore to give us an overall 'topography' of provision (Barrett *et al.* 1992a; Whitty *et al.* 1992; Miles *et al.* 1993). What the survey revealed was a large and highly complex national system with some local variation. As an introduction to this chapter we therefore present a brief overview of the system as a whole. We then look in more detail at the changing nature of conventional BEd and PGCE courses before turning in the next chapter to examine innovative courses that were being established at the time.

The 'topography' of provision – a national system with local variation

Our first national survey demonstrated that, at the time of our research, almost 99 per cent of all initial teacher education was offered through higher education institutions – colleges of higher education, polytechnics and universities[2] – with the other 1 per cent being through the Licensed Teacher scheme offered by LEAs. Within higher education there were 317 different courses and over 45,000 students spread across 88 different institutions: 31 universities, 22 polytechnics and 36 colleges of higher education. However, the influence of the universities was broader than these figures suggest in that two-thirds of courses in the colleges were validated through universities, with the remainder being validated through the CNAA. All of the polytechnic courses at the time were validated through the CNAA.

There was a strong relationship between phase of training and training institution. Colleges of higher education for example recruited 42 per cent of all teacher training students, 79 per cent of whom were training to be primary school teachers. By contrast, universities offered 31 per cent of provision but 84 per cent of their students were training to be secondary school teachers. Overall, they trained 53 per cent of all of those entering secondary school teaching. Polytechnics recruited the remaining 27 per cent of students and had a more even balance between primary and secondary trainees and between undergraduate and postgraduate awards.

The courses available varied considerably in size, one-third of all courses having an intake of less than 25 students per year and one-third having over 100. However, smaller courses were more likely to be for secondary rather than primary teaching and at the postgraduate rather than the undergraduate level. They were also more likely to be in the universities than in the other two sectors, though interestingly the universities also had the largest number of courses with an intake of over 100.

At secondary level we also noted some sectoral specialization in terms of the subjects taught. Mathematics was the most frequently offered subject in all institutions but in the colleges, religious education (RE) was the next most widely offered subject whereas it was relatively rarely offered in polytechnics and universities. Universities tended to focus on the traditional 'grammar school' curriculum while, in polytechnics, courses in craft, design and technology and business education were amongst the most common.

Our survey also revealed details of student intake. Particularly significant was the percentage of courses recruiting mature students. The standard higher education definition of mature students was those over 24 years of age and, on this basis, 60 per cent of all students were mature. Perhaps more significant is the fact that almost one third of students were estimated to be over 31 years of age. In addition, over one-third of all courses reported that they recruited non-standard entrants to their courses and 23 per cent of courses reported that such students represented more than 10 per cent of their student intake.

Clear patterns in the student population emerged in relation to gender and ethnicity. Two-thirds of the student intake were women but this overall fact concealed a more complex picture. We separated returns into courses with an intake of over two-thirds female and those with an intake of more than two-thirds male – 'female dominated' and 'male dominated' courses. One hundred and forty-four courses were female dominated while only 28 were male dominated. Given the overall proportions of men and women in courses overall, this balance is not surprising. What was less expected however was that female dominated courses were more likely to lead to the award of PGCE (56 per cent) than to BEd (44 per cent) while the male dominated courses were more likely to lead to an undergraduate qualification (64 per cent) than to a postgraduate qualification. Students on male dominated and female dominated courses had distinctly different age profiles. The student age ranges on female dominated courses paralleled the national average while the age range on male dominated courses was significantly older, with 41 per cent being over 31 years. Two-thirds of the female dominated courses were leading to primary age qualifications.

In relation to ethnicity, one-third of all courses reported that they did not recruit any ethnic minority students and only three of these were actively trying to do so. Over half of the 181 courses that reported that they did recruit ethnic minority students had less than 5 per cent. Only 15 courses included more than a third of students from ethnic minorities. Eleven of these 15 courses were run by polytechnics; only one was in a college. The 15 courses were located in 11 different institutions, all in areas which had significant minority ethnic populations, suggesting that such courses probably had a local recruitment base.

An analytical framework

So much for the general pattern of provision – but if we were to understand the implications of that provision for teacher professionalism then a more detailed analysis was essential. In Chapter 1, following Hoyle and John (1995), we suggested that challenges to traditional visions of professionalism were likely to involve struggles around three central issues – knowledge, autonomy and responsibility. As we also indicated in Chapter 1, a great many other policy initiatives in the field of education since the late 1980s (the introduction of the National Curriculum, league tables, appraisal, etc.) have done much to challenge the autonomy of the teaching profession and thereby their ability to define for themselves how they should act with responsibility. Most changes in initial teacher education, however, work on the other dimension of professionalism – that of knowledge (and we would add skills and values too). The central concern of our research was therefore to understand how the changes introduced by different policy texts had served to transform the opportunities student teachers had to acquire different forms of professional knowledge, skills and values during their training.

In undertaking this analysis we therefore drew on and developed earlier work by Furlong et al. (1988). They too argue that approaches to initial teacher education can be differentiated in terms of the skills, knowledge and values to which students are exposed. Differences in course structures (for example the number of days students spend in school as opposed to university) obviously affect what students are expected and have the opportunity to learn in terms of knowledge, skills and values. Also influential is the content of training. However, as Furlong *et al.* (1988) argue, this varies not simply in relation to what appears on the curriculum of different courses. What students are intended to learn is also influenced by those responsible for teaching them a particular topic. Different personnel – lecturers and teachers – tend to make available to students different forms of professional knowledge (theoretical and practical) about the same topic. Moreover, different course structures can then affect the opportunities students have to integrate such different forms of theoretical and practical knowledge. Who is responsible for teaching students and the way in which different courses provide opportunities to integrate different elements can therefore be very significant in what is actually learned.

All of these factors – course structure, curriculum, personnel and forms of integration – will, in different courses, influence what student teachers have the opportunity to learn in terms of skills, knowledge and values. In other words they will influence the forms of professionalism they have the opportunity to develop. In examining the impact of different policy initiatives, we will therefore be looking at how they served to reconstruct these different elements of courses.

Course structures

Time in school

One obvious fact that affects the forms of professionalism students are expected and have the opportunity to develop is the amount of time they actually spend in school as opposed to higher education institutions. As we have already indicated, Circular 24/89 (DES 1989a) extended this for all courses – to 100 days for four-year BEd degrees and 75 days for all other courses apart from Articled Teacher Schemes.[3]

Our data revealed considerable variation in the amount of school-based experience offered to students both within and across these different routes into teaching. When we came to look at courses where the requirement was 75 days, we found that, while all courses provided the minimum, some course types typically offered significantly higher levels, especially two-year PGCE conversion courses and two-year BEd courses. Two-thirds of all one-year PGCE courses provided more than 81 days of school-based training.

When we broke down the one-year PGCE courses by age phase, we found that, of the 31 courses which offered more than 50 per cent (90 days) of school-based experience, nearly three-quarters were courses that led to a secondary phase qualification. These data suggest that *phase of training* was a key factor in the provision of school-based training, at least as far as the one-year PGCE course was concerned; 83 per cent of the primary PGCE courses offered less than 90 days of school-based experience. Students on conventional one-year PGCE courses spent an average of 50 per cent of their time in school. However, our data also reveal that 65 per cent of one-year PGCE courses exceeded the minimum requirement of 75 days by more than five days and 28 per cent of such courses exceeded it by more than 15 days.

Of the four-year undergraduate courses that were required to provide at least 100 days of school-based training, a third offered more than 30 per cent above this amount. Here though the phase differences observed in the school-based training offered by one-year PGCE courses did not apply; a third of both primary and secondary courses provided more than 131 days of school experience.

Overall therefore, by 1991, all courses conformed to the 1989 circular in relation to time spent in school and the majority actually exceeded the requirement. As we will see in Chapter 4, in 1992, the amount of time to be spent in school was to be substantially increased again. However, it was clear from our research that, by 1991, students were already spending significantly more time in school compared with courses of a decade earlier (Wilkin 1996).

Patterns of school experience – serial and block practice

The pattern of serial and block practice established is also highly significant in that, as Furlong *et al.* (1988) argue, it potentially affects the opportunities students have to integrate different forms of professional knowledge. As HMI (1991: 20) noted at the time, 'a carefully planned balance of serial and block practice may be a more important factor in increasing the quality of training courses than increasing the number or pattern of days spent in schools'. From our survey it appeared that, in many courses, complex patterns of serial and block practice had been established with students moving regularly back and forth between school and their training institution.

Of the 112 one-year PGCE courses in our sample, two described school experience as entirely serial experience, with no identified 'block practices'. Of the remaining 110 courses, 15 courses provided one block practice, 72 provided two block practices and 23 provided three block practices.

The majority of four-year courses provided four block practices: 56 of the 84 courses. Two course leaders reported that they provided only two block practices and 28 courses offered three block practices. Few courses (11) offered long block practices of 11 weeks or more; typically the pattern was three balanced periods of between two and six weeks of block practice during the course, with a fourth practice lasting between seven and 10 weeks. In relation to additional 'serial' days in school, we found that two-thirds of all courses offered students between 11 and 30 days of serial school experience, with one-year PGCE courses and four-year undergraduate courses typically providing between 11 and 20 additional days.

We can therefore see that complex patterns of serial and block practice were the norm on PGCE courses, both primary and secondary. One primary PGCE course tutor in maths explained the aims of this sort of course structure.

> We prepare them here and then while they are here they go on one day visits and report back. Then we help them prepare schemes of work in the light of their preliminary visits – they go and do it and then they come back and talk about it.

With such structures, the flow of ideas was not always one way. As a history tutor on the same primary course noted,

> With the introduction of the National Curriculum for History the schools are putting quite a lot of pressure on students. They come to me and say, 'I've got to do ancient Egypt, floating and sinking and electricity'. I try and emphasize the attainment targets rather than the content, but when your audience is being driven by the schools which are being driven by content, it is difficult.

Typically, because of the demands of subject studies, BEd degrees had a simpler structure, though there were some examples of more complex patterns in undergraduate degrees too. For example, one four-year primary BEd degree could only be described as 'aggressively concurrent'; students spent half of each week throughout their whole four years in schools, working in six different schools overall. The strain on the students of constantly moving between two very different institutional cultures was considerable. However, the explicit aim of this course structure was to ensure that all aspects of students' college work were linked to the work of the school.

Overall therefore the structure of courses revealed by our first MOTE project was highly significant. As Circular 24/89 (DES 1989a) had intended, students were spending an increased amount of time in school on all courses. Moreover, through the development of complex patterns of serial and block practice and the location of other elements of their training, they were being provided with the opportunity, at least potentially, to integrate their higher education and school-based work.

Course content

As we indicated above, one of the central demands of Circular 24/89 (DES 1989a) was for higher education institutions to develop a close working relationship with schools. As we have seen, this resulted in students being required to spend substantially more time in school than in the past. However, this requirement also influenced college-based parts of courses. Indeed it would seem that, at the time of our case study fieldwork (1992), many courses had placed far more emphasis on revising the nature of the college-based parts of their course than the school-based parts. This became particularly apparent when we came to examine course content.

We explored the content of college-based courses under the headings identified within Circular 24/89 – that is, curriculum courses, subject studies and educational and professional studies. In almost all courses there was strong evidence of explicit attempts to link each of these areas of work directly to the world of schools.

Curriculum courses

The vast majority of curriculum courses undertaken within higher education were highly practically oriented. As noted above, a common strategy employed was to exploit serial and block experience in order to integrate college-based and school-based work. Lecturers frequently used curriculum courses to prepare students for work in school by setting them assignments and by encouraging them to analyse and reflect on their school experience when they returned to college the following week. Even in courses where the pattern of school experience was more conventional, however, there was much evidence of the practical nature of curriculum work. For example, the students on one four-year primary BEd course, which had a fairly traditional pattern of teaching practice, described their curriculum courses in very positive terms.

The college gives you lots of ideas and ways of doing things.

They give us so many ideas for lesson plans. We could have a whole scheme of work for five weeks just from what we've done.

Curriculum tutors confirmed their overwhelmingly practical orientation. For example, the curriculum studies tutor on a design and technology degree, which also had fairly conventional teaching practice arrangements, explained,

The whole time one is able to see the student against an imaginary background of the school and try to emphasize the difficulties they will have in coming to terms with the curriculum of design and technology in school, its assessment and with discipline and control.

Subject studies

Subject studies necessarily form a central element in all two, three and four-year undergraduate degrees and on two-year conversion PGCE courses. On many such courses, students take their subject studies alongside students studying for other degrees, and the move towards modularization has increased this practice. In these circumstances, the opportunities for linking subject studies to the work of school are limited, though not impossible. For example, a tutor in one small college that ran a limited programme of 'non-education degrees' explained that other students 'simply have to put up with slightly "educationally oriented" subject studies'. A large polytechnic, which placed BEd students in a number of different faculties for their subject studies, adopted a different strategy in an attempt to maintain coherence for students: the polytechnic had agreed a series of 'permeating themes' (race, class and gender) that would be covered in all undergraduate courses. (The history course, for example, included work on the rise of Nazism and the role of women in pre-war communist society). It was intended that these themes would then be followed through in different ways into curriculum and other educational courses and into the classroom, but as one subject studies lecturer admitted, 'How clearly this is pulled together in the student's mind I wouldn't like to say.'

However, in courses where subject studies teaching was organized directly through education faculties, there were necessarily many more opportunities to link to the work of schools. Our case study courses included a number of examples where subject studies courses had been explicitly constructed so as to mirror the National Curriculum closely. For example, on one four-year primary BEd course, 'main subject' geography had been redesigned to follow the National Curriculum. As the senior geography lecturer explained,

> Previously, the geography course was designed in relation to the expertise of the lecturers, and what we thought geographers needed . . . but it was essentially human geography being done, there was no physical geography. Since the National Curriculum has come out it talks about human, environmental and physical geography . . . and we have therefore designed a course that equips them with these skills. That is not incompatible with degree level geography. We can now say that we are producing geographers in a rounded sense with all the dimensions that that subject calls for and secondly we are providing the basic knowledge and skills to allow them to deliver the National Curriculum.

Educational and professional studies

The aspect of course content most thoroughly transformed in recent years has been educational and professional studies. Evidence from the early 1980s (Patrick *et al.* 1982; HMI 1983) shows that, at that stage, educational and professional studies was still commonly addressed through the teaching of the separate disciplines of education – sociology, psychology, philosophy and history of education. In 1992, the disciplines were noticeably absent from the courses we examined. Instead, educational and professional studies was almost universally taught in a highly school-focused manner, usually being constructed explicitly to address the professional issues set out in Circular 24/89 (DES 1989a). Although there were some examples of specialist teaching, a more common strategy was for a single lecturer to take responsibility for teaching the whole educational and professional studies curriculum to their particular group of students.

One striking feature of many such courses was that the taught sessions were explicitly designed to meet a range of educational objectives. These included covering cross-curricular themes, providing a link between curriculum courses and school, modelling teaching strategies as well as preparing students directly for school experience. Some courses tried to achieve several of these aims at the same time. For example, on one four-year BEd primary course, the substantive focus of educational and professional studies was cross-curricular themes, but as the tutor in charge of the course indicated, there were many other aims too.

> Part of my own agenda is to get them to look at themselves as learners and also to prepare them practically for teaching. For example this week we are looking at the programmes of study in cross-curricular themes and how they would do things in the classroom. Next week I am going to introduce them to debates on subject study and look at Alexander's work . . . and then go into a very practical session about what we want children to learn and then how you would organize the classroom appropriately through the study of National Curriculum cross-curricular themes.

Given the range of professional topics to be covered and the complexity of educational aims being pursued, the demands on lecturers were often considerable; several lecturers we interviewed, like the one quoted above, realized that they could not claim to be experts in everything they were expected to cover and expressed concern at the possible superficiality of some of their work.

As we have already indicated, noticeably absent from the vast majority of educational and professional studies courses was any explicit concern with disciplinary theory. The tutor quoted above was also responsible for introducing such residual aspects of disciplinary theory that still existed in this particular course.

> It's also our job to put the 'education' into their course. They don't get as much sociology and psychology as they would have had a few years ago – they get it indirectly in that when we ask them to reflect we do make reference to Piaget, Bruner and Vygotsky. But I am unhappy they don't get more of this because they garble it back in essays in an undigested form and I wonder if it would be better not to introduce it at all rather than in the limited way we have to. It concerns me that we have to spend so much time looking at how we should implement the National Curriculum rather than examine how children learn.

Pedagogy

Significantly, links with schools were not only made through course content; the pedagogy utilized by lecturers was important too. Lecturers, it seemed, seldom lectured; indeed those who did often apologized for doing so! Most tutors deliberately employed a range of teaching styles that students might come across in school; they deliberately used their sessions as an opportunity to 'model' teaching for students.[4]

> I have used every strategy you could possibly think of; basically it is anything that I would use in the classroom.

> We have a deliberate strategy of exposing students to different teaching and learning styles in our sessions.

The significance of such modelling was clearly exposed in one course where it was missing. In one mathematics two-year conversion PGCE course, main subject maths was provided by the university's mathematics department. This led to some problems, as a course tutor noted,

> Working with the BSc maths students adds credibility to the course because they are doing the same lectures, but the teaching styles they are being exposed to are traditional maths lectures rather than 'education' maths.

One of the mentors associated with this course confirmed that this led to difficulties when the students were in school.

> There are problems with the maths faculty input because they are teaching them in a way which we [in school] encourage them not to use.

In addition to modelling, some tutors deliberately put their students in the role of pupils as a way of exploring teaching issues within their subject. For example, the maths tutor on a different two-year secondary maths course explained,

> They work on developing their own mathematics and observing themselves doing it so it is a matter of developing that understanding of how children learn while they are actually learning as well. For many of them it is a different way of learning than they ever experienced before. We don't lecture, we give them problems to work on and they work as a group on these problems – that creates a powerful dynamic of them realizing what they always just accepted in the past . . . it means that they start thinking about it and that raises their awareness of what it means to teach maths in school.

In this course, a carefully chosen and sophisticated pedagogy became possible because main subject study in mathematics was provided within the education faculty itself.

Assignments

A final strategy for linking college and school-based work was through the use of school-based assignments. Typically these assignments involved investigations of school or classroom practice on some issue, or the development and trialing of materials. So for example, 64 per cent of all primary courses and 69 per cent of all undergraduate courses reported that the development of curriculum materials was one of their main methods of assessment. Interestingly it was the courses that included an above average amount of time in school that utilized these types of assignment most frequently. On such courses, school teachers were also more likely to be given a role in their assessment.

The primary aim of this form of assignment was the integration of college and school-based work. For example, the curriculum tutor on a primary PGCE explained his course's procedures as follows,

> None of the course tutors are long out of the classroom so the work and assignments all have a tendency to be focused on the classroom and they all have an element of preparing materials for use in schools . . . The assignment is an adhesive – it gels the course.

Another commented,

> We design the activities, the teachers organize the situation in the classroom and the teachers then help the students to get it done – they talk to the students about it.

In the majority of courses, as in this one, the selection of topics for investigation was directed by the training institution; students typically chose their assignments from a range suggested by course leaders. There were however some examples of courses where a more collaborative approach was evident. In one secondary PGCE, for example, the idea that the schools should benefit from the course was built into the whole course design, including assignments.

> School-based investigations are not just for the benefit of the student but are intended to contribute to the school. It also gives schools more ownership of the course because assignments are negotiated according to schools' needs and concerns. The fact that the schools must benefit is the *sine qua non* of our partnership scheme.

Personnel – a growing role for teachers?

As we have already indicated, what student teachers learn during their initial training is as much influenced by *who* is responsible for teaching them as it is by the content of the curriculum. This is because teachers in schools typically have access to different forms of professional knowledge from teacher educators based in colleges and universities. They may also subscribe to quite different values too. Exploring the way in which Circular 24/89 (DES 1989a) influenced with whom students had the opportunity to work during their training therefore became an important question for us. In particular we were interested in the growing role for teachers themselves in the training process. As HMI (1991: 6) noted at the time:

The idea of partnership is crucial to the concept of school-based training. The extent to which a course is school-based cannot be determined adequately just by counting the hours students spend in school; the more influential role for teachers implied by the criteria needs to be evident, too.

One way of exploring the growing role for teachers was to examine the location of particular course elements.

Location of other course elements

Course leaders were asked on our questionnaire where the teaching of various aspects of their courses took place. As might be expected, the teaching of subject studies on undergraduate courses and PGCE conversion courses took place predominantly in higher education institutions; on the vast majority of these courses (97 per cent) the higher education institution was the main location for this aspect of the course. Non-conventional secondary courses seemed to be the exception in this, as in other, respects.

Nevertheless, it was clear that, on many courses, aspects of training in addition to school experience were being based in schools as well as in universities and colleges. The traditional pattern in which school experience was clearly separated from the higher education-based elements of a course was hardly typical of the courses surveyed in 1991. Only half the course leaders (137) said that educational and professional studies were taught *mainly* in college and fewer than half (101) described subject application work as taking place *mainly* in college. A rather larger proportion (65 per cent) said that higher education was the main location for the teaching of primary curriculum courses. Where elements were not based mainly in higher education, they were likely to be taught jointly by lecturers and teachers.

Involving teachers

In trying to assess the growing role for teachers, we explored a number of other issues besides location of training. For example, we asked course leaders to describe the involvement of school teachers in the interviewing for entry to the courses – whether teachers were involved at all or whether they had a joint or leading role in the process. All but 16 courses reported regularly involving teachers in this task but their degree of responsibility varied. Of the 16 courses that did not involve teachers in interviewing at all, most (11) were small courses.

Students applying for entry to a primary course were more likely to be interviewed by a teacher who had joint or primary responsibility for student selection than those applying for entry to a secondary course. Thirty-eight per cent of all primary courses, compared to only 20 per cent of secondary courses, described teacher involvement in interviewing in this way. The 77 courses that described teachers as taking joint or primary responsibility for interviewing were also more likely to be postgraduate courses than undergraduate courses (18).

There is some evidence that teacher involvement in interviewing students for entry to the course was related to more general teacher involvement in course planning, teaching and assessment. On those courses where teachers were described as taking joint or primary responsibility for interviewing students, teachers were also likely to have been described as taking joint or primary responsibility for other aspects of teacher training.

Teachers as mentors

The national survey collected data about the role of teachers in the planning, supervision and assessment of courses. What became clear was that their involvement varied across different course elements, though overall they were more likely to have a role teaching and supervising students than in course planning and assessment.

Perhaps unsurprisingly, teachers' strongest role was in relation to school experience – their role as a 'mentor'. Within our 45 case study courses it was possible to identify three rather different approaches to the support of students' school-based learning, each of which implied a different vision of the role of the mentor.

The first, and by far the most common, pattern of support for students was the traditional one where lecturers, rather than teachers, took formal responsibility for overseeing students' school-based work through their weekly or fortnightly visits. A tutor on a two-year PGCE course expressed an 'ideal' version of this model as follows,

> Integration between school and college work comes about principally from the strength of support we are able to give to students when they go into school – the preparation we go through with them here and the support we give them when they get in. At the moment we are able to spend time talking to students after visiting them in schools and therefore we can bring these issues back into college for general use.

As this tutor makes clear, in this model, 'training' takes place within the college; tutors then support students as they learn to 'apply' that training within the real world of the school. The formal role for the teachers in this process is relatively minor. They make their classrooms available for teaching 'practice' and generally keep an eye on things between the tutors' visits; they are supervisors rather than 'mentors'.

A number of case study courses had, either by necessity or design, moved to a less frequent pattern of school visits by tutors. As a consequence, in these courses the role of the teacher in supporting students was increased. One BA (QTS) degree called their supervising teachers 'associate tutors'. As the course leader explained:

Associate tutors are largely a response to the fact that we are a small department and we have vastly increased numbers – PGCE numbers have quadrupled and undergraduate numbers have doubled and the staff have stayed the same. We cannot cope with the school visits. We have therefore sworn in as deputies, 12 associate tutors who are senior teachers who are well known to us and they act as though they were main subject tutors on their own site. They carry out the support, advice and assessment of the students . . . I just visit them once a term.

What was distinctive about this course, and others like it, was that, although the role of the teacher in supporting students was enhanced, the fundamental model of training had not been changed. Students, it seems, were still being 'trained' in the HEI and then 'applying' their learning in school by working under the supervision of a teacher who took on the role of the lecturer. It is significant that in this course, and other case study courses that employed a similar model, very little had been done to support teachers in the execution of their extended role; in each case there was 'the course document' and an annual meeting but little more. What it meant to be an 'associate tutor' was seen as relatively unproblematic.

Both of the above models contrast sharply with those courses where there had been a sustained attempt to develop the role of the mentor. Such courses, had, to different degrees, begun to reassess their model of training; they were moving from an 'applications' model, where training took place elsewhere, to one where the school was seen as a key training site in itself. In courses following this model of training, teachers, acting as mentors, had significant responsibilities for planning and supporting the development of students' practical teaching competence. As a consequence, mentors had to be fully involved in the planning of students' training, and the flow of information between the schools and the college was vital. Moreover, such courses had to establish some means to help students integrate their school-based learning with their work in the college; integration had to go both ways.

When we came to look at assessment we found that overall, on 87 per cent of courses, teachers were described as taking joint or primary responsibility for the supervision and assessment of students on school experience. However, while there were examples of courses where assessment of practical teaching competence was seen entirely as the responsibility of the school, it was more common for college tutors to retain a strong role as moderators and mediators. The following comments from a mentor on a secondary PGCE expressed a common position.

Well, I would say that it is up to me up to a point. I fill in the half-termly reports and if I have got any particular concerns I can contact the tutor from the college and the tutor can come in and discuss with the students what the concerns are . . . One feels very much in a school department that it is hard to take responsibility for the failure of a student. You can't help but feel it is a failure within the department. And so I think you feel that final responsibility should lie with the college.

There was evidence though that power relations were shifting in a number of courses. As the tutor on another secondary PGCE said,

> It's very difficult to pass a student now if the school says they should fail.

Despite the growing role of teachers in this aspect of their work, they were not always central to the planning of school experience. Less than half (47 per cent) of course leaders described teachers taking joint or primary responsibility in planning school experience.

Teachers in other roles

Teachers have traditionally had some role in relation to school experience. However, by 1991/2 they were also becoming involved in other course elements that have traditionally been the sole province of those in higher education. For example on 60 per cent of courses, teachers were described as regularly assisting with, or taking joint or primary responsibility for, the teaching and planning of subject application. They were, however, less likely to be involved in the assessment of this element, with three-quarters of course leaders saying that teachers were not involved or only occasionally assisted with it. Nearly half the primary courses reported involving teachers in the planning and teaching of curriculum work, though they only had an assessment role in 20 per cent of courses. When it came to educational and professional studies, teachers on more than half the courses were described as giving regular assistance with the teaching and planning of this element of the course though on only about one-quarter of courses did they have any significant assessment role. The area of work where teachers at this time had little direct involvement was in relation to subject studies; in over 90 per cent of courses, it was claimed that they were not involved in teaching, planning or assessment.

Given that teachers were being given more responsibility in the training process, particularly in relation to school experience, the question of the training and support they were given is important. At that time, only about half of all courses (137) indicated that they offered in-service training to teachers working in collaboration with them and only in about half of those courses (77) was it accredited in some way. Training was more likely to be offered and accredited by colleges of higher education (CHEs) than universities; it was also more frequently available in supporting non-conventional courses, particularly the articled teacher courses, as we will see in Chapter 4.

Course leaders were also asked to describe any other 'significant supports', apart from training, available for teachers who worked regularly with students. Most course leaders referred to meetings between college-based tutors and school staff, and to the importance of providing clear documentation on all aspects of the course. Course leaders also described the provision of non-contact time and involvement of teachers in college-based in-service training programmes, not directly connected with their supervisory role, as of importance. Secondments of teachers to HEIs, where available, were considered to offer significant support to schools when supervising students, and the involvement of teachers in course selection procedures was also felt to support teachers in their supervisory role.

Models of professional training

The reflective practitioner

When asked whether the course was based on any particular philosophy or model of professionalism, 81 per cent (218) of course leaders said 'yes'. There was no significant relationship between a course employing a particular model of professionalism and phase of training. There was a relationship, however, between institutional sector and course models. Courses that were located in the university sector were *less* likely than courses in other institutional sectors to employ an agreed model of professionalism. While 88 per cent of courses in polytechnics and 89 per cent of courses in CHEs reported that they used an agreed model, only 65 per cent of courses in universities responded 'yes' to this question.

The overwhelming majority of course leaders who responded 'yes' to this question described the agreed model as that of reflective practitioner. A typical example was a primary BEd course leader who described the philosophy of their course as one of developing 'the primary teacher as a highly educated, professionally competent and reflective individual.' Almost three-quarters of the 207 respondents who provided details of course philosophy described the course model in this way. In some cases these respondents elaborated on the model of the reflective practitioner with, for example, the 'interactive, analytical practitioner' or qualified it with references to another model of teacher professionalism (e.g. the competency model). For example a primary articled teacher course coordinator wrote: 'Reflective practitioner plus competency based assessment – believed by team not to be incompatible.'

The percentage of courses employing the reflective practitioner model was remarkably consistent across all phases and course awards. Thus, 72 per cent of secondary and primary courses reported that they were based on the model of reflective practitioner, while 70 per cent of undergraduate courses and 73 per cent of postgraduate courses described this as their course model.

Only 13 courses (6 per cent) explicitly subscribed to what they identified as a 'competency model' of teacher professionalism. Of these, nine were primary undergraduate courses. Ten per cent of all undergraduate and primary courses that used an agreed model of professionalism reported the use of a competency model, compared to only 3 per cent of secondary and postgraduate courses.

Eight secondary courses and seven postgraduate courses employed what they termed a 'theory into practice' model of professionalism, compared with only two undergraduate courses and one primary course. Primary undergraduate courses were more likely to employ a model of the 'teacher as researcher' – four primary undergraduate courses, compared with only one secondary postgraduate course.

A 'problem-solving' philosophy was cited by four secondary courses and two primary courses. More postgraduate courses (seven) than undergraduate courses (two) described their model of the teacher as one of the 'developing professional'. For example one secondary PGCE course leader wrote:

> Teachers need to be able to integrate the high quality decision-making of preparation with the low quality decision-making of classroom inter-action. To do this, and survive, requires an awareness of what is pos-sible, extensive opportunity to make errors in a supportive situation and an opportunity to improve.

Nine courses reported a 'practical' or 'school-based' philosophy; these included five secondary postgraduate courses and four primary undergraduate courses. Other models reported by course leaders included 'eclectic model' (four postgraduate and undergraduate courses at the same institution), 'teacher as manager' (one secondary and two primary postgraduate courses), and 'active learning' (two secondary postgraduate courses) and a 'child-centred' model (a primary postgraduate course).

Competences

During the early 1990s, statements of competence were increasingly being used as a basis for the assessment of professional practice in many fields including initial teacher education (Jessup 1991). Our survey asked about the use of competences in profiling and in other aspects of ITT courses in 1990–91 – prior to the new regulations which required it (DfE 1992). The responses indicate that, even then, the use of competences was by no means restricted to the 6 per cent of courses that claimed to be underpinned by a 'competency model' of the teacher. Even though 'reflective practitioner' and 'competence-based' approaches are sometimes seen as incompatible, many of those courses that had adopted a 'reflective practitioner' model were among those that reported using competences in their profiling systems or for other purposes. As one secondary PGCE conversion course leader wrote,

> I don't see how an effective course can be run without analysis of competences. It permeates the work, but its greatest use is in self-analysis of students' practical experience.

Over three-quarters of the course leaders (115) who used a profiling system stated that they had included competences in the profile; the aim was to help identify areas of strength and weakness within students and to assist in course planning. For example one primary Articled Teacher Scheme coordinator wrote:

Areas of weakness/uncertainty are identified and the course programme attempts to overcome some of these (not always possible, even with just 10 students!)

Similar comments were made by other course leaders. A secondary PGCE course leader explained:

Our 36-week PGCE course is a developmental one. Competences and skills are listed at different stages of the course – if certain skills are not shown, the course then seeks to develop or strengthen these weaknesses.

A four-year BA/BSc (QTS) course leader wrote:

All candidates for the course are asked for self-rating on a list of competences. These are used to inform planning for specific input for years 1 and 2.

Course leaders reported a variety of uses for competences, in addition to their being used as a basis for profiling. On 47 courses, competences were being used as a basis for course planning or for defining course aims and objectives. They were also frequently used in order to assess students' individual needs (22), or to assess teaching practice (20). Twenty-two courses were using competences in order to evaluate course provision and on three courses competences were being used to improve working practices between the higher education institution and schools, and thereby develop the notion of 'partnership'.

Conclusion

In this chapter we have concentrated on the way in which the vast majority of courses responded to the introduction of Circular 24/89 (DES 1989a). As we argued at the beginning of the chapter, much of the thrust behind the circular was a concern with two key policy objectives – the interest in recreating a national system of initial teacher education and the idea of challenging conventional notions of professionalism, particularly through 'opening up' provision to the 'realities' of schools. However, Circular 24/89 was not the only policy text to affect initial teacher education in the early 1990s. Also significant were a number of initiatives designed explicitly to deal with the government's third policy priority – maintaining an adequate supply of recruits into the teaching profession. The late 1980s, just like the late 1990s, was a period of considerable shortages in recruitment. This stimulated the development of a range of policies aimed at establishing a number of 'new routes' into the teaching profession. By the time we undertook our research, these policy initiatives had begun to be put into operation. It is to a consideration of these policies that we now turn.

Notes

1 When we asked HMI for a list, they referred us to lists drawn up by the professional associations (UCET, NATFHE); this is apparently what they used!
2 Interestingly, this figure has not changed significantly even today, despite the development of School Centred Initial Teacher Training (SCITT) schemes. See Chapters 5 and 6.
3 The Articled Teacher Scheme was an experimental two-year PGCE course in which students received a bursary and spent 80 per cent of their time based in schools. Further details are given in Chapter 4.
4 For a discussion of the importance of 'modelling' in student teacher learning, see Furlong (2000).

4 New populations, new professionalism?

The Government's aim is to provide a diversity of routes into teaching, offering a variety of choices to people with different skills, knowledge, experience, background and family circumstances. Taken together, innovative, non-conventional routes to qualified teacher status (QTS) will soon account for more than 10% of the annual intake to ITT.

(DES 1991)

Introduction

As we indicated in Chapter 1, maintaining an adequate supply of teachers is always an important issue for any government. In 1991, the year when we conducted our first national survey, 23,796 students entered initial teacher training courses in England and Wales; in 1996/7, at the end of our research, the number entering training had increased to 30,660 (DfEE 1998c). Given the sheer numbers involved, maintaining an adequate supply of recruits is necessarily challenging. However, the difficulties of maintaining recruitment are not consistent. In some years, particularly when the economy is buoyant and there is a strong demand for graduates from elsewhere, recruitment into teaching tends to dip; in these periods recruitment emerges as a key policy issue for governments. At other times, when there is less competition from other forms of employment, the issue of recruitment seems to command less importance within the policy process.

During the period covered by the two MOTE studies, we witnessed peaks and troughs in recruitment. The end of the 1980s and the end of the 1990s were periods of severe shortages; both periods therefore saw a growing number of policy initiatives focusing explicitly on recruitment. By contrast, the early and mid-1990s was a period of stable recruitment, mirroring the general downturn in demand for graduates elsewhere in the economy. As a result, during that period, recruitment was a less significant issue within the policy process.

Given the time lag in policy implementation, it was the initiatives of the late 1980s that were beginning to be influential at the time of our first MOTE study. The economic boom of the late 1980s meant that those in higher education found it progressively more and more difficult to fill their courses. As a result, during that period, the government encouraged the introduction of a range of 'new routes' into teaching, partly at least with the aim of attracting new populations into the teaching profession (Barrett *et al.* 1992b). As we argue below, however, some of these new routes had a double purpose in policy terms. The structure of some of the new training programmes that were devised had as much to do with challenging conventional models of professional preparation as bringing in new populations. Particularly significant in this regard were the Articled and Licensed Teacher Schemes. We therefore chose to make a particular study of these initiatives in our research. However, before turning to these courses in detail, we will present the findings from our survey of all the 'non-conventional' courses established at the time.

New routes, old models?

During the late 1980s, higher education institutions were encouraged to develop a range of new course models to complement the traditional four-year undergraduate and one-year postgraduate courses. At undergraduate level, the four-year Bachelor of Education (BEd) or Bachelor of Arts/Science (BA/BSc) with qualified teacher status (QTS), were joined by shortened two- and three-year undergraduate courses. For students who already had a degree, a variety of routes to the award of Postgraduate Certificate in Education (PGCE), in addition to the conventional one-year course, became available. In 1991–92, higher education institutions in England and Wales offered 83 of these non-conventional courses. In addition, as we will discuss in more detail below, a new and potentially non-graduate Licensed Teacher route to QTS was also available through local education authorities (LEAs) in some parts of England. The alternative routes into the teaching profession available in 1991–92 are described in Table 4.1.

In the first MOTE project, we were particularly interested in examining these different modes of teacher education and chose to include a wide range of such non-conventional courses in our case study sample (see Appendix for more details). Overall it seems that these courses were relatively successful in broadening the base of recruitment. Many of the students recruited onto them would not have considered a career in teaching without the more flexible entry requirements and training arrangements that were made available. So, for example, our survey showed that non-conventional courses were generally more successful at attracting older students. While mature students comprised over two-thirds of the student intake on only 9 per cent of all courses, 40 per cent of the non-conventional courses recruited over two-thirds of students aged 31 or over. The gender profile of students on non-conventional courses was also distinctive. The proportion of female-dominated courses (i.e. courses where more than two-thirds of the students were female) reflected the overall figures – roughly half of all courses. The proportion of male dominated courses however was significantly different

Table 4.1 Alternative routes to qualified teacher status available in 1991–92

Route and award	Length	Distinctive features
Undergraduate:		
Shortened BEd	2 years	For students with relevant experience and at least one year's successful higher education study (e.g. HND/HNC)
Shortened BA/BSc (QTS)	3 years	Reduced emphasis on certain aspects of subject study. Route open to students with HNC/BTec
Postgraduate:		
Part-time PGCE	2 years	Mostly secondary shortage subjects
Conversion PGCE	2 years	Mostly secondary shortage subjects. Students had a degree in a subject other than that for which they were training
Articled Teacher Scheme (PGCE)	2 years	LEA involvement. Students spent 80 per cent of their time in schools and 20 per cent of their time in the higher education institution
Non-graduate:		
Licensed Teacher Scheme	2 years	LEA schemes. Licensed teachers based full-time in schools with release for training. Can be non-graduates

from that of the total sample: 34 per cent of non-conventional courses, compared with only 1 per cent of teacher training courses overall, reported that more than two-thirds of their student intake was male. These courses were mostly two-year PGCE conversion courses and two-year BEd courses. Non-conventional courses were also more likely to attract students from ethnic minority groups; 16 per cent of the non-conventional courses, compared with only 5 per cent of courses overall, reported that over a third of their students were from ethnic minority groups.

Despite all of these achievements, it needs to be recognized that actual student numbers on these alternative courses were small, totalling only 1193 in higher education provided courses and approximately 700 licensed teachers in each of the first two years of the scheme. Survey data collected from 74 of the 83 non-conventional courses on offer during 1991–92 (see Table 4.2) illustrate the size of the particular routes. These figures need to be set against the total intake for conventional courses at the time of around 24,000; they therefore represented approximately 5 per cent of the total.

If we add these data to the topography of teacher education described in the previous chapter, a highly complex pattern of national provision is revealed. At the time of our first MOTE study, different types of courses and different higher education sectors were attracting rather different types of

Table 4.2   Non-conventional higher education courses: by sector and
student numbers (MOTE survey data)

Route	Number of courses			Total	Number of students			Total
	Univ.	*Poly.*	*CHE*		*Univ.*	*Poly.*	*CHE*	
2 year BEd	3	17	6	26	21	428	138	587
3 year BA/BSc	2	0	0	2	11	0	0	11
Part-time PGCE	7	4	1	12	72	65	10	147
PGCE conversion	7	1	3	11	59	21	23	103
Articled Teacher Schemes	9	5	9	23	102	59	184	345
Total	28	27	19	74	265	573	355	1193

students in terms of age, ethnicity, gender and previous experience. The aim
of the diversity of provision within the system seemed to be closely related
to the issue of student recruitment, which varied significantly between different types of courses and different types of institution.

However, despite the search for 'new populations', our case study work
highlighted the fact that most of the non-conventional courses that were
developed did not in themselves constitute a significant challenge to the
conventional approaches to teacher education nor therefore to conventional
models of teacher professionalism. In the majority of cases, the content of
training offered these new populations differed little from that made available in mainstream courses.

There were, however, two exceptions to this conclusion. These were the
Articled and Licensed Teacher Schemes. In sharp contrast to other non-
conventional routes, these initiatives, we would suggest, were designed deliberately to link the search for new populations with the piloting of new
ways of training teachers. Although they were small in number they were
given a high profile, thereby demonstrating the government of the day's
interest in reshaping the nature of teachers' professionalism. It is to a consideration of these two types of training that we now turn.

The Articled Teacher Scheme

Articled Teachers are pioneers of the school-based approach. It is an
important experiment which should be put in perspective. The Government's aim is to provide a diversity of routes into teaching offering a
variety of choices to people with different skills, knowledge, experience,
backgrounds and family circumstances.

(DES 1991)

The Articled Teacher Scheme, which ran from 1989–94, was an entirely
new form of school-based PGCE. Students, who had to be graduates, spent

two years, rather than one year, in training with 80 per cent of their time in school. Somewhat counter to government trends at the time, schemes were to be established by local education authorities (LEAs) working in consortia with higher education institutions. The scheme as a whole was relatively generously funded; articled teachers were given a bursary rather than a means-tested grant and school-based mentors were paid for their work with students in schools.

Officially, the scheme, which was announced on the same day as the Licensed Teacher Scheme, was designed as a recruitment strategy. As the letter inviting tenders from potential consortia put it, 'Our objective will be to support a variety of types of course under the scheme while giving priority to schemes designed to address teacher shortage' (DES 1989c). In the secondary area, it was confined to shortage subjects such as mathematics, science and modern languages and this, combined with the generous nature of the funding and the involvement of LEAs, meant that the scheme certainly had the potential to address shortages.

The slightly more generous funding to students meant that the scheme could attract some entrants who would otherwise find it financially impossible to take up training. This point was confirmed by many of the articled teachers (ATs) to whom we spoke. Students were certainly attracted to the school-based nature of the training, the majority seeing it as a more effective introduction to the profession.

> The other thing was I didn't think I'd like to go through a one year course and then be thrown in at the deep end. I liked the idea of growing, paddling if you like rather than swimming.

For many of them, however, the money was important too, as in the case of this secondary AT:

> Finance was the reason as well. The main reason was that you spent more time in school but the financial aspect was important as well.

A primary student made essentially the same point:

> The money was a very big incentive and basically it was everything I was looking for, spending time in the classroom . . . I really wanted the first hand experience.

The involvement of LEAs also meant that schemes and training places in schools could be targeted in areas where there was little training provision or where the shortages were most severe. The fact that 80 per cent of time was to be spent in a local school meant that, potentially at least, the Articled Teacher Scheme was particularly attractive to non-mobile mature graduates, such as women at home with family responsibilities.

However, in policy terms, the Articled Teacher Scheme was not only of relevance to teacher shortages. The fact that so much of the course was to be based in schools meant that at the ideological level it had real significance in challenging conventional models of teacher education. As the quotation from the DES at the opening of this section indicates, as a scheme it was pioneering – it was a generously funded experiment to produce a high quality school-based route into teaching.[1] Whether in reality it was that radically different was something that we were interested in exploring.

The Articled Teacher Scheme officially began in September 1990 with 16 consortia and 410 trainees. As the figures in Table 4.2 show, in our national survey, we collected data from 23 schemes with 345 trainees. We also included two secondary and three primary Articled Teacher Schemes within our 50 case studies courses, visiting schools, higher education institutions, observing and talking to students, teachers and lecturers as with other courses.

Course size and recruitment

Most of the schemes we surveyed were small – only three of the 23 courses had more than 25 students. As a strategy for recruiting secondary students in shortage areas, the scheme was not particularly successful and at the end of the first year there was evidence of such courses finding real difficulty in filling their places (a point confirmed by Ofsted 1993a in their review of the scheme). However, we found that Articled Teacher Schemes were far more likely to be targeting 'non-standard' students than conventional courses. Overall, 89 per cent of ATs on primary courses and 60 per cent on secondary courses were women – slightly higher proportions of women than on conventional courses. In our national survey of all courses, we found that only 24 out of the total of 317 nationally had targeted mature students; eight of these 24 were Articled Teacher Schemes with over two-thirds of their students over 31 years of age.

Overwhelmingly then articled teachers were women and many of them mature, but they were also overwhelmingly white and born in the UK. Some schemes were intended to be particularly targeting minority ethnic groups but in this regard the Articled Teacher Scheme was not particularly successful. As the course coordinator of a primary scheme in a polytechnic explained:

> There just isn't a big enough pool of appropriately qualified people who meet the target . . . we are in sympathy with the targeting policy, especially as the one-year PGCE does not produce ethnic minority teachers, but it is extremely problematic and is affecting course viability.

Because of such problems a number of Articled Teacher Schemes that had been specifically targeted at minority ethnic recruitment had to close down after the first intake.

Training in school

As we have already noted, ATs spent 80 per cent of their time in school and unlike licensed teachers (see below) they were to be supernumerary throughout their two years. Designated mentors were appointed in each

school, trained and paid for their work. This was a highly significant innovation in that although at that time there was a growing recognition of the
importance of mentors in supporting students' school-based learning
(McIntyre *et al.* 1993), our national survey showed that in the vast majority
of schemes the role was not properly defined and in only about 12 per cent
of courses were they paid directly for their work – even then it was usually
only a very modest honorarium.

By contrast, designated mentors involved in the Articled Teacher Scheme
were twice as likely to be paid as those supporting other schemes. Moreover,
they often received significant payments for their work – between £500 and
£1000 a year. Training was also more widely available. From our national
survey we found that training for teachers to support their work with students was only available in about half of all courses. In the Articled Teacher
Scheme it was available in 22 out of the 23 courses surveyed.

One consequence of the different pattern of attendance with 80 per cent
of time in school was that mentors felt much more committed to 'their'
articled teacher. As one mentor explained:

> You didn't have the contact with the [conventional] students. They
> were picked up by coach at 3.30 when school ended. Here they are
> members of staff really and they join in activities. At lunchtimes they
> may drift in for a chat so it's a different sort of relationship altogether –
> you kept contact with them even when they went off on their other
> teaching practices. We went in to see them so we were constantly in
> contact – and liaised with the teachers in charge of them then which
> was nice too. The usual PGCE students are here for a month – they
> then go off for a second practice somewhere else and often we get them
> back for a third in the summer term but not always. It's quite detached
> in that respect.

Another made a similar point:

> We never felt sort of ownership of students in that sense; these ones I
> feel totally responsible for if things go wrong. Whether it's my fault or
> not I feel that it's my responsibility to sort things out because they've
> got this two-year commitment to the school and it's totally reciprocal.

However, in looking at the role of schools in the training process, it is
important to recognize that in the Articled Teacher Scheme, higher education was intended to retain a strong role. Although trainees were to be
based in school for 80 per cent of their two-year course, their training was
not intended to be provided entirely by teachers. As the letter setting out
the detail of the scheme put it:

> They would receive most of their formal training in school and such
> training would be delivered both by the institution's academic and pro-
> fessional tutors and by selected members of the staff of the school.
> Schemes should allow for the training needs of such staff.
>
> (DES 1989c)

Despite the 80–20 split in terms of time then, it was in reality much more of an equal partnership in training. As one mentor on a primary course put it:

> It's a very happy marriage the relationship that we have now, the sort of hand in glove, the almost *equal partners* – that is very good and works very well.

In all of the courses we visited, staff in higher education still played a very important part in leading the formal aspects of the training – even when it was undertaken in school. A teacher in a primary scheme described what was in fact a common approach:

> They were structured from the very beginning of each term. Work would be done in college and we would be told in advance what the work would be and then if there was something to be followed up, obviously we would take it from there. Very much the formal seminar was based on what had been done in college with obviously special relevance to the school which you were working in.

Outside the formal, college-driven part of the work, mentors took on a more generalized role – perhaps more detailed but not fundamentally different from mentors working in conventional courses. As one teacher explained,

> Certainly it's pastoral – it's everything, it's health, personal problems, problems of discipline, all sorts of ways in which we've counselled them and spoken to them.

Significantly absent from this list was any mention of subject work, but as one AT explained:

> I find that the questions I really need to ask aren't really related to the subject anyway – questions are usually on classroom control and management.

Tutors, on the other hand, continued to bring a different and sometimes challenging perspective on classroom practice:

> I think the different perspective can be helpful. The college tutor came in and I was teaching the lesson quite happily and I thought it was fine but at the end he said, 'Yes, but how much time did you spend talking to the girls in the class?' I nearly fell through the floor and then when I looked back over the lesson I found I hadn't actually picked myself up on that, and I knew about the problem of boys dominating, I knew about it, I was conscious of it and yet somehow the lesson had swivelled in their direction and I had failed to realize that the girls had been marginalized. I was really – I'm not saying I'm a very good feminist or anything – but I really was annoyed with myself as a woman to have allowed myself to let that happen. And it was only picked up by my [college] supervisor – no one else seemed to have picked that up.

In 1992, HMI carried out their own evaluation of the Articled Teacher Scheme by visiting five consortia. HMI concluded that, in the vast majority of cases (90 per cent), ATs' progress was satisfactory or better and 50 per cent were judged to be good or very good. A small percentage were judged to be truly outstanding, achieving standards seldom seen amongst trainees; however, the overwhelming majority were not considered to be significantly better than students trained on a conventional PGCE course. Where they did score strongly though was in their confidence and in their understanding of whole school life. As HMI said:

> Almost invariably, Articled Teachers adopted a professional attitude. They had a better understanding of the pattern of school life and the role of the teacher and took a more active part in the life of the school than many students trained by other means.
>
> (Ofsted 1993a: 7)

This confidence was something that we picked up too in our interviews with students. The ATs we met on school visits were very much part of their school, acting as members of staff with access to and responsibilities in all aspects of school life. In this regard, they were very different from the majority of student teachers at the time. This was an advantage that the ATs themselves noticed, as was explained by this secondary student:

> We feel more at home in the profession – I've spoken to PGCE people here about it and the fact that we've done the whole school, we've done the parents' evening, the whole lot and you feel more confident . . . we know exactly what it's all about, the whole school aspect.

Nevertheless, HMI did report some important weaknesses (Ofsted 1993a). One problem was variability. The quality of the training within each of the consortia they visited varied considerably and this led, in their judgement, to highly variable standards of attainment. The degree of inconsistency was, they argued, considerably more evident than in conventional PGCE courses.

A further significant weakness was that many primary students were coming to the end of their course with insufficient knowledge in particular subject areas, and in secondary courses, despite having a degree in their subject, some students remained ignorant about key parts of the National Curriculum. As HMI commented: 'The extra time available through this form of training is spent in schools which are not resourced to offer the necessary curriculum and specialist subject training' (Ofsted 1993a: 4). In other words, the increased time devoted to initial training was, in the view of HMI, something of a lost opportunity because so much of it was devoted to school experience. It might have been making them more confident and more encultured into the school, but it was not necessarily, at least in HMI's judgement, making them better teachers.

The Articled Teacher Scheme and professionalism

> The Articled Teacher Scheme is a forerunner of the move to make initial training more school-based.
>
> (Ofsted 1993a: 23)

The Articled Teacher Scheme was an experiment. The fact that it cost almost twice as much to train a teacher than by a conventional PGCE course meant that it was never likely to become established as a permanent way forward. Once HMI had reached the conclusion that its graduates were not fundamentally different in quality from those coming through more conventional courses, the writing was on the wall and the scheme came to an end in 1994. However, as we will see in the chapters that follow, by 1994 the Articled Teacher Scheme had already served its purpose in that new secondary and primary regulations issued in 1992 and 1993 (DfE 1992, DfE 1993a) meant that all courses had to move to a school-based model – without the luxury of additional resources and additional time in school.

Despite its short life, the Articled Teacher Scheme was extremely significant in establishing a more practical and professionally oriented form of initial teacher education. Its importance lay both at the ideological and at the practical level. Ideologically it demonstrated that schools could take on far greater responsibility in the training process than had hitherto been regarded as possible by many people. This was a message that was important both for the schools and for those in higher education.[2] As such, it did much to attract a growing number of teacher educators to the *principle* of school-based teacher education.[3]

Its real influence, however, was at a practical level in that it provided the DfE with many lessons that were to influence future policy: the need for funding in schools if they were to be involved; the need for training school mentors and other teachers if they were to have the ability and the confidence to do the job; the practical necessity and educational value of developing a whole school commitment to the training process; the need for a single curriculum running across both higher education and the school; the need to develop new and more effective forms of quality control if teacher education were not to become an entirely fragmented affair. As we will see in Chapters 5, 6 and 7, all of these were issues that were central to many of the policy initiatives that formed the context for our second MOTE project. In many ways then the Articled Teacher Scheme, despite the fact that it was relatively small and short-lived, did much to pave the way for changes in initial teacher education in the mid-1990s.

The Licensed Teacher Scheme

The Licensed Teacher Scheme was launched in 1989 (DES 1989b) on the same day as the Articled Teacher Scheme. Because of this and because both schemes involved trainees spending much of their time in school, the two schemes were often confused by teachers and by the media. In reality they were very different, with the Licensed Teacher Scheme being a far more radical departure from conventional training routes. Whereas the Articled Teacher Scheme was a PGCE with a systematic and structured training programme organized through higher education, the Licensed Teacher Scheme allowed mature entrants with a minimum of two years of higher education to be recruited directly to positions in schools and provided with any necessary training by their employers 'on the job'. The first licences were granted in spring 1990 and, by July 1992, 1500 licences had been issued. By the time Ofsted undertook its first report on the scheme in 1992 (Ofsted 1993b) 500 teachers had qualified by this route.

Under these new regulations, the requirement for a teacher entering employment to have a recognized teaching qualification was thus waived. Instead, licensed teachers, who had to be at least 24 years old and have at least two years unspecified higher education, were to be given a licence for up to two years.[4] They were to be appointed to paid posts and provided training 'on the job' by their employer – either an LEA or, in the case of grant maintained schools, the school governors. It was up to the licensed teacher's employer to decide how that training was to be organized – whether it was to be entirely school provided or involve periods of formal training with the LEA or at an institution of higher education. At the end of the period of the licence, the trainee was to be assessed for readiness for the award of qualified teacher status.

Officially, it was claimed that the main purpose of the Licensed Teacher Scheme was to 'tidy up' non-standard entry routes to qualified teacher status. However, it was very quickly recognized by LEAs as providing an opportunity for dealing with teacher shortages; many LEAs therefore gave the proposals their support. Significantly though the strongest support came from neo-conservatives who saw it as at least implicit government support for the model for school-provided initial teacher education they had been arguing for. For example, the Hillgate Group's *Learning to Teach* argued that the licensing route was a far better way of producing good teachers than many existing courses.

However, the fact that the Licensed Teacher Scheme introduced a non-graduate route into teaching, and that it took training out of the hands of higher education, caused considerable anxiety among many sections of the teaching profession itself. Within a week of the publication of the Green Paper announcing the scheme (DES 1988a), both of the major teacher unions came out strongly against the proposal. The National Union of Teachers (NUT) deplored the development and argued that 'the absence of a professional qualification for all teachers cannot maintain, let alone improve standards in education' (Doug McAvoy, quoted in *TES* 25 May 1988). The National Association of Schoolmasters and Union of Women Teachers (NAS/UWT) described it as 'an attempt to get through the problem of shortages by dilution instead of responding to market forces by increasing pay to attract better teachers. They want to pedestrianise the teaching profession' (Nigel De Gruchy, quoted in the *TES* 25 May 1988). As the *TES* sardonically put it, 'putting them [the middle aged refugees from industry and commerce] into schools without preliminary training is not, on the face of it, a particularly good idea' (Leader comment, *TES* 25 May 1988).

It was against this background that the MOTE team decided to make a detailed study of the new scheme in 1992.[5] As in our main study, the licensed teacher survey involved two elements: a national questionnaire of providers, and in-depth case studies of a stratified sample of five schemes. The questionnaires were completed by a representative of the scheme organizer – usually an LEA officer; returns covered 70 per cent of all trainees nationally. Case studies included interviews with LEA personnel, headteachers, mentors, licensed teachers and others directly involved in the running of the schemes. A total of five LEA staff, 10 headteachers, 10 mentors and 10 licensees (five primary and five secondary) were interviewed (further details of the sampling and methodology are given in the Appendix).

Significantly, our survey revealed some rather unexpected characteristics of the national intake to the Licensed Teacher Scheme. As in other routes into teaching, about two-thirds of all licensees were women; however nearly half were from minority ethnic groups. The data also called into question the image of the licensed teachers as poorly qualified non-graduates. Overall, 44 per cent of the intake were first degree holders, one in 12 had postgraduate qualifications of some sort and just under half were overseas trained teachers. Only 12 per cent were indigenous non-graduates. There were nearly equal numbers of primary and secondary licensed teachers but three-quarters of all primary trainees were based in London. Individual licensees reported very different personal reasons for applying to participate in the scheme. For many it was the only feasible route into teaching in view of their existing qualifications or financial commitments.

The MOTE survey results suggested that there were two rather different types of scheme in operation: those initiated and managed by LEAs and those managed by LEAs but not initiated by them. These schemes were set up in response to pressure from individual schools. The former 'LEA led' schemes tended to be larger (up to 41 licensees) and more frequently in the major conurbations, particularly London; the latter schemes were typically smaller (sometimes as few as one licensee) and based in the shire counties. Two-thirds of the schemes (41 out of 59) were small, recruiting under 15 licensees; at the other extreme, four large LEA schemes accounted for one-quarter of all licensees.

The most frequently reported reason for individual schools taking on a licensed teacher was in response to staffing shortages, which were acute at the time. The headteacher of one secondary school in the southwest described the situation he faced as one of 'desperation'. Another said, 'I have never appointed a licensed teacher when a qualified one has been available . . . That is a comment on teacher supply here.' LEAs also indicated that their most common reason for initiating a Licensed Teacher Scheme was to respond to teacher shortages. However, their second most common reason was to secure the qualification of overseas trained teachers. Overseas trained teachers accounted for one-third of all licensees in our survey, nearly a half (63) of these being Americans working in London-based schemes. As one LEA official explained:

> There were a lot of teachers in the authority who were working in schools without QTS – mainly overseas trained. It started off being limited to those people . . . the only instance when it's not overseas-trained teachers is where people have been in the LEA for a large number of years. One person has been here [unqualified] for 17 years.

This finding lends some credence to the official view that the Licensed Teacher Scheme was 'a tidying up procedure'. Another common reason for establishing a scheme was to encourage ethnic minority and/or bilingual teachers into the classroom. As one Jamaican licensed teacher said:

> At the outset I was wondering why is it that having been trained in Jamaica . . . I was wondering why it is that I have to come here to gain QTS. But having looked at it I realized that I am coming out of a different system. A culture that is completely different and I need that time.

As we have already indicated, at the time of our survey nearly 50 per cent of licensees were from ethnic minorities, most of them on LEA-led schemes deliberately designed to recruit and train them.

Initially there was some concern that the appointment of licensed teachers might lead to conflicts with other staff. However, once appointed to schools, any initial resistance nearly always melted away. Most licensees we interviewed reported being well-received in their schools and, with a few exceptions, they were positive about the training they were receiving. As one primary head explained:

> The next hurdle was telling the staff . . . I was a bit anxious about this – there had been a lot of negative publicity about the licensing scheme that year. I decided to tell them the whole truth so I explained that she had taken a training course and done everything except her finals. They all said, 'Oh, poor girl, what a shame that she's having to do two years' probation.' So that was OK.

In looking at the character of the training schemes devised, data from the MOTE research suggested that there were as many variations as there were LEAs and schools participating. However, our findings strongly suggested that the size of the scheme was a very significant factor in defining the character and quality of the training offered. In large, LEA-initiated schemes, officers tended to take a strong role in overseeing recruitment and in providing 'off site' training. For example an Assistant Education Officer in one large LEA-led scheme said:

All our licensed teachers have previous teaching experience and all are graduates. They are all actually teachers rather than career changers. The selection procedure is rigorous because we have maintained the criteria of graduate status and teaching experience. A significant number of our licensed teachers have qualifications above graduate level and substantial teaching experience.

Another LEA representative explained:

The Teacher Associations were keen that the scheme should not dilute the profession through non-graduate entry. We therefore worked with them in developing the scheme – and laid down the criterion that licensed teachers should be graduates.

In schemes that were not LEA-led there was much greater variability in who was recruited. Some heads and governors insisted on graduate status and previous teaching experience, others did not. As an LEA official explained in one such scheme:

We do have less control over those licensed teachers who are nominated by schools. Ultimately these schools make the appointments and all the LEA can do is try to strengthen the quality of these appointments by including them in the training programme and trying to get QTS for them.

There were also substantial variations in terms of the 'off site' training offered. In one scheme, all licensees attended a specially devised training course lasting a term in a local polytechnic, but at the other extreme one licensee was provided with an Open University course and told to get on with it. Elsewhere, licensees joined existing higher education-provided courses, though in some cases these were ill-suited to their particular needs.

However well, or badly, organized the 'off site' training was, in reality much of the responsibility for day-to-day training lay with individual schools. Yet the nature and quality of what schools were willing and able to provide also varied substantially. For example, in the larger LEA-led schemes, mentors received carefully structured training and worked closely and consistently with their licensees. Others had received no training for their role whatsoever, were given no time to carry out their duties and at best could only offer ad hoc support when the licensee asked for it. Some schools, it seems, were able and willing to give their trainees high quality support; others – for a variety of reasons – were not.

As the first Ofsted report on Licensed Teacher Schemes noted, most licensed teachers were appointed to LEAs and schools with some recruitment difficulties. Some LEAs 'tried not to use very poor schools as placements but the priority was nearly always to cover a vacancy rather than to find a good training school' (Ofsted 1993b: 7). Our own survey confirmed that nearly three-quarters of LEAs surveyed indicated that they were prepared to make

Licensed Teacher Schemes available to *any* school that requested. Perhaps unsurprisingly, Ofsted (1993b: 3, 8) concluded that a significant number of the training placements were problematic:

> Although most training placements were considered adequate, only 15% were considered good. Many of those Licensed Teachers who were performing poorly were in schools which were considered unsatisfactory for the training of teachers . . . Hardly any of those Licensed Teachers in poor placements were better than satisfactory and poor teaching was often linked to a poor placement.

Licensed teachers and professionalism

We argued above that the main legacy of the Articled Teacher Scheme was the detailed insights it gave into the practicalities of running school-based teacher education. By contrast, the impact of the Licensed Teacher Scheme for teacher professionalism was, we would suggest, primarily ideological. In its early stages it had a high national profile and was publicly supported by a number of neo-conservatives with a ready access to the media and the government of the day (e.g. Lawlor 1990). The fact that this route provided a legitimate way to gain qualified teacher status without a degree and without taking part in a training programme organized through higher education was itself extremely significant. It certainly served publicly to undermine the claim that forms of knowledge traditionally made available through higher education were a necessary part of professional preparation.

As we have seen, though, the reality was not as straightforward as this. At the time of our research only a minority of British trainees (12 per cent) had no degree and for the overwhelming majority (89 per cent) forms of systematic, non-school based training were provided either by LEAs or through higher education institutions. It is clear that many individual headteachers and certainly many LEAs saw themselves as promoting similar forms of professionalism to those made available within traditional higher education-based courses. The majority refused to take non-graduates on principle and nearly half of the schemes claimed that they were based on a similar range of course philosophies to those found in higher education-based courses (the competent teacher, the reflective practitioner etc.).

However if we look at the structure and content of training (including the personnel and forms of integration typically made available) we can see that despite these traditional aspirations, what was in reality offered to licensees was significantly different from that made available in more conventional courses. Even in the small number of courses with substantial out-of-school training, the majority of the trainees' experience was actually doing the job of teaching – in a particular context with a particular group of children. This provided a very different basis for training from traditional schemes which emphasize 'indirect' rather than 'direct' practical experiences

(Furlong *et al.* 1988). In supporting learning through this 'direct' practical experience, school-based mentors were critical to the scheme. They themselves had little training and little formal opportunity to develop and provide a broader perspective on their work. They were also seldom provided opportunities to work in collaboration with those providing out-of-school support; the opportunities for trainees to integrate different forms of professional knowledge, even where they had access to it, were therefore strictly limited.

The reality was that licensees were provided with a rich and extensive *experience*; whether they were provided *training* was more problematic. Yet as one Education Officer suggested:

> For the scheme to have credibility it has to be seen that training does take place. It doesn't even matter if most of it takes place in school – the place doesn't really matter as long as people are seen to be doing it.

However, our observation of the Licensed Teacher Scheme would suggest that when schools were working with only one or two licensees, and when they were provided little in the way of support and few resources, their chances of turning 'experience' into 'training' were limited. In these circumstances the best hope, as many headteachers realized, was to try and select high quality licensees who already had substantial experience. One secondary school headteacher from London spoke for many when he said:

> Theoretically we are happy with this as a route. But we have been able to choose the candidates and have also restricted the number of licensed teachers we take. The consequences of schools taking greater numbers of licensed teachers or losing control of selection would be enormous.

Models of integration – professionalism re-formed?

In the final part of this chapter we want to reflect on the extent to which the forms of initial teacher education we documented in our first MOTE study did indeed constitute a new approach to professional preparation likely to produce a new model of professionalism. As we saw in Chapter 1, many of those in the 'context of influence' close to the government of the day did want a new form of professionalism: one where the forms of pedagogic knowledge traditionally made available through higher education had markedly less significance than in the past – a model of professionalism that was closely geared to the practical realities of day-to-day school life. Moreover, policy texts of the time were clearly influenced by those aspirations. As we have seen, both Circular 24/89 (DES 1989a) and the Articled Teacher Scheme placed great emphasis on practical, school-based work. The higher education-based work that did remain had to be much more closely 'integrated' with the world of school than in the past (Ofsted 1993a). The Licensed Teacher Scheme, potentially at least, marginalized the role of higher education entirely. But to what extent were these aspirations actually realized

Figure 4.1 Models of integration and partnership in initial teacher education (1992 data)

	Integrated models			
Traditional HEI-led models X	HEI-led/school-focused agenda	Weak school base A	Strong school base C	New school-led models Y
	Jointly led/joint agenda	B	D	

in practice? We will attempt to answer this question by examining different models of 'integration' in initial teacher education.

Looking back over the data presented in this and the previous chapter, we would suggest that, by 1992, initial teacher education courses in England and Wales had put significant effort into 'integrating' their college and school-based programmes. However, not all courses were adopting the same strategy for integration. We would further suggest that it is possible to identify a number of different 'ideal typical models' of integration that were in use at the time. These are set out in Figure 4.1.

Models X and Y in Figure 4.1 represent the extremes of a continuum in that they involve no integration whatsoever. Model X is the traditional higher education-based model of the type that was the focus of the reforms of the 1980s (DES 1984, 1989a). University and college lecturers would define the content of the course, selecting the skills, knowledge and understandings to which students were introduced. As a result of that control, course content would be largely theoretical in character, firmly divorced from the world of the school; teaching practice would be about the application of theories learned in college. As a consequence, teachers would have little, if any, formal input into the course; responsibility for the supervision and assessment of students' practical teaching competence would remain firmly with those in higher education. As the results of our national survey clearly demonstrated, by 1991/2 no such model existed in practice (if it ever did).

Model Y, at the other end of the continuum, represents those models where the skills, knowledge and understandings promoted within the course are defined by and focused entirely on the school. Neither the staff of any university or college, nor the forms of professional knowledge to which they have access, form part of the training programme. Some of the smaller and less organized Licensed Teacher Schemes we discussed earlier in this chapter were approaching this end of the continuum, although, as we have seen, the vast majority of Licensed Teacher Schemes did attempt to maintain a role for higher education.

Models A, B, C and D, which have as their basis some form of integration between higher education and school-based programmes, represent the overwhelming majority of courses in England and Wales in 1991/2. Within these different models there appeared to be three key variables that influenced the forms of integration achieved: the degree to which courses were physically based in school; the degree to which school staff were involved in leading the course (planning, teaching and assessing); and the degree to which teachers contributed to the definition of the content of the course.

At the time of our fieldwork, Model A was by far the most common approach to integration. In such a model, those in the college remained in clear control of the course, defining its content, teaching its courses, and assessing the students. Teachers were seen as relatively distant, having little input to the course apart from the traditional role of supervising students on teaching practice. The move towards integration was primarily achieved through redesigning the college-based programme to become school-focused and practical in its nature. As we saw in Chapter 3, many of the courses we visited had fundamentally reformed the structure, content and forms of assessment of their college-based programmes so as to relate more directly to the world of the school, and tutors deliberately adopted forms of pedagogy that would model teaching styles that could be used in school. By the use of these strategies, many of the courses we examined had become highly practically oriented, despite little evidence of attempts to restructure the nature of school-based work. The form of training offered by such courses was therefore 'indirectly practical' (Furlong *et al.* 1988), defined and delivered by those in higher education but intentionally distant from the real world complexities of the school and the classroom.

Model B represented a modified version of this common approach. Here, there was still a relatively weak school base, though there was a more sustained attempt to ensure that at least some aspects of the course were jointly devised and jointly led. Assessment of practical teaching competence and of other assignments were also more likely to be a shared responsibility. This was the philosophy of Initial Training – Inservice Education of Teachers (IT–INSET) (Everton and Impay 1989) which represented a distinctive approach to integration. Topics such as lesson preparation or curriculum development that might traditionally have been addressed exclusively within the training institution, were planned and led in school by teams of teachers and lecturers working together. Despite the involvement of teachers, however, the training as a whole remained firmly controlled by the college; it was they who constructed the course and located the opportunities for collaborative work within it. Moreover, the intention of the collaborative work was not necessarily to induct students into the workings of one particular school. In comparison with more recently developed school-based models, the aims were more generally conceived. The specifics of what students learn on any one topic may be located in one particular context, but it was the task of the tutor, who is firmly part of the teaching team, to place that learning in a broader framework for the student.

A four-year primary BA (QTS) course provided a useful example of this model:

On eight school visits, the tutor is there all day with the students. The tutor's role is to make the links and forge the integration; they are not there as a supervisor but as a link. Ten students work in each school and five in a classroom, so we work with two teachers . . . the tutor is part of a team working in a school and assessing that experience. We jointly plan, with the teachers, what our contribution should be on a topic. Then we always meet as a team to review what we have done at the end of the day. These are particular schools that particularly want to be involved in this work which is based on IT-INSET. They felt they got something back from it.

Or as a BEd course leader explained:

The teachers become very involved with what the students are doing. We design the activities – the teachers organize the situation in the classroom – the teachers help the students to get it done – they talk to the students about it. That seems to happen without any difficulty.

Model C was different again. In this model students spent a greater proportion of their time in school, though significant aspects of the curriculum remained organized and directed by the college. Interestingly, a number of the articled teacher courses we visited followed this model. Despite the fact that students were placed in schools for 80 per cent of their time, their college remained a significant force, planning the course as a whole, retaining control of key aspects of training and maintaining a strong role in assessment. For example, in one course, the LEAs involved insisted that each cohort of articled teachers were placed in a new consortium of schools in different parts of their counties. At the time of our fieldwork, a third group of schools was being prepared to take on students. This strategy certainly maximized the LEAs' opportunities to recruit non-standard entrants into local schools. However, it left the college clearly in control of the scheme as a whole; they were the only constant partner. Yet even some other schemes that were based on more permanent relationships with schools still seemed largely college-led. For example, on one course, tutors still managed the programme as a whole and visited the students once a week in the first year. As a tutor explained,

If you ask me, the college trains them and the school provides the opportunity for them to practise . . . The responsibility lies with the college to direct, but the schools have been marvellous in providing them with massive opportunities and lots of guidance and support because they don't want the responsibility beyond what they can cope with.

Clearly, increasing the amount of time students spend in schools does not necessarily introduce a reconceptualization of the training process, nor does it necessarily result in a school-led course.

The final model, Model D, was the one that most closely resembled the partnership approach that was to emerge after the next round of reforms announced in 1992 (DfE 1992; DfE 1993a). As noted above in our discussion of mentoring, this model depended on courses reassessing their conception of training; they had to move from an 'applications' model, where training took place elsewhere, to one where individual schools were seen as key training sites in themselves. In courses following this model of training, the development of students' practical teaching competence was accorded prime importance; moreover, the development of that competence was seen as being best achieved by students receiving their training in *particular* schools. The emphasis was on 'direct' rather than 'indirect' practical training (Furlong *et al.* 1988).

Clearly the most likely place for the development of such a model was within the Articled Teacher Scheme and indeed some of these courses were moving in this direction. However, there were other examples within our sample of conventional courses developing in this way too. For example as the course leader of one four-year BEd course described developments in his course:

> We are now building up much stronger networks between students, schools and tutors, keeping the students in the schools with serial practice for the continuity. Schools are given a tremendous amount of information about what's going on. We have a tremendous partnership with schools and it operates in so many different ways. Teachers are involved in selection, teachers are involved in delivering courses, we pay for supply, teachers are involved in our scheme. We have an annual conference for schools . . . We take stock with them, we share with them any ideas we are having, their ideas and much of the documentation about school experience is rewritten as a result of work with schools.

In another secondary PGCE course, students were attached to one school for the majority of their school year and much of their training was organized through that school attachment. Mentors and college lecturers were accorded 'equal but different' responsibilities, the mentors being given primary responsibility for supporting 'their' students as they developed their practical teaching skills throughout the year. Close contact was maintained between the college tutor and the mentor, rather than merely between tutor and student. Careful and regular communication meant that mentors were fully aware of the structure and content of the college-based course and were able to tailor their programme of work with the student in ways that complemented the college-based programme.

Conclusion

In conclusion we can suggest that in the early 1990s many courses, including many Articled Teacher Schemes, continued to be influenced by visions of professionalism made available by those in higher education. In the vast majority of cases, it was still those in universities, polytechnics and colleges who planned the structure and content of courses; it was they who defined what knowledge, skills and values students were expected to learn and develop. Certainly course content was more closely integrated with the practical world of school than in the past, but in the vast majority of cases those practicalities were interpreted through the visions of professionalism, particularly the notion of the 'reflective practitioner', made available by higher education tutors.

The Licensed Teacher Scheme was somewhat different for two reasons: first, because, in its early years at least, it was subject to so few external controls. The schemes produced were therefore immensely variable, some of them being systematically led by LEAs, others being largely ad hoc; second, because, however schemes were organized, the reality was that licensees spent the vast majority of their time actually doing the job of a teacher. As a result of their responsibilities, 'experience' was inevitably prioritized over 'training' and other forms of professional knowledge, whether made available by LEAs or through higher education, were likely to be marginalized. Despite the aspirations and hard work of some LEAs, we would suggest that at at the time of our research, the Licensed Teacher Scheme did imply a different vision of professionalism, one that was highly pragmatic and rooted entirely in the experience of particular schools. As such it served, if only modestly, to challenge traditional visions of professionalism sponsored by higher education.

The story of the early 1990s was nevertheless more one of continuity than of change. As we will see in Chapter 8, students were perhaps more satisfied with their training than in the past and it was certainly seen as more practically relevant, but there was a sense in which the models of training actually developed in the early 1990s were simply better or at least more effective ways of doing what many in higher education had wanted to do anyway rather than something entirely new. This is because the policy texts that were produced at the time were, in Bowe and Ball's (1992) terms, highly 'writerly'. What 'integration' meant was not defined. It was still accepted, by government and by Her Majesty's Inspectorate, that there were many different ways in which teacher education could be organized. Any of the ideal typical models defined above (A, B, C or D) were acceptable. As a result, most course leaders chose Model A, which left them firmly in charge.

Significantly, it was a recognition that perhaps not as much had changed as some of those in the 'context of influence' had intended that led to the next round of reforms begun in 1992. As Lawlor (1990: 21), one of the most outspoken New Right critics of teacher education, wrote at the time,

Contrary to the intentions of the 1980s' reforms, general theory continues to dominate at the expense of individual practice; and students are not encouraged to approach classroom teaching with an open mind or to develop individually as teachers. Instead they are expected to bring to the classroom, and to apply to their teaching, the generalised educational theories which they have been taught.

While we would not agree with her interpretation of the role of 'general theory' we would agree that perhaps less had changed in teacher education by the early 1990s than was intended. However, as we will see in the next chapter, things were about to change significantly.

Notes

1 As the DES official responsible for developing and managing the scheme said in a private communication, 'We read the findings from the Cambridge research on school-based teacher education that we commissioned in the early 1980s (Furlong *et al.* 1988) which talked about the value of school-based training if it was properly funded. In the Articled Teacher Scheme, we wanted to try and do it right.' (The implication may be that in the Licensed Teacher Scheme, which was announced on the same day and for which he was also responsible, the primary aim was not 'to do it right'!)
2 It is significant, however, that despite the success of the Articled Teacher Scheme, School-Centred Initial Teacher Training schemes (SCITT) which followed, where consortia of schools were given total responsibility for training, proved far less popular. The majority of schools have not been willing to take on the responsibility for training without the involvement of those in higher education. See Chapters 5 and 6.
3 Whether they were attracted in practice to the particular form of school-based teacher education that was thrust upon them in the middle 1990s is, of course, quite a different matter.
4 Originally, licensees had to be at least 26 years of age except for the case of overseas-trained teachers for whom the minimum age requirement was waived. Circular 13/91 (DES 1991) amended these regulations and reduced the minimum age to 24 years. The same circular allowed overseas-trained teachers with a year's teaching experience to teach under licence for as little as a term before being recommended for QTS.
5 For a fuller report of the MOTE study of the Licensed Teachers Scheme, see Barrett and Galvin (1993).

5 The policy context of MOTE 2 – the middle 1990s

Now is the time to press ahead with getting teacher training right. I meet too many young people who don't go into teaching because they are put off by the length of the course. Or they go on a course and give up because they are put off the idea of learning too much theory and not enough practice. I want to see students actually getting into a classroom for much more of the time while they train. I want them to learn how to control a noisy class of 30 kids by actually having to do it with the help of an experienced teacher and using their training courses to sort out the problems.

(Clarke 1991)

New policies – new challenges

The economic downturn of the early 1990s had a positive effect on recruitment into initial teacher education courses. As a result, concerns over supply, for the moment at least, became of secondary importance to the government, allowing other policy issues (re-forming professionalism, re-creating a national system) to come to the fore.

The quotation above comes from a speech made by the then Secretary of State for Education, Kenneth Clarke, to the Conservative Party conference in September 1991. Four months later, in January 1992, Mr Clarke kept his promise and issued a major new set of proposals for the reform of initial teacher education in England and Wales (Clarke 1992). These proposals were radical in many ways, most particularly in their suggestion that secondary students should spend 80 per cent of their time in school, thus significantly curtailing the role of higher education in the training process. After a period of consultation, however, this particular suggestion was modified to 66 per cent. Despite this concession, the new criteria for secondary (DfE 1992) and primary courses (DfE 1993a) involved a major restructuring of the organization and the curriculum of initial teacher education. It was against this background that the MOTE team applied to the ESRC for a further research project to monitor the implications of these changes.

Once again, our research included a further national survey (undertaken in 1996) and a more in-depth qualitative study of a subsample of 50 courses (undertaken in 1995) (see Appendix for more details of the methodology of MOTE 2).

As indicated earlier, in applying for a further grant, we recognized that the proposed changes were significant. What we were not aware of at the time was that 1992 would in retrospect be seen as a major watershed for teacher education in England and Wales. Mr Clarke's intervention marked the beginning of a very different, and much more confrontational period of reform; much of the confrontation was with those in higher education. Over the next three years, new policies came thick and fast, each of them seeming more radical than the last. These changes included the establishment of the Teacher Training Agency (TTA) and the abolition of the Council for the Accreditation of Teacher Education (CATE), the transfer of funding for teacher education from the Higher Education Funding Council for England (HEFCE) to the TTA, and the development of a new Ofsted inspection framework for teacher education. Other policy changes that affected the research included the ending of the Articled Teacher Scheme, and the establishment of School-Centred Initial Teacher Training (SCITT) schemes and The Open University distance learning scheme. Meanwhile, additional pressures on HEIs, such as the Research Assessment Exercise (RAE) and moves to semesterization and modularization, were also significant.

The post-1992 reforms had a number of aims but two stand out as particularly significant. First, there was a much more concerted attempt than hitherto to curtail the power of those in higher education in initial teacher education and increase the role of schools. Within the policy texts of the time, these processes were seen as two sides of the same coin – unless schools agreed to take on more responsibility in the training process, the role of higher education could not be reduced. Almost equally important, however, was the concern to increase direct control of the curriculum and the assessment process, whoever was responsible for delivering them. The policies of the mid-1990s therefore had implications both for schools and for those in higher education. In the next chapter we will focus on our research findings in relation to the implications of the reforms for the work of schools; in Chapter 7 we will look at the consequences for higher education. However, before turning our attention to the findings from our work, we need to examine some of these key policy changes in more detail.

The first moves – the new circulars and SCITT

In 1992 and 1993, two new circulars were introduced – 9/92 (DfE 1992) covering secondary courses and 14/93 (DfE 1993a) covering primary courses. The greater involvement of schools in the training process was perhaps the most significant change introduced by these policy texts. In a deliberate attempt to challenge the monopoly of those in higher education, all schools, both maintained and independent, were given the 'right' to apply to be partners in initial teacher training if they so wished, with a threat of withdrawal of accreditation from institutions that treated any such applications 'arbitrarily or unreasonably'.

Once the parties are involved in a partnership, the circulars stated that 'the government expects that partner schools and HEIs will exercise a joint responsibility for the planning and management of courses and the selection, training and assessment of students' (DfE 1992: para. 14) and this joint responsibility was further emphasized throughout the detail of the document. For example, the amount of time students should spend 'on the premises' of partner schools was defined as 66 per cent of most secondary courses and around 50 per cent of most primary courses. More significant than the specification of time though was the fact that the future division of responsibilities between the two partners was explicitly defined. Schools were to 'have a leading responsibility for training students to teach their specialist subjects, to assess pupils and to manage classes; and for supervising and assessing their competences in these respects' (DfE 1992: para. 14), while HEIs were merely to be 'responsible for ensuring that courses meet the requirements for academic validation, presenting courses for accreditation, awarding qualifications for successful students and arranging student placements in more than one school' (DfE 1992: para. 14). In addition, the two circulars insisted that in the future there should be an appropriate 'shift of resources' from HEIs to schools to pay for their additional role. In the secondary field this came to mean approximately 25 per cent of the fee income, a change which, as we will see in Chapter 7, had a significant effect in destabilizing the staffing of many training institutions.

In both primary and the secondary circulars, in line with New Right thinking (Lawlor 1990), 'training' was explicitly presented as involving only two elements: subject knowledge, which was largely, though not exclusively the province of higher education institutions, and practical teaching skills, which students were to learn in school. In an explicit attempt to tighten central control of the curriculum, the standards that newly qualified teachers needed to achieve in both of these areas were expressed in the form of a comprehensive list of 'competences'.

Measuring outcomes – a new role for competences

The notion of specifying competences or standards for professional education has by no means been confined to initial teacher education nor to the British context, as we shall see in Chapter 10. Competence-based and performance-based approaches to teacher education also pre-date the 1990s reforms. They were popular in the USA in the 1970s and had some impact on the further education (FE) sector in the UK in the early 1980s (Tuxworth 1982). However, they were given fresh impetus during the 1980s by the influence of the National Council for Vocational Qualifications (NCVQ) and by a wider debate about quality in education and training (Jessup 1991). While these developments were not centrally concerned with teacher education, their potential relevance was recognized by a number of FE teacher training courses which sought to model themselves on the National Vocational Qualification (NVQ) approach.

The use of competence-based approaches in teacher education for the school sector in Britain developed somewhat later. Eraut (1989) pointed to their potential and a few BEd and PGCE courses were beginning to show signs of their influence in the late 1980s. Far more significant than these moves among teacher educators, however, were the external critiques of conventional approaches to initial teacher education and the growing demands that they develop some means to demonstrate their effectiveness. In 1989, Circular 24/89 (DES 1989a) had included exit criteria for a few specific activities within courses of initial teacher education, notably those relating to information technology, and courses had to meet these in order to be recommended for accreditation by the Council for the Accreditation of Teacher Education (CATE).

By the early 1990s, the growing official interest in linking qualified teacher status to the achievement of specified competences initiated a flurry of activity on the part of various agencies and institutions to explore the potential of competence-based approaches to teacher education. With the introduction of the new circulars in 1992 and 1993, the use of competences in designing, undertaking and assessing initial teacher education ceased to be optional in England and Wales. Circular 9/92 (DfE 1992) required higher education institutions, schools and students to 'focus on the competences of teaching throughout the whole period of initial training'. A similar phrase was used in Circular 14/93 on primary training issued the following year (DfE 1993a). These circulars contained 'official' lists of competences organized under headings such as the following:

Secondary list
   Subject knowledge
   Subject application
   Class management
   Assessment and recording of pupils' progress
   Further professional development

Primary list
   Curriculum content, planning and assessment
   (a) Whole curriculum
   (b) Subject knowledge and application
   (c) Assessment and recording of pupils' progress
   Teaching strategies
   (a) Pupils' learning
   (b) Teaching strategies and techniques
   Further professional development

Significantly, the competences that were developed were in reality quite broadly defined. Thus for example under 'class management' just four general competences were listed:

> Newly Qualified teachers should be able to: 2.4.1 Decide when teaching the whole class, groups, pairs or individuals is appropriate for particular learning processes; 2.4.2 create and maintain a purposeful and orderly environment for pupils; 2.4.3 devise and use appropriate rewards and sanctions to maintain an effective learning environment; 2.4.4 maintain pupils' interests and motivation.
>
> (DfE 1992, Annex A)

Although it was indicated that the statements of competence were not intended to provide a complete syllabus for initial teacher education, they were intended to define the issues on which courses would be accredited by the government. In other words, individual courses were free to devise syllabuses that went beyond the competences listed but that fact would not be of relevance in the application for accreditation. In order to ensure conformity to the new competency framework, the remit of Her Majesty's Inspectorate in teacher education was extended to include the inspection of schools.

More new routes

Under the terms of these new circulars, initial teacher education was therefore expected to become narrowly focused, functional and technical. The loss of autonomy for higher education was now publicly stated; according to Circular 14/93, courses had to be explicitly designed to serve 'the Government's policy objectives for schools' (DfE 1993a).

In 1993, the challenge to the role of higher education was taken a stage further with the proposal to introduce two new routes into teaching. The first was the proposal to create a new, one-year non-graduate training scheme for early years teachers. These courses, which were to have been explicitly directed at parents and others with experience of working with children, constituted the most fundamental challenge yet to the idea that teaching involves the development of an expert body of knowledge made available through higher education. In line with New Right thinking, the 'common sense' of parents was portrayed as equal to that of the expert teacher; the proposals were branded by the press as 'the Mums' Army'. However, after overwhelming opposition from teachers and others, in 1993 the proposals were dropped by the government.

The second initiative, which turned out to be politically much more significant, though in practice only marginally more successful (DfE 1993b; Anderson 1994; Ofsted 1995b; *TES* 1995, 1998), was the launching of the 'school-centred' teacher training initiative (SCITT) which allowed schools to opt out of links with higher education provision entirely and receive direct government funding to run their own postgraduate training schemes. Within SCITT schemes, small groups of schools work together as consortia, buying in higher education expertise and/or accreditation if and when they see fit. Even if they do choose to involve higher education, it is the school or consortium, rather than the HEI, that initially receives the funding for such courses. The aim of the scheme, according to the government, was to give the teaching profession itself control over training. As the Minister of Education responsible for launching the scheme said at the time: 'Under the school-centred teacher training scheme, schools will have real power to decide how members of the teaching profession should be trained' (DfE 1993d). Those in higher education saw it rather differently. Anderson, who made an early study of the scheme, for example wrote, 'Behind this move is an attempt to undermine the alleged over-theoretical and "producer" dominant role of university schools and institutes of education' (Anderson 1994: 20).

The early 1990s was a period of considerable influence for New Right thinkers in relation to initial teacher education. Their stated aim was the suppression of 'lengthy, doctrinaire and demoralising' training courses (Lawlor 1990) and the creation of a 'neutral' system, in which teachers, rather than teacher educators, prepared students on a list of pre-defined competences. Their hope was that, by these means, they would see the rise of a different generation of teachers, whose professional values were untainted by views of the teacher education establishment. As we have indicated above, much of the thrust behind the 1992 and 1993 circulars and the creation of the SCITT scheme seemed to be in accord with these aspirations. However, the passing of the 1994 Education Act and establishment of the Teacher Training Agency (TTA), meant that the next five years were to see some significant changes in this policy agenda.

The rise of the TTA

The Teacher Training Agency was established by the 1994 Education Act and took over most of the functions of CATE, as well as the funding of all initial teacher education in England. Indeed, one rationale used by the government for the setting up of the TTA was a need to find a way permanently to fund SCITT schemes. It was because such schemes, which were central to the government's vision of the future of teacher education, were outside existing funding arrangements, that a new agency had to be invented. As a 1993 consultation document put it:

> The Government expects the numbers of school-centred courses to increase steadily during the rest of this decade. The role of schools as partners can also be expected to grow under the Government's existing reforms and proposal. For the future, new arrangements will be needed to ensure that school and higher education courses can be considered together and that the appropriate balance can be struck each year in the

distribution of students and funding as between courses of different types. To meet this need, the government proposes to establish a new statutory body, the Teacher Training Agency, to administer all central funds for initial teacher training in England.

(DfE 1993e: 6)

In a sense, the agency was established as part of the government's ongoing challenge to the role of higher education. It was fundamentally based on the assumption that higher education did not have a *necessary* and *distinctive* contribution to make to initial teacher education; that is why a new national body was needed. John Patten, the Secretary of State in 1993, put that challenge more explicitly when announcing the new agency:

Higher education institutions will maintain an important although changing role in initial teacher training. Teacher training will be a joint venture in which they must work alongside schools. *Where schools choose to run their own courses, they will be able to take the initiative and work with higher education institutions of their own choice and on their own terms.* By establishing one body to administer all the funds we will ensure that there is a co-ordinated approach to the provision of places and an appropriate balance between the different types of training.

(Patten 1993, emphasis added)

The 1994 Education Bill which set up the TTA was highly controversial (Ambrose 1996), though much of the debate did not focus on the agency itself but on the principle of whether or not initial teacher education should necessarily include a higher education element. The new body was to be given three core responsibilities in relation to initial teacher education: teacher recruitment and supply, the funding of teacher education in England (though not in Wales), and the accreditation of courses.

With the establishment of the TTA, funding for initial teacher training in England was formally separated from the funding of other forms of higher education by the Higher Education Funding Council for England. Universities and colleges bidding for funding were, in the future, to be treated as 'service providers' rather than a professionally autonomous group. Of course, the very idea of establishing an agency to take over the entire sector of educational provision can be seen as an example of the neo-liberal marketization of education. As such it needs to be understood as part of a broader process of restructuring public administration (Mahony and Hextall 1996). This is an issue that we discuss in more detail in Chapter 10.

When the new agency was formally established in September 1994, its board included two prominent New Right activists – Professor Anthony O'Hear and Baroness Caroline Cox. In many ways this incorporation of prominent critics of initial teacher education was significant for, together with the increasing marginalization of higher education, it signalled an important change in the policy process. No longer was there to be a vocal 'context of influence' separated from those actually formulating policy texts. With its new responsibilities and its formal separation from the DfE, the TTA seemed increasingly to develop its own policy, while voices in the broader context of influence were silenced.

The initial remit letter for the TTA from the Secretary of State was broad and by 1995 the TTA was assuming responsibility for an ever-widening range of activities (Mahony and Hextall 1996). In relation to initial teacher education, two requirements in the remit letter were particularly important. The first, giving sustenance to New Right ideas, was the formal requirement for the TTA to promote SCITT. The result has been that, despite the extremely small numbers involved (never more than 1.5 per cent of provision), and the apparently negative reports on quality by the Office for Standards in Education (Ofsted 1995b), SCITT schemes have continued to enjoy official support. The second concerned the requirement to develop a strategy for linking funding to quality. It was this formal requirement that became the main strategy used by the TTA to gain progressively more control over the system as a whole. In theory, despite the constitution of its board, the primary concern of the TTA, at least in its early years, was not simply the advancement of the New Right agenda. Rather it could be seen as an aggressive attempt, led by its senior officers, to rebuild a national system in which the agency itself was the definer and guardian of 'quality'. In practice, the distinction was often not so clear, particularly as the TTA often had to compete with Ofsted, and Her Majesty's Chief Inspector in particular, for the ear of government ministers.

An early attempt by the TTA to gain control was the proposal to launch a detailed competency-based career entry profiling scheme. If it had been successful, the content of the profile would inevitably have become the content of the teacher training curriculum. However, trials showed the proposed strategy to be unworkable and the approach was drastically modified. A second, and in the event much more successful, strategy was to utilize the formal requirement to link funding to quality. It was this requirement that during the mid-1990s was utilized by the TTA to increase control over the structure and content of courses.

In developing this control, inspections and inspection frameworks used by Ofsted, which was charged with working with the TTA on this issue, became increasingly important tools. Between 1993 and 1995, nearly all teacher education courses were inspected by Ofsted and 'quality' ratings applied; these inspections did much to encourage rapid conformity to the 1992 and 1993 circulars. (As inspections became even more significant in the later 1990s, more details of the process are given in Chapter 9). As we have already noted, the TTA was unusual in being responsible for funding, as well as policy and management within the system and the accreditation of courses. Following a very public enquiry into funding (Coopers and Lybrand 1995) the somewhat chaotic funding structure was simplified and rationalized. The TTA was then in a position to develop mechanisms that linked Ofsted 'quality ratings' directly to funding. Again, we will examine this process in more detail in Chapter 9.

This then was the changing policy context within which we undertook our second MOTE study. In the early phases of our work, SCITT schemes were being established and higher education-provided courses were in the process of implementing the 1992 and 1993 circulars. Later in the project, courses were having to come to terms with the workings of the TTA – with new accreditation arrangements, with new funding arrangements and with progressively more specific inspection regimes. If we again utilize the concepts of 'readerly' and 'writerly' texts, then we can suggest that this period was characterized by a concerted attempt by the government and later by the TTA to move to more 'readerly' policies. Those in higher education and in schools were intended to have less and less autonomy in how to interpret their responsibilities.

Meanwhile, the government was encouraging a further competitor to both traditional providers and SCITT schemes through The Open University's courses of initial teacher training by distance learning. For some years, The Open University had collaborated with other higher education providers to produce support materials for teacher education, but now it entered into direct competition with them. It began to offer both primary and secondary PGCE courses in which students arranged their school experience in schools in their own locality, while they and their mentors were supported by distance learning materials and staff in regional offices.

The potential implications of this plethora of new policies for teacher professionalism and professionality were complex. What Maclure (1993) said of one of the government's proposals may well have been more generally true:

> The first thing to remember about Government plans for teacher training is that there is a plot and a sub-plot. The plot is straightforward. Give practising teachers a bigger part to play in the professional preparation of their future colleagues. This is a good idea. The sub-plot is more sinister. It is to take teacher training out of the universities and colleges and ultimately to sever the connection between the study of education in higher education and its practice in schools. This is a deeply damaging idea and must be fought tooth and nail. The [proposals] must be examined closely for insidious attempts to dismantle the traditional defences of teaching as a profession.

But how, in practice, did the succession of policy initiatives actually change provision for professional preparation during this period? Commentators, many of them professionally involved in teacher education in traditional higher education contexts (Edwards 1992; Adams and Tulasiewicz 1995), expressed alarm. Were their fears actually realized? In the next two chapters we present the findings from our second national survey and our continued case study work undertaken during this period. Initially, in Chapter 6, we look at the impact of the reforms on the involvement of schools in the training process; in Chapter 7 we examine their impact on those in higher education.

6 Partnership – the changing role of schools

Introduction

Despite the aspirations of the government, the SCITT experiment did not take off in any significant way. During the time of our research, students training through this route amounted to no more than 1.5 per cent of the total and the vast majority of courses continued to be provided through higher education. As we indicated in the last chapter, in response to the circulars being implemented at the time (DfE 1992, 1993a), most courses were now having to re-establish themselves in terms of 'partnerships' between those in higher education and local schools (Ofsted 1995a). As this was the dominant form of provision at the time of our research, we have chosen to use the concept of 'partnership' as a central theme in this and the next chapter. Where appropriate, however, we contrast our findings with evidence from the school-led SCITT experiment.

In Chapter 3 we argued that in 1992, immediately prior to the emergence of the new criteria, with one or two well publicized exceptions (e.g. Benton 1990), the majority of teacher education courses in England and Wales were based on the principle of what we termed 'integration' rather than partnership. What courses were aiming to integrate was the students' training experience in college or university with the world of the school. However, we suggested that in most courses the responsibility for achieving this integration lay largely with those in higher education. Tutors presented sessions within college that were highly practically oriented; they adopted pedagogies that were designed explicitly to model classroom teaching; they set and marked school-based assignments for students to undertake while they were in school; they took overall responsibility for supervising students on teaching practice and they had primary responsibility for assessing students both in their written work and in their practical teaching competence. Although much of the course was closely related to the world of school, for the most part, the formal responsibilities of teachers in the planning and provision of training were minimal. Even their role in the assessment of teaching practice was often only an advisory one.

One thing that our second round of research indicated was that in nearly all courses, that model of training had all but disappeared. Teachers were now significantly involved in a range of different aspects of courses, including planning, teaching and assessment. However, what also became apparent was that there were many ways of organizing partnerships (the detail of what was to be involved was not specified in the circulars); different models had significantly different implications for what the role of schools and teachers should be. They also had implications for the forms of professionalism they were designed to engender in students. Exploring different models of partnership therefore became an important dimension of our research.

'Ideal typical' models of partnership

From our research we would suggest that as a starting point it is useful to identify two 'ideal typical' models of partnership at each end of a continuum. At one end of the continuum there is 'collaborative partnership'; at the other there is 'complementary partnership'. We originally described this latter version as 'separatist' (Furlong *et al.* 1996; Whiting *et al.* 1996), but now feel that 'complementary' is a more appropriate term for this approach. However, as we shall see, some aspects of this approach can appear separatist in practice. Meanwhile, it is important to emphasize that these models are indeed intended to be seen as ideal typical. Any one individual course might well embody aspects of each of these models – either in different parts of the course or for particular groups of students. The position is therefore complex. Nevertheless we have found it valuable to begin by suggesting such a continuum as represented in Figure 6.1.

Figure 6.1 sets out a continuum of possible relationships between higher education institutions and schools. One end of the continuum represents the 1992 position – with higher education-based models of integration. At

Figure 6.1 Possible relationships between HEIs and schools showing ideal-typical models of partnership

HEI	School
HEI-based schemes (1992)	SCITT
A continuum of models of partnership	
Collaborative ------------------------------ Complementary partnership	partnership

the other end of the continuum there are those SCITT schemes where those in higher education have no formal responsibility (though they may be brought in on an ad hoc basis). Neither model can be characterized as partnership in that partnership necessarily, we would suggest, involves some degree of joint responsibility for course provision. The two idealized models of partnership between these two extremes represent very different strategies for linking work in school and higher education. They are discussed in more detail below.

Complementary partnership

At one end of the continuum is what we would characterize as 'complementary partnership'. The school and the university or college are seen as having separate and complementary responsibilities but there is no systematic attempt to bring these two dimensions into dialogue. In other words there is partnership but not necessarily integration in the course; integration is something that the student him or herself has to achieve. This is the model of partnership that is put forward within government Circulars 9/92 (DfE 1992) and 14/93 (DfE 1993a); the vision of the circulars is of a division of labour between schools and those in universities and colleges rather than integration.

Within our sample of courses it seemed that such a model might emerge either from a principled commitment to allowing schools the legitimacy to have their own distinctive area of responsibility or as a pragmatic response to financial constraints. For example, the leader of one secondary PGCE course which had passed major responsibility to schools explicitly claimed to be following the spirit of Circular 9/92 (DfE 1992):

> The main responsibility for recommendations to the Exam Board are the [deputy head] and [teacher] mentors; the schools are responsible. . . . It is not normal practice to observe and assess on a 'flying visit' from college . . . It's not normal practice [for tutors] to visit [at all]. Occasionally there are visits but they are for specific purposes. Routine visits do not take place . . . The schools themselves have actually taken ownership and taken professional responsibility for postgrads and recognize the seriousness of their role. I haven't pushed them.

More frequently, though, the complementary model seemed to be emerging as a pragmatic response to limited resources, as another secondary PGCE course leader explained:

> This university is in the situation where we have no reserves to sustain PGCE at the same level that we have at the moment. So the strategy that we've taken as a department is to recognize that staff who are presently engaged in the PGCE secondary will have to look to other

things to earn their keep . . . Principally we have taken the area covered by the professional course and transferred responsibility for the assessment of that entirely and part of the provision to schools so that means that as far as we're concerned, the role of the link tutor has disappeared . . . the nature of visits that we make to schools will [also] change – because teachers will have the assessment role – we won't any more. The kind of time that we spend on assessment will change . . . because we are going to have to count it within the hours and be very restrictive.

From our own fieldwork we would suggest that there are a number of strategies that can be utilized in any course in the development of partnership. We would suggest that the principal features of a complementary model of partnership might be as shown in Table 6.1.

Table 6.1   Complementary partnership – key features

Planning	broad planning of structure with agreed areas of responsibility
HE visits to school	none or only for 'troubleshooting'
Documentation	strongly emphasized, defining areas of responsibility
Content	separate knowledge domains, no opportunities for dialogue
Mentoring	mentoring comes from knowledge base of school
Assessment	school responsible for teaching assessment
Contractual relationship	legalistic, finance led with discrete areas of responsibility
Legitimation	either principled commitment to role of school or pragmatic due to limited resources

The implications for the professional socialization of students are clear. Work in school is intended to be undertaken separately from that in higher education. What students have to learn about the practical business of teaching is defined and assessed by those in school with little or no reference to more 'theoretical' forms of knowledge traditionally made available through higher education. Universities and colleges retain an important role, but largely as the organizers of the scheme as a whole. Their time with students and therefore their sphere of influence is significantly curtailed.

Collaborative partnership

Among teacher educators at the time, however, a very different model of partnership was being proselytized – one that we would characterize as 'collaborative'. The best known example of collaborative partnership at the time was that developed by the Oxford secondary PGCE (Benton 1990, but see also Furlong *et al.* 1988). As McIntyre (1991) argued, at the heart of this model is the commitment to develop a training programme where students are exposed to different forms of educational knowledge, some of which come from school, some of which come from higher education or elsewhere. Teachers are seen as having an equally legitimate but perhaps different body of professional knowledge from those in higher education. Students are expected and encouraged to use what they learn in school to critique what they learn within the college or university and vice versa. It is through this dialectic that they are expected to build up their own body of professional knowledge. For the model to succeed, teachers and lecturers need opportunities to work and plan together on a regular basis; such ongoing collaboration is essential if they are to develop a programme of work for the student that is integrated between the higher education and the school. Below are some of the principles of this model of partnership taken from McIntyre (1993a):

- integration – one curriculum;
- complementarity;
- access to different kinds of knowledge;
- no need for consensus about good practice;
- critical questioning of all ideas about good practice;
- emphasis on student-teachers' understanding of how they can learn;
- progression individualized;
- mentoring as a new role to be explored;
- college tutor – also a new role to be explored.

Some of these principles were expressed by our respondents. For example, one secondary course lecturer said:

> In maths, I used to spend my time trying to give the students a vision of mathematics and education that would last them throughout their careers. They then went off to school and hit the reality of school life. They promptly forgot most of that. I would visit the school and help them try to win the battle to keep the ideas alive but in most cases it was a non-starter. Now we are much more realistic – we can no longer pretend the realities of school don't exist and we have to find ways of working with that. Now I am talking to teachers as equals and I'm actually much more aware of what is going on in school. They are much more likely to tell me about the problematic nature of what is going on at school and the things they can do and I feel there is a real sense of partnership . . . and they are starting to gain in confidence as they start to understand the agenda for professional development that we have developed together for initial teacher training – they see the relevance to their own professional development.

A teacher mentor working in a primary partnership said:

> The whole ethos of working in this cluster is collaborative and I think there is a very good level of cooperation and understanding – both. As

Table 6.2 Collaborative partnership – key features

Planning	emphasis on giving all tutors and teachers opportunities to work together in small groups
HE visits to school	collaborative to discuss professional issues together
Documentation	codifies emerging collaborative practice
Content	schools and HE recognize legitimacy and difference of each others' contribution to an ongoing dialogue
Mentoring	defined as giving students access to teachers' professional knowledge – mentor 'training' as professional development, learning to articulate embedded knowledge
Assessment	collaborative, based on triangulation
Contractual relationship	negotiated, personal
Legitimation	commitment to value of collaboration in ITE

far as I'm concerned there has been a big effort . . . to power share if you like and there has been a genuine movement of responsibility.

In Table 6.2 we set out how in ideal typical terms this model would be interpreted in practice. This then was the 'idealized' model of partnership that was favoured by professional teacher educators in the early and mid-1990s. Its popularity with those in higher education lay at least in part in the fact that, while it formally met the demands of recent reforms (schools were to be given a strong and valued role in the training process), it maintained a strong role for higher education too; a view captured by one primary PGCE course leader to whom we spoke:

I believe strongly in the fact that we are in partnership – that the schools are as responsible for the training of the students as we are. So they are part of our planning and what they can provide, the hands-on experience we can't and I think they also accept that what we can provide they can't. They haven't got the time, they haven't got the resources, they haven't got the expertise that we have here and so I do feel that it is a strong partnership.

Significantly, this vision of partnership, rather than challenging the forms of professionalism traditionally made available through higher education, potentially at least, made them more achievable. By encouraging ongoing forms of collaboration between students, lecturers and teachers, the model held out the possibility of developing an effective and principled strategy for developing reflective practice where theory and practice were interrelated. Its implications for the professionalism of student teachers were therefore significant.

These then were the two very different models of partnership that were being put forward at the time. The collaborative model was widely espoused, especially by those in higher education; government regulations encouraged a different approach. But what model was in fact being realized nationally as courses changed to meet the new requirements? Were teachers becoming contributors to teacher education, independent of those in higher education? Alternatively, were they being drawn into the process as 'collaborators'? In exploring these questions we will look first at the growing role for teachers in the training process and second at some of the challenges faced by the system in developing effective partnerships. At the end of the next chapter, after we have looked at the impact of these changes on those in higher education, we set out a third ideal type of partnership which we feel more accurately characterizes what we found in practice.

A growing role for schools and teachers

Time in school

Perhaps the simplest way of documenting the growing role of schools in training is to examine the amount of time students actually spent in schools on serial and block practices. As we have seen, the new arrangements that were introduced during the course of the project specifically extended the amount of time that was required. All secondary courses should have been complying with the new arrangements of Circular 9/92 (DfE 1992) at the time of the survey; primary courses were not required to comply until the term after we undertook our survey – September 1996.

On one-year PGCE courses, the new requirement was 90 days per year in school for primary students and 120 for secondary students. Our findings showed that by 1996 all secondary courses were at least complying with the new requirements though a significant number of primary courses had not yet increased their time in school to the new minimum. Those on SCITT courses were necessarily based in school for their whole year, which in most cases was around 40 weeks. The aim here was to immerse trainees in the culture of schools as thoroughly as possible. As one SCITT course leader explained,

> In terms of what our trainees look like at the end . . . when it comes to someone coming through a year in a school . . . it says a lot more about them than someone who's come through a traditional route.

On four-year undergraduate courses, the minimum for both primary and secondary courses was 160 days in school. Here we found that all but three secondary courses were complying to this requirement and these three were working under special arrangements. Half of the primary courses were already providing more than 130 days and five had already met the new requirement. However a large majority of primary courses had still to adjust to the new criteria.

In comparison with our 1991 survey therefore, students were on average spending significantly more time in school. However, as we saw in Chapter 3, in 1991 many courses were giving students more time in schools than the minima required. Now, courses were not generally exceeding the specified minima, indicating that, even for those course leaders committed to a school-based model, the maximum time in school had been reached. This seemed particularly so in the case of primary, where many courses seemed to have put off complying with the new requirements until it was absolutely necessary.

Location of training

Another way of assessing the involvement of schools in the training process is to look at the physical location of the teaching of various course elements. In the national survey, course leaders were therefore asked to rank each main course element on a five-point scale ranging from 'all in the HEI' to 'all in school'. The main course elements were defined as follows:

- undergraduate subject studies (for undergraduate and conversion courses only);
- main subject application;
- core curriculum (for primary only);
- other curriculum (for primary only);
- education/professional studies (EPS);
- school experience/working with children.

From the results of this question we found that only 'school experience/ working with children' seemed to be taking place mainly in school. Predictably, over 85 per cent of course leaders described undergraduate subject studies as taking place wholly in the college or university. However, even main subject *application* was still seen by very few as taking place mainly in school. Around half regarded it as a joint venture between school and higher education, but a substantial percentage overall (32.6 per cent) saw it as taking place mainly in the university or college, and 10 per cent suggested that it all took place there. Educational and professional studies (EPS) showed a similar pattern: although 60 per cent said that EPS took place jointly between higher education and school, the remainder still indicated its location as being mainly or completely in higher education. Despite the growing amount of time being spent in schools there had not been any dramatic shift in the forms of training being undertaken there as opposed to what was offered within higher education.

Teacher involvement in courses

We also collected data on levels of school-based teacher involvement in various aspects of course delivery. These included:

- course planning, management and leadership;
- teaching students (subject studies, subject application, curriculum subjects, EPS, school experience);
- assessing students (essays, practical teaching, school-based investigations, curriculum materials);
- profiling students (formative and summative, using and not using competences).

Course leaders were asked to describe the level of involvement of school-based teachers on a rating scale of 1–6. A rating of 1 indicated that they considered teachers were not involved at all. The scale between 2 and 5 implied different degrees of joint responsibility. A rating of 6 was for when course leaders considered teachers were firmly in charge.

The figures that follow show the overall pattern of involvement as assessed by course leaders across all modes of training. However, the commentary based on more detailed analysis of the returns indicates that it was almost invariably secondary one-year PGCE courses which involved teachers most of all.

Figure 6.2 Primary and secondary teacher involvement in course leadership, recruitment and management

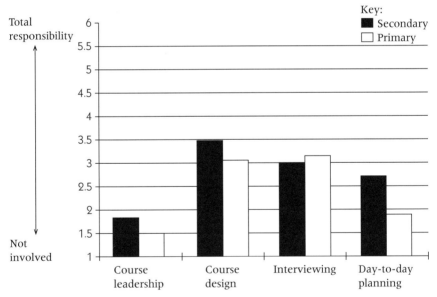

Course planning, managing and leadership

As Figure 6.2 shows, the mean ratings for course planning, managing and leadership activities nowhere went above 3.5 (the level would have indicated real joint 'responsibility' rather than mere 'involvement'). The only area where this was starting to happen was in course design and interviewing.

Elsewhere the ratings indicated involvement, but not responsibility. It seems surprising that course leaders' rating of teacher involvement in day-to-day planning was not higher overall, although on one-year secondary PGCE courses it was given a rating of 3.5. However we would interpret this as indicating that it was only a small number of teachers who were becoming involved in the management of courses and in interviewing; when it came to the broad range of day-to-day course activity, teachers' involvement was significantly less developed. In secondary courses, it was the one-year PGCE rather than the four-year undergraduate that recorded the higher ratings of 3 or more – but in primary courses there was no such distinction. Course leadership clearly remained the responsibility of university and college tutors on all types of course.

Figure 6.3 Primary and secondary teacher involvement in teaching students

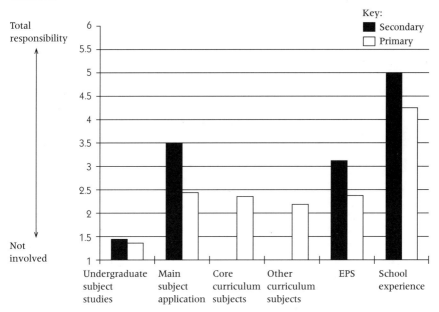

Teaching students
In relation to teaching, as Figure 6.3 demonstrates, teachers were rated by course leaders as having joint or primary responsibility for teaching students in the area of school experience or working with children. In secondary courses in particular, teachers were seen as taking the lead in this aspect of the work and secondary one-year PGCE courses showed a rating of 5. Given the increased amount of time students were now spending in school, this therefore represents a significant change in the balance of responsibilities between those in schools and those in higher education.

Much of this move is captured in the change of title for teachers from 'supervisors' to 'mentors' that happened at this time. (Our first national survey revealed that at that time about 14 per cent of teachers working with students were formally designated as 'mentors'; by our second survey this figure had risen to nearly 60 per cent in secondary courses.) As supervisors, teachers had been traditionally responsible merely for overseeing students. As mentors, most courses expected them to take on a much more active role – a change well captured in this quotation from a mentor within a primary PGCE scheme:

> Up until a couple of years ago the class . . . you just had a role as the class teacher really and supported them and talked about how they'd done and gave suggestions and advice, whereas now it's much more a tutoring role because we're a partnership school . . . and we've actually gone through training as student mentors and have a particular file and set procedures to go through.

A mentor in a different scheme illustrated the demands as well as the rewards of the new role:

> I find it quite demanding but I also find it very rewarding. Erm, I really enjoy it. It gives me a kick up the backside quite honestly when I see what some marvellous ideas they come up with . . . We spend a lot of time talking – every day after school – twice a week I give them at least an hour or two hours of my time so that's nearly four hours plus there's always before school, after school. There's lunchtimes – even if they're doing a full-time block and they're teaching full-time I'm always there if they want me, either as a classroom assistant or to talk to.

Historically, as the leader of a SCITT scheme pointed out, this change of role was the legacy of the Articled and Licensed Teacher Schemes that we discussed in Chapter 4:

> The key thing about both the Licensed Teacher Scheme and the Articled Teacher Scheme is they effected a fundamental shift in teacher education, away from the idea of supervision to mentoring. The thing about mentoring is that it's labour intensive [but] it is profoundly developmental from both sides. The genie's out of the bottle . . . we can't go back to before now.

Teachers were then being asked to take on much more responsibility in relation to the developing of students' practical teaching competence. However, in other areas of teaching, they were seen as having less involvement, though teachers in secondary courses were moving towards taking some responsibility in main subject application, particularly in PGCE courses. This again accords with the data on the location of this element of courses as reported above. However, there was much less evidence of teachers taking responsibility for curriculum subjects in primary courses. There was more involvement in core subjects than in other curriculum subjects, but even this did not merit a 'regularly involved' rating. In secondary educational and professional studies, teachers were moving towards taking shared responsibility, again on PGCE courses in particular.

Teachers were also seen as taking virtually no role in assessing essays and examination scripts, though they had some involvement in assessing school-based investigations and curriculum materials. As one four-year BEd course leader explained:

> They are involved in commenting on reflection activities, the sort of things that the student teachers are obliged to do, but not in terms of actually assessing them; they're involved in, sort of, negotiating a focus and whether it's sort of a worthwhile thing to be doing, maybe if somebody's looking at special needs and special needs policies or whatever special needs teaching, and at the end the mentors are asked to make a comment on it, in terms of, you know, it's validity within that school context. But the ultimate assessment, is actually done, final assessment is done by college staff.

However, in the assessment of practical teaching they were beginning to take primary responsibility – especially on one- and three-year secondary courses.

Moreover, in the area of profiling (both summative and formative), teachers were being given even more responsibility. This was especially so in secondary courses that used competences, where teachers were moving towards taking primary responsibility for both formative and summative profiling. Teachers were also regularly involved in forms of profiling which did not make use of competences. Although the mean ratings on primary courses were lower than for secondary, they were all above 3.5, indicating that course leaders saw teachers as taking joint responsibility.

SCITT course contributors

In the SCITT questionnaire we asked course leaders to rank the contribution of a range of groups (e.g. course leaders, other teachers, higher education staff, LEA staff) to different elements of their course. From the responses it was evident that, in the area of course management in particular, the balance was very different from the higher education-based courses. In addition to high school involvement in the various taught elements of the courses, schools were rated as taking a leading role in course design, leadership and day-to-day planning; higher education was rated as making a very low contribution to each of these areas. It was also clear that course administration was being carried out almost totally by the school-based course leaders. Nowhere in the higher education column was a mean rating reached, indicating that the partnership role of universities and colleges in this case was clearly much reduced. In relation to teaching, it seems that SCITT course leaders themselves had a strong role, taking joint responsibility in secondary courses for main subject application and EPS. Within our three primary

SCITT courses, LEAs appeared to have a significant role in teaching main subject application.

This strategy of SCITT consortia taking major responsibility for their own teaching with only occasional support from other external specialists was well illustrated by one secondary course leader who explained:

> There is no involvement of HEIs except for the fact that the external examiners we use happen to be employed by X University though we employ them in a personal capacity. We have also bought the occasional session from someone based in an HEI. Other consultancy-based inputs include some from NCET [National Council for Educational Technology] and from 'Somerset Thinking Skills'. The rest has been provided by the consortium – we have the necessary expertise ourselves; for example, one of our mentors was an advisor before we poached her back into teaching. We are very lucky to have her.

Overall, therefore, we can see that the role of schools did increase significantly during this period. Students were spending more time in school and teachers were taking progressively more and more responsibility for mentoring and assessing their practical teaching competence. However, what our data also reveal is that this increased role for teachers was largely confined to this traditional area. Nationally we can see that, outside the SCITT experiment, schools were not significantly becoming involved in the management of courses or in teaching and assessment of issues other than practical teaching competence.

Forming partnerships

However, the fact that students were spending more time in school and that teachers were more involved in their supervision and assessment tells us little about the model of partnership and therefore the form of professionalism that was being developed in the mid-1990s. As we indicated above, the idealized complementary partnership is dependent on schools making a strong and independent contribution; by contrast the collaborative model is dependent on lecturers and teachers having regular opportunities for joint planning and teaching. Clearly, either model is difficult if schools are unwilling partners, if the number involved is too high or if resources to support the scheme are limited. We can therefore gain some further insight into the model of partnership that was being developed at this time by examining these factors.

Numbers of schools

The number of schools with which a course works is likely to affect the nature of the partnership into which it can enter; certainly close collaboration is challenging with large numbers of schools. As Table 6.3 shows the

Table 6.3 Numbers of schools used by one- and four-year courses

Number of schools	up to 30	30–50	51–70	71–90	91–110	111–130	131–150	151–200	201–300	301–400	mean
Postgraduate secondary	8	19	12	9	3	3	0	0	0	0	58
Postgraduate primary	9	24	4	6	1	2	1	0	1	0	56
4-year secondary	12	4	3	0	0	0	0	0	0	0	48
4-year primary	2	4	1	3	2	1	0	1	19	6	190

numbers of schools used by the primary undergraduate courses in particular were very large, with most using over 200 and several up to 400. This was partly because of the high numbers of students on such courses, approaching an average of 150 per course, but also because student–school ratios were low. Most primary schools took only one or two students and were reluctant to take more. One BEd course tutor, explaining the difficulties of moving to the new partnership model, said:

> We're having to press the schools to take on more than they want . . . some are very reluctant [to take on more] – they're tremendously interested in what we're doing but they're keen not to spoil what's there already because they think that they already have a very good link with us and not to overreach themselves. So many of them, if we allowed them to, would like to carry on as they are now.

The issue of numbers of schools was particularly acute in the Open University distance learning course, which placed students one at a time in two different schools. Across its primary and secondary schools it was using almost 2000 schools.

On conventional primary and secondary postgraduate courses, there were on average more students per school – between three and five was normal. Thus, although intakes on secondary PGCE courses in particular were high, school-based work was concentrated on fewer schools (the mean number was 58 schools), arguably making partnership easier.

By contrast, the numbers of schools in our respondent SCITT consortia ranged from just 4 to 11. The average student–school ratio for both primary and secondary courses was 2.7 to 1. The small number of schools involved in these consortia helped facilitate collaboration between the participating schools. As the coordinator of one SCITT scheme explained:

> There is no concept of a 'lead school' here – that is merely a financial arrangement . . . [but] being a member of a consortium has certainly been of benefit to those acting as mentors because it has enhanced their own professional development . . . There are also other spin offs, like helping our NQTs get jobs.

Selecting schools

Respondents to the national survey were asked to state the criteria used by their courses for selecting partner schools. Examples of desired criteria included previous relationships and good track records with students, trained mentor availability and, for secondary courses, suitable subject departments. Primary course leaders often mentioned matching philosophy or ethos within the schools and the HEI and availability of National Curriculum expertise.

Figure 6.4 Percentage of courses reporting difficulties in recruitment of schools

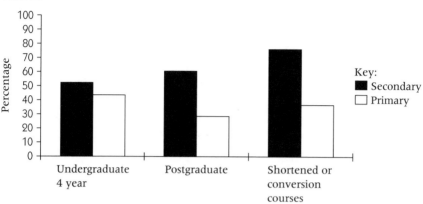

Selection criteria were often written into partnership agreements. However, as Figure 6.4 reveals, difficulty in recruiting schools meant that these criteria could not always be applied. It is not possible to know from this survey how many schools were actually selected according to the stated criteria, but it may be significant that the most common criterion of selection cited by respondents was 'willingness' to be a partner and to sign up. This was particularly true of the secondary courses and even more so with those courses concentrating entirely on shortage subjects.

In additional comments, many course leaders said that their desired criteria, although carefully thought through and often documented, were difficult to apply in practice; they often had to take what was offered. The following comments are from both primary and secondary undergraduate and postgraduate course leaders:

Selection is a luxury we cannot afford.

We are not in a position to be able to reject many schools who offer to be involved!! The chance would be a fine thing.

All who have applied have been accepted.

This year, because of huge student numbers, desperation! Anyone will almost do.

These views were confirmed in our interviews. As one secondary two-year BEd course leader explained.

The main reason is that in this current climate – financial climate – with the teacher–pupil ratio changing, so many teachers don't have time to work with students and headteachers are saying – 'No the teachers have enough to do – we can't take on more.'

In many areas those schools that did participate were therefore in a powerful position and able to call the shots, as another secondary course leader explained:

> To be frank, a lot of the schools where we are not particularly happy with the level of support, they respond one of two ways – to hold their hands in the air and say, 'Yes, we are sorry, we have not been doing what we should', and the other is to say, 'Well, we're not going to have students any more.'

As a result, some course leaders felt it inappropriate to make any significant demands on schools in their negotiations. As this primary BEd course leader explained:

> Our major concern is that we don't want to frighten off schools who may be saying, 'Well, we don't want any more than we are dealing with at the moment.'

While there were continuing difficulties in finding enough secondary school placements, some institutions reported a lessening of the problem in PGCE partnerships which were in their second year. Overall, however, more difficulties were reported with secondary PGCE courses than with undergraduate courses, although there was a mention of some schools being unwilling to take undergraduate students.

In some areas, competition from other universities and colleges had exacerbated problems with placements – sometimes because schools had signed up to a sole partnership with another institution, sometimes because they were offering better terms. Where there were schools taking students from more than one university or college, it had sometimes caused complications or even withdrawal of partnership. Many secondary course leaders suggested that some schools were unwilling to take on the added responsibility involved in partnership schemes, especially when funding did not reflect the time and effort required.

This was expected to apply even more to primary courses, although some respondents acknowledged that the difficulties had not always become apparent. Accordingly, there was concern about what would happen when the fuller partnership model became mandatory in September 1996. Primary schools were often said to be happy with old arrangements and not to want full partnership and the additional responsibilities it implied. As a primary PGCE course leader said, in pointing out the problem of last minute withdrawal, 'Schools' needs come first.'

Contracts

As a further indication of the character of partnerships, we asked about the contracts that had been set up. Significantly, some universities and colleges reported having to enter into different levels of partnership with different schools. For example, in 28 secondary courses, course leaders reported that they had solved the problem of recruitment of appropriate schools for particular subjects by maintaining high university or college involvement. Schools could be in partnership in one of two (or more) ways: a full partnership or into what was called a 'level 2' or 'associate' partnership. At the second level of partnership, schools were involved with students at a lower level of responsibility or commitment and received a lower level of remuneration. In many ways, their role remained closer to that of pre-partnership practice. As one secondary PGCE course leader explained:

> We weren't able to recruit enough schools who would come into full partnership with us offering us staffing on professional tutor and subject level and so this means that we had to perpetuate something of the old course, which is very much based on the subject link.

At the time of the survey, many primary courses were still relating to their schools on a basis of custom and practice and goodwill, but comments suggested that many would be operating through differentiated contracts the following year.

Finally, although we did not specifically ask about turnover of schools, a number of respondents mentioned the difficulty of turnover in the 'additional comments' on the questionnaire. For example two BEd course leaders, one primary and one secondary wrote:

> There is likely to be significant turnover of schools.

> Turnover in schools, departments and mentors is a problem.

Of course when a school or even an individual mentor left the partnership there was not only the difficulty of finding another to take its place, the higher education institution also had to invest again in training a new group of mentors. It is to training and support that we now turn.

Supporting partnerships

As we have indicated, the collaborative model of partnership is dependent on close and regular contact between lecturers and designated teachers in schools; it also demands the development of new skills, particularly on the part of designated mentors who have to take significantly greater responsibility for key aspects of the training. The same is true in complementary partnerships, although the skills involved might be different in certain ways. In our national survey we therefore asked about forms of regular contact and training.

Only 153 out of 211 course leaders responded to our question on training, but our data show that the majority of respondents reported that around half of all designated teachers were trained, but that only 20 courses were training all or almost all these teachers. Nearly 90 per cent of those who answered the question claimed that 50 per cent or more of their designated teachers were trained and 72 per cent said that 80 per cent or more were trained.

Some training was therefore widely available for designated staff in partnership schemes. However, it was also apparent that such training was generally not available to other class teachers who were working with students on a day-to-day basis but lacked a designated role. Training for such staff largely came from school staff who were already trained, though it was not clear whether time or resources were made available for this. As one mentor explained:

> I did find the training [at the university] was very helpful because I did come back and I'd got all these competences, responsibilities, who's responsible for this, who's responsible for that, who has the greater responsibility . . . and it meant that I could come back and say to class teachers, these are the areas where we have specific responsibilities during this practice and to ensure that we offer students opportunities which we can offer in school which they cannot have at the university.

Despite such positive comments, when course leaders were asked how many days' training were available, the limited character of what was offered in most schemes, even to designated mentors, became apparent. Our evidence showed that the numbers of training days available ranged from one to 15 but that, in the vast majority of cases, the training offered was limited to three days at most. Comments from course leaders indicated that a smaller numbers of days (say, one to three) were compulsory for new mentors, while higher numbers were often accounted for by an option to develop training into a certificate or module leading towards a higher degree within the HEI. As one mentor explained:

> I've very much enjoyed it and feel much more confidence about doing it now, but I'm very aware that there are tutors in college who have far more experience and expertise than I do, for instance, and that they've got the breadth of having visited hundreds of different schools, you know, and they're able to sort of compare student practice across all of those different environments. I'm very conscious of that but I think the training that we've had has been probably the best it could be to actually prepare us for what we actually do in the school.

SCITT courses, although offering almost 100 per cent of designated staff training, gave them an average of only two days' training, with a range of one to five days. In other words, they did not appear to have significantly more training than that provided for teachers working within HEI-based courses. They were also less likely to offer accreditation for the training – only three of the nine respondent courses said accreditation was possible at the time, although those with courses validated by one particular institution said that this was being considered.

What about other forms of contact? How did partners keep in touch with each other? Large numbers of course leaders reported the following mechanisms: briefing meetings (173 courses); tutor visits (203 courses); collaborative planning (176 courses); representative committees (191 courses). Other reported strategies included the following: newsletters, cluster meetings, telephone contact, and annual conferences or meetings. One course leader mentioned computer links (specifically e-mail) and it is known that at least one other institution was piloting this approach at the time. However, it was also apparent that the amount of routine personal contact had, in most courses, decreased. As the mentor from one primary BA (QTS) course explained:

> We have a link tutor who's an overall link and somebody who's there to visit the second years and make sure they're OK because they don't actually get the observations and things, and just for us to ring up, you know, if there's a problem or we're not sure about something so that there's that link between school and college all the time. But there isn't a college tutor that would come in weekly.

Another mentor was more critical:

> I think we need more time alone with the tutors before the students come or during the time they're here. We do get offered certain meetings in college at certain times – usually towards the end of the course. My student now has a tutor called X who I've only met on one or two occasions . . . I don't know her very well.

Of course it is the character and the quality of those links that is as important as their quantity. Many mentors we spoke to considered that they were in a strong position to provide high quality support for their students, as this quotation from a mentor in a secondary scheme illustrates:

> I think the school takes a pride in being involved in bringing new professionals into business and I think . . . that being involved with the university gives a considerable input to the departments who are actively involved in a number of ways. The responsibility of the subject mentor has been proved in the school to be useful professional development. Erm . . . simply the injection of the students themselves into a department I think is clearly demonstrable, that that brings in fresh ideas to the department and a self-reflective quality into the department.

Others mentors, however, saw their changed role less positively, as did this deputy headteacher involved in a large secondary PGCE course:

> The situation now is that you've got the same personnel at the university department trying to do their level best to keep standards up but [the students] arrive here after four weeks as opposed to seven weeks of the old course and they are not so well-informed and do not have

the same skills. I feel, and the other mentors agree, that we keep an eye on them but we don't give them the same attention as the tutors would have done in college . . . this is because we simply don't have the time.

Course leaders were also asked if current patterns of training and contact were likely to continue. Although 85 per cent of courses anticipated carrying on with the same basic training patterns, there was obvious concern as to how this would be paid for. Special 'transitional funding' had been used to initiate and develop partnerships, including the funding of mentor training, but respondents were concerned that this would be an ongoing cost which had not been allowed for. As the course leader of a secondary scheme explained:

There's been a constant need to train staff up to work with our students and equally, even with schools staying inside partnership, it won't necessarily be the same staff every year who look after the students.

A primary course leader was also worried:

My real concern is the issue of continuing training for teacher-tutors once the initial sum of money allocated is gone . . . I have fears that the 'cascade' effect ultimately becomes so watered down that it is less than effective. If training is not funded in the future then the whole partnership concept is threatened.

Conclusion

From the evidence of our second national survey and case study work, it is therefore apparent that, by the mid-1990s, the role of schools in initial training was changing significantly. Students were spending longer on school premises and teachers were being given significant responsibility for the day-to-day supervision and assessment of practical teaching competence. However, it was also clear that the forms of partnerships that were being developed between schools and those in higher education, were, for the most part, not those set out in either of the idealized models described earlier.

In only two of our case study courses were schools being given the degree of autonomy envisaged by the complementary model, though a number of other courses were moving in this direction – usually because of the constraints of finance rather than out of principle. In the overwhelming majority of cases, however, schools were unwilling to take on a more substantial role. As we will see in the next chapter, this left those in higher education with a considerable degree of responsibility in particular for the management and organization of the courses, including the organization of school-based work.

On the other hand, a small number of colleges and universities were working with a stable group of schools and had been able to select those schools in relation to their chosen criteria; they also seemed to be in a position to offer substantial training. In such conditions, it would have been possible in principle for them to develop collaborative forms of partnership with close and regular personal contact between teachers and HEI tutors – and a few did. However, the majority of courses found themselves having to form partnerships on much more adverse terms. They were working with large numbers of schools with some turnover; difficulties in recruitment of schools meant that they had little chance of imposing their own criteria and some at least were forced to enter into different forms of contract with different groups of schools; the majority also had only limited resources for training. In these circumstances the chances of establishing genuine collaboration were substantially reduced.

Some of these findings can be contrasted with SCITT courses. Here we found relatively secure relationships developing between small numbers of schools working in consortia. However, as we have also seen, they too failed to provide the opportunities promised by the collaborative or the complementary model of training. The opportunities for working with professionals outside their designated schools were extremely limited – indeed much of their training was provided by one or two key teachers. Moreover, the professional development opportunities made available to those teachers who were involved were also found to be limited.

So much for the changing role of schools in the mid-1990s. In the next chapter we turn our attention to the implications of the reforms for the changing role of those in higher education. We also present a rather different model of partnership – one that more closely matches the reality that most institutions found themselves in when responding to the new criteria.

7 Partnership – the changing role of higher education

> Well we know from the national data that HEI staff are still holding the baby in all sorts of ways – that is what partnership means nationally.
>
> (course leader, secondary PGCE)

Introduction

In the last chapter we documented how, in response to the policy changes introduced in the early 1990s, schools took on a much more active role in initial teacher education. Our national survey of 1996 revealed that students were spending substantially more time in school, and when they were in school, in comparison with the past, teachers were taking a much more active role in supporting and assessing their practical teaching competence. The change in title from 'supervisor' to 'mentor', we suggested, captured much of the spirit of these changes. However, implicit in the findings that we presented was the fact that, despite the aspirations of New Right commentators, those in higher education retained an important, if changed, role too (Furlong 1996; Furlong and Smith 1996). In the vast majority of courses, initial teacher education was now being organized through some form of partnership.

As we saw in Chapter 6, we came to recognize that it was possible to develop more than one form of partnership between schools and those in higher education. Moreover, those different forms of partnership could well influence notions of professionalism being engendered in this new generation of teachers. As a way of illuminating the forms of partnership that were developing, we therefore compared our findings concerning the growing role for schools with two ideal typical models of partnership that were important at the time. The first we called the complementary (originally separatist) model, and this was the one that was implicit within government circulars. The second was the collaborative model, which was widely proselytised within the professional literature at the time. However, we suggested that neither of these models seemed to fit the changes in practice that we saw emerging in the majority of courses at the time.

In this chapter therefore we want to do two things. The first is to explore in more detail how the development of the partnership approach to training did indeed change the role of those in universities and colleges. Having done this, we will then return to consider the form of partnership that was in practice emerging in the mid-1990s and its implications for changing models of professionalism. To begin with, in order to understand the impact of the recent changes on the role of the higher education tutor, we briefly examine how that role has been constructed in the past.

The changing policy context

The 1950s, 1960s and 1970s – the expert emerges

In 1981, Bell published a useful paper exploring the changing nature of teacher education in England and Wales during the 1950s, 1960s and 1970s. Three types of institutions succeeded each other during these decades – the teacher training college of the 1950s was transformed into the college of education of the 1960s, which was itself later transformed into the institute of higher education or polytechnic. On each occasion, as Bell notes, there was substantial disruption and the nature and conditions of teacher educators' work were changed. At the same time, however, there was a slow and progressive move towards the establishment of the teacher educator as an 'expert' with academic expertise in the field of children's education and hence in teacher education itself.

In characterizing the changes that took place during the postwar period, Bell draws on Weber's (1948) ideal typical account of developing educational structures to suggest that the vision of teacher education (and therefore the work of lecturers) in each type of institution was different. Teacher education in the 1950s in the teacher training colleges, he argues, can best be characterized as being 'charismatic' education. Lecturers were primarily concerned to produce the 'good teacher'; training was fundamentally a 'moral' exercise. Colleges were typically small, single-sex and physically and intellectually isolated – all factors that helped to create a moral community. The curriculum was largely undifferentiated and, as far as the students were concerned, the most important person was their education tutor who had responsibility for education theory, curriculum work and for supervising their teaching practice.

Following the Robbins Report (Robbins 1963), teacher education in the 1960s was, as we noted in Chapter 1, massively expanded and relocated within the higher education system proper and the new BEd degree was born. The increased size of the institutions, the reduction in tutor and student residence and the coeducational nature of the institutions meant that relationships were less personal. In addition, the curriculum became more differentiated, academic and removed from the direct world of the school. Moreover, in order to satisfy the demands for academic rigour of the validating universities, new disciplinary specialists in sociology, psychology, philosophy and history were recruited to replace generalist education tutors. These moves were justified largely in terms of the liberal education of the students. Studying the disciplines was conceived of as 'part of the education of the scholar, who happened to want to be a teacher' (Bell 1981:13); teacher educators became 'academic experts'.

The 1970s saw further upheaval in teacher education. Large numbers of colleges of education were closed and amalgamated and there were substantial job losses. Following what many considered to be the 'rape' of the teacher education system (Henke 1977), initial teacher education increasingly took place in highly diversified institutions – the monotechnic college gave way to the polytechnic and institutes of higher education. Following the James Report of 1972 (James 1972), the academic approach of the 1960s was increasingly brought into question. What James had argued for was for a form of training that was 'unashamedly specialised and functional' (1972: 23). The educational disciplines of sociology, psychology, philosophy and history should only be studied in so far as they were of practical use in developing effective teaching. The 1970s, according to Bell (1981), therefore saw the emergence of Weber's final ideal type of education – 'specialized expert training'. Experts in curriculum, classroom interaction, geographical and mathematical education now taught students in college, but they were indeed 'experts' – sophisticated theoreticians in one specific aspect of professional practice.

The 1980s – the expert re-formed

As we saw in Chapter 1, from an ideological point of view, the Thatcher government was strongly influenced by New Right thinking (Gamble 1983; Whitty 1989) which suggested that the central problem in teacher education, as in other areas of 'state monopoly', was 'producer capture'. Thus according to O'Hear (1988b: 6) 'a large vested interest has arisen in the form of a teacher training establishment which runs, directs and assesses the courses in teacher training'. Reform of teacher education was therefore dependent first and foremost on challenging those in control of the teacher education establishment – the academic experts.

The first challenges, as we have seen, were the establishment of CATE and the issuing of Circular 3/84 (DES 1984) both of which attempted to open up teacher education to the 'realities of the market' – bringing it closer to the world of schools. However, whatever the ideological aspirations of those in the context of influence, it is clear that those who drafted the circular and indeed CATE itself saw their aim not as undermining the expertise of teacher educators but of 're-forming' it – promoting what they thought of as the best professional practice of the day. In reality what CATE sought to promote was not that different from the vision of training set out by the James Report of 12 years earlier. When the circular insisted that lecturers should periodically return to school for 'recent and relevant' experience, or when it insisted that main subject studies should be related to the curriculum of the school, its intention was not to challenge the expertise of teacher educators per se. Rather its aim was to insist that what teacher educators taught was appropriately related to the real world of school. The expertise of teacher educators was to be defined for the first time, but the right of teacher educators to be 'the experts' was not in itself questioned.

The policy changes of the late 1980s were however more contradictory, as New Right critics arguing for the complete abolition of higher education's role in training became increasingly influential. Within Circular 24/89 (DES 1989a), it is possible to identify elements associated both with the 'expert training model' (probably promoted by CATE and HMI) as well as neo-liberal and neo-conservative views. For example, the circular increased the minimum time students should spend in school and insisted on a far greater involvement of teachers in the training process. At the same time, however, it maintained a strong role for 'expert trainers'. It reasserted the importance of studying pedagogy, educational and professional studies and insisted that school experience should be closely related to these more 'theoretical' dimensions of preparation.

A similar dualism was apparent in the two new routes set up – the Articled and Licensed Teacher Schemes. As we saw in Chapter 4, articled teachers spent 80 per cent of their time in school, but for much of the training it was the expert view of the teacher educators that was to the fore. The Licensed Teacher Scheme was, however, quite different and the role of higher education was largely marginal.

The 1992 reforms – the expert suppressed?

This then was the context into which the reforms of the early 1990s came. As we have already seen, Circulars 9/92 (DfE 1992) and 14/93 (DfE 1993a) formally at least, significantly weakened the position of those in higher education, insisting that training was handled through a partnership and insisting on the transfer of significant portions of the teacher education budget to schools for their contribution. The failed idea of the 'Mums' Army' and then the SCITT experiment were even more of a challenge in that they denied in principle that those in higher education had any distinctive contribution to make to initial teacher education. This denial was then formalized with the development of the TTA, which was charged with the responsibility of 'managing' initial teacher education, wherever it was provided. How then did those in higher education respond to these changes? In the next section we draw on our research evidence to consider how their work was in reality changed by these interventions.

Who are the teacher educators and under what conditions do they work?

In exploring the changing role of higher education tutors it is important to recognize that by the mid-1990s they were not a uniform group; those recruited to the profession as well as those who moved (or were moved) out of it were heterogeneous in their professional and academic biographies. What became clear during our research was that the structure and forms of expertise of the higher education teaching force to an important degree reflected the changing conditions under which initial teacher education had been organized in England and Wales in the past. When institutions had had the opportunity to appoint new staff, they had usually done so in ways that responded to the demands of the time. For example, the criteria used by institutions in making appointments prior to Circular 3/84 (DES 1984) were often very different from those utilized afterwards. Since that date, successive circulars and other pressures, particularly the Research Assessment Exercise (RAE), continued to influence recruitment policies. As a result, at the time of our second round of fieldwork we could identify the following groups of staff, each of which was recruited at different times and with different criteria in mind.

Those recruited prior to Circular 3/84 were:

- 'disciplinary' based academics who were sociologists, psychologists, philosophers or historians. They were mainly recruited for their academic expertise in the parent discipline;
- subject studies specialists who were mainly recruited for their academic rather than school expertise in the subject area;
- curriculum/methods specialists who were mainly recruited for expertise in schools in the teaching of particular subjects and/or primary age phases. However, they frequently had higher degrees in the teaching of their specialist area.

After Circular 3/84, institutions continued to recruit subject studies specialists and curriculum/methods specialists but disciplinary experts were no longer recruited in substantial numbers. Moreover, in virtually all appointments after this circular, 'recent and relevant' classroom experience was a recruitment criterion that was given far greater importance than in the past: in many cases it was given equal significance to that of established academic expertise. For many recruited in this period, a higher degree was something to be achieved after, rather than prior to appointment. Subject studies specialists often chose to undertake their higher degrees in 'education' rather than in the parent discipline as many of those recruited prior to 1984 had done.

Within higher education institutions, therefore, changing recruitment criteria had resulted in there being a range of different groups of tutors in post with contrasting professional and academic backgrounds. The challenge for those with responsibility for managing faculties of education in the mid-1990s was therefore how to deploy these different groups of staff in a context of rapidly changing national guidelines. All types of higher education tutor, whatever the reason for their original recruitment, were now fewer in number than in the recent past. Largely as a result of the transfer of funds to schools, virtually all institutions reported that they had reduced numbers of staff directly involved in initial training. This 'wastage' had occurred through a variety of mechanisms including: redundancies, retirements, promotions, movements to other education courses, and movements to other faculties (e.g main subject departments). The following response from the course leader of a two-year conversion PGCE course was typical of many:

> How does that [the transfer of funds] affect your staffing actually in the university then – the people that were working with them [students] in the previous term say – what will they be doing then?

> Well they are not here is the simple answer. First of all our staffing was such that nobody was only involved in teaching PGCE work. So our staff was also . . . we've always had a mixed economy. So people's posts are justified by a diverse range of work. But in fact we're able to take advantage of people leaving either for a variety of reasons so that we've actually been able to reduce . . . or to put it another way round . . . we've been able to release funding to pass across to the schools without having to forcibly reduce our staffing. Just for the record I suppose we may have lost the equivalent of something like six staff – their posts have been turned into money that is now in schools.

Many of those who had left direct involvement with initial teacher education were older staff with more traditional academic biographies. Those who remained in post found the nature and the conditions of their work had changed significantly. Many of the teacher educators we spoke to reported that in comparison with 1992 there had been a greater 'intensification' of their work, but what does intensification mean in this particular context?

Increasing central control of the curriculum

Designing a curriculum that fitted the demands of the new criteria was an increasingly difficult task – particularly in primary courses. The number of hours to be spent on each of the core subjects was now centrally specified as well as time in school. The result was that more and more issues had to be packed into less and less time. The following quotation from the director of a newly developed three-year primary BEd degree well illustrates the demands and the complexities of curriculum planning under the new arrangements. It also demonstrates how, in the face of government prescription, curriculum planning was becoming an increasingly technical affair.

> The programme totals 949 hours, the days in school somewhere about 133 days. The English contact now is 112 and 38 directed in school, that goes for English, maths and science. The other three are 72 hours each, art, history and design technology with 19 connected to the school,

that makes 85 hours. Physical education is 40 hours, of which we have got 26 at Key Stage One and 14 at Key Stage Two. RE is 10.5 hours. Geography is 23.5; this will come within the primary curriculum then, 13 in the first year in Key Stage One and 10.5 for Key Stage Two. Expressive arts, which is dance, music, drama, is taught only once so it has got to do both areas, that is 26 hours. Child development is 26 hours in Year One. Equal opportunities is 13 hours, that is really one of the few education bits we have got left. Special needs provision is – there's two components – it is called dimensions of exceptionality, special needs itself is 10.5 plus the permeation which we have all got to take on board and highly able provision is 10.5 and they both work together. And the class in classroom organization, management, the nuts and bolts we have upped considerably and across the whole course to 66 hours – philosophy, sociology went six to seven years ago; there is only psychology left.

Financial and other pressures

The introduction of payments to schools had led directly to financial pressures on education faculties (this is in addition to financial pressures affecting the whole of higher education at the time for other reasons, e.g. so called 'efficiency gains'). This pressure had necessarily affected staffing levels. However, we found that obtaining precise and comparable data on staffing across different teacher education programmes was highly problematic. Courses utilized their staff in different ways. As the earlier quotation illustrates, sometimes they were deployed on one course, sometimes on many; staff–student ratios also varied substantially and increasing course sizes masked some of the worst effects of reduced funding. Nevertheless, our evidence suggests that financial pressures had resulted in:

Increased staff–student ratios (SSRs) – Our survey indicated that the mean SSR for primary and secondary courses nationally was 1:21.5. However, often the ratios we observed during our field work were considerably worse than this. For example, one educational and professional studies (EPS) tutor was required to lead a 'discussion' with 140 students while in another institution a curriculum tutor led a 'practical' creative arts session with 40 students. Additional comments on our questionnaire indicated that, with the transfer of funds to schools, there had been a substantial worsening of SSRs over the past few years from about 1:15, brought about both by increasing student numbers and/or reducing staff numbers.

Pressure to diversify – In addition to increased SSRs there has been diversification. For example, in one secondary PGCE, staff had been informed that initial teacher education now only paid for two days per week of their time; as a result all staff were expected to take on substantial additional teaching duties on other courses in order to 'cover their costs'. What 'diversification'

actually came to mean varied considerably depending on the i
context. In some institutions it meant working on other initial te
cation programmes (secondary curriculum tutors taking subjec
work in primary programmes), in others it involved working in o
ties, while in yet other institutions it involved working overseas (
of other programmes.

For example the course director of a secondary undergraduate course
described the pressures in her context:

> The university originally said it was fine and [payments to schools]
> were being taken into account, but in fact with the TTA, they are
> beginning to say, 'This course has to be cost effective and it's costing
> £X'. We are having to pay £1000 next year. We are waiting for final
> approval from the Finance Department on main campus . . . There have
> been comments like, 'get out there and earn the money that's being
> paid to schools'. It is very difficult and although you might think we
> have more free time, in fact we don't. We are being expected to do
> more and more and take on the workloads of colleagues who have
> taken early retirement.

Casualization – Casualization can take two forms: an increasing number of
staff appointed on part-time contracts and/or a greater proportion of full-
timers being appointed on temporary contracts. Once again, comparable
data were very difficult to obtain but, as an example, it may be helpful to
examine one institution where the dean of initial teacher education reported the following staffing structure for the secondary PGCE in 1992 and
1995:

> In 1992, we employed 14 full-time permanent members of staff on this
> course, plus a large number of additional part-time casual support for
> EPS and some school supervision. Now [in 1995], although the course
> has expanded by about 20 per cent, we only employ 12 full-time staff,
> but three of them are on temporary contracts. In addition there are five
> part-timers who are actually leading curriculum groups. All other part-
> time support stopped in 1993.

As a direct result of these financial pressures, many teacher educators
reported feeling increasingly insecure about their position and their future
in the profession. As the course director of one four-year primary BEd
course tellingly put it:

> Extra pressures, larger classes, reduced funding and eroded salaries have
> seriously affected [the morale of staff] together with redundancies over
> the past 18 months. Individuals who have been totally committed to
> ITT no longer view it as a viable career.

RAE pressures – Although the Research Assessment Exercise (RAE) was not a
central focus of our research, during 1995 and 1996 it was clearly a vitally
important issue for many of the lecturers we interviewed, particularly those

in universities. Significantly the RAE affected different groups of staff in initial teacher education in different ways. For some, the 'research successful', successive rounds of the RAE had led to increased status and greater institutional opportunities; the RAE had also provided a route out of initial teacher education teaching for some. For others, particularly those recruited after Circular 3/84 (DES 1984), the RAE had been a major challenge. As was noted above, many lecturers recruited to universities in that period had not themselves completed research degrees or, sometimes, even masters' degrees. As a consequence they were less able to compete for external and internal research funding and found themselves pressured to deliver on publication targets while studying for their own degrees and facing continually increasing teaching workloads.

Institutional contexts

In understanding the impact of all of the above pressures on individual lecturers, our research illustrated the importance of institutional contexts. In some institutions, the impact of reduced finance on individual lecturers was significantly affected by the mix of other subjects within and outside education faculties. Monotechnic faculties with a very limited range of education programmes were perhaps most vulnerable to funding changes. The wealth of the institution was also important. In those colleges and universities experiencing general financial pressures, there were additional demands which resulted in almost insurmountable problems for those in education. Another factor was the financial model of the institution (top-slicing etc.).[1] At the extremes, in one case study institution, top-slicing, taken before any other costs, amounted to nearly 50 per cent of student fee income. In another, central costs were calculated at 30 per cent of any residue after all costs, including staffing and fees to schools, had been paid. This, in combination with widely varying student fees between institutions resulted in substantial variation in the income to individual faculties and courses. All of these pressures also varied in how they were mediated to staff by the institutional cultures. For example, some old universities continued to protect their culture of individualism and lecturer autonomy while other institutions were subject to various versions of new managerialism. It was apparent in our research that the strengths and weaknesses of each model of partnership significantly affected how individual lecturers experienced the demands being made on them.

The changing nature of the teacher educators' work

Professional ideals

The conditions under which those tutors who remained in higher education worked were therefore materially worse than in the previous period; there were fewer of them, their staff–student ratio had substantially worsened and they were subject to a range of other pressures – financial, the RAE etc. Despite this, we found that, in the vast majority of cases, their professional ideals had changed very little. As the course leader of one four-year BEd course put it:

> The problem is that a lot of the changes that have happened haven't actually affected one's philosophy but have removed the chance of achieving it – have made one much more reactive than proactive . . . Crisis management – lack of time to actually do the job properly, lack of time to actually talk to the students, increasing student group sizes, lack of money for hard resources – we can't replace our computers when we need to, for example.

As we saw in the last chapter, the planning of courses remained largely a responsibility for those in higher education. We can therefore gain some further insight into the nature of the ideals of those in higher education by looking at 'course philosophy'. When course leaders in our national survey were asked whether their course was based on any particular model of the teacher, 137 out of 211 course leaders said 'yes' (65 per cent). Of those who elaborated on this in the open-ended section of the question, 98 (46 per cent) mentioned the word 'reflective', 86 of them using the term 'reflective practitioner' (41 per cent). Twenty-three used the word 'competent' or 'competence' (11 per cent).

Course leaders were also asked to choose three words from a list which would best characterize the sort of teacher their course aimed to produce. The three most common responses were 'reflective', 'professional' and 'competent'. Significantly, SCITT course leaders answered in a similar fashion; 'reflective' and 'competent' again being the most popular choices, together with 'professional' in secondary courses, and 'collaborative' in primary.

Overall therefore, the responses suggest that the dominant model of professionalism in initial teacher education at the time had remained that of the 'reflective practitioner' – though it was somewhat less dominant than at the time of the previous survey. Some of the other 'orthodoxies' that government and media commentators often associate with higher education-based provision, such as being over concerned with 'theory' or being 'child-centred', were rarely in evidence in the responses.

As we have seen, however, despite the continuity of ideals, the reality was that teacher educators now had to work within a competency framework defined by government and they also had to work in partnership with schools. How did they respond to these new constraints?

Working with competences

As we noted in Chapter 4, a key part of the government's strategy to reform initial teacher education was the development of competences. Circulars

9/92 and 14/93 (DfE 1992; DfE 1993a) set out a list of competences which both primary and secondary initial teacher education courses were required to focus on 'throughout the whole period of initial training'. The list of competency statements within the circulars was also to form the criteria against which students were to be assessed.

Initially, some British teacher educators had rejected the whole idea of using competences in teacher education on the grounds that it would encourage an overemphasis on skills and techniques; that it ignored vital components of teacher education; that what informed performance was as important as performance itself; and that the whole was more than the sum of the parts. This rejection was partly a reaction to American checklists of teacher behaviour, such as one scheme in which 121 separate teacher behaviours had to be checked off by an independent observer and fed into a computer to produce a competency level (see Gitlin and Smyth 1989).

However, other teacher educators who were equally scathing about such behaviourist approaches, argued that a 'reflective practitioner' model of teaching, which often claims to be the very antithesis of a technicist and behaviourist view of teaching, could itself be expressed in competence terms. Hextall *et al.* (1991: 15), for example, argued that 'teaching is not reducible to a set of technical operations' but then went on to say that they were not 'running away from the issue of the systematic appraisal of teaching competence' and that even the quality of reflectivity could be formulated as a series of competences that could be monitored.

When the Council for National Academic Awards looked at the early use of competences in teacher education course submissions, it found that there was considerable confusion about the use of the term (Whitty and Willmott 1991; CNAA 1992). A few courses did indeed define competences in terms of a series of behaviours or performances, the execution of which at an acceptable level could readily be identified by observation. However, although the superficial attractions of this approach were considerable, it took little account of the fact that in real life a competence can be applied only within specific contexts. These will vary considerably according to circumstances, and in order to perform successfully a practitioner needs to be able to respond to new situations in a way that goes beyond a decontextualized set of practised procedures. The approach was also open to the criticism that such a varied and diffuse activity as teaching could not properly be seen as nothing more than the sum of a number of discrete behaviours.

As a result, the CNAA found that most courses assigned much greater importance to the part played by knowledge, understanding and attitudes as central to the whole process of developing professional competence, and viewed these as permeating and affecting practice in an integrative and holistic way. One advantage of applying this perspective to teaching was that it could be seen to accommodate a strong dimension of values. It could thereby provide the basis for elaborating a more fully developed concept of the reflective practitioner (McElvogue and Salters 1992). Unlike simplistic checklists of teacher behaviour, this approach avoided seeming to place inappropriate constraints on the professional judgement of teachers and teacher educators.

It is usually argued that national vocational qualifications (NVQs) entail the first approach, while a high level professional occupation like teaching can only operate with this broader approach to competences. A narrow definition based on observable workplace skills is certainly in some tension with the rationale of a liberal education and with the notion of the reflective professional. However, because there was apparently little pressure to force everything into an NVQ or behaviourist straitjacket, many British teacher educators eventually took the position that, if they could find ways of working with competences that met the government's criteria without sacrificing a commitment to deeper professional values, they would be prepared to do so. More positively, some argued that, properly used, competences could actually help to enhance the quality of the professional education of teachers and help to remove some of the mystique that had too often surrounded university-based teacher education in the past.

This growing willingness among teacher educators to employ competences was evident in the findings of both our national survey and our case study visits. In our national survey of 1996, course leaders were asked whether they were using competences at the time (primary courses were not formally required to introduce them until the following year). The responses showed widespread use of competences across all types of course, both primary and secondary, though some courses (13 per cent) were using threshold competences (achieved/not yet achieved) and others (74 per cent) favoured developmental competences (noting different levels of achievement). Competences had also come to take on a major role in the management of courses – in planning, in partnership, in profiling, in assessment and in quality control.

We were particularly interested in the extent to which the existence of an official list of competences, which has often been criticized for embodying technical rationality and neglecting more reflective and critical competences, was actually changing the model of the teacher espoused by teacher educators. Although the idea of competences had become a major element in many aspects of initial teacher education (planning, teaching and assessing) only 7 per cent of courses felt that the government list of competences was sufficient in itself. Seventy-seven per cent of courses reported that they had supplemented government competences with their own; the remaining courses reported that they had developed their own competences entirely. In other words, most courses had retained considerable freedom to decide on the particular approach they took to competences.

The officially stated view in the circular was that the specific competences listed in the circulars 'do not constitute a complete curriculum for teacher education' nor can 'all aspects of a course . . . be described or assessed in [competency] form' (DfE 1992). This was consistent with our fieldwork, which indicated that there was little continuing objection to the idea of competences among course leaders, but only because they felt that reflective competences could indeed be added to the official list in order to sustain a broader definition of professionality. Course leaders appeared to believe that they could defend extended notions of professionality while still conforming to government policy. Overall our findings on competences would support Landman and Ozga's (1995: 32, 35) suggestion that, even though there was a shift between Circular 24/89 (DES 1989a) and Circular 9/92 (DfE 1992) from 'open-ended requirements . . . to the rather more technical competences', there remained considerable 'room for constructive interpretation'.

Working in partnership

Partnership was also now mandatory and this, potentially at least, had significant implications for the role and responsibilities of those in higher education. In many ways, their work with students had been curtailed. As the course leader of a two-year BEd degree said:

> In many ways all the business of developing the actual classroom prac-
> tice is largely down to the school . . . Whereas in the past I would go
> into a school and watch a student and give them feedback on the lesson
> and debriefing, obviously I am not doing that any more – the school is.

A secondary PGCE course leader said:

> Principally we have taken the area covered by the professional course
> and transferred responsibility for the assessment of that entirely and
> part of the provision to schools so that means that as far as we're
> concerned, the role of the link tutor has disappeared . . . the nature of
> visits that we make to schools will [also] change – because teachers will
> have the assessment role – we won't any more. The kind of time that
> we spend on assessment will change . . . because we are going to have
> to count it within the hours and be very restrictive.

As a result of such changes it was also apparent that the opportunities for lecturers to achieve their ideals had been substantially reduced. As one BEd course leader explained:

> Considerable chunks of HE input [are being] reduced, particularly
> subject expertise; we're reducing main subject hours considerably
> because we have to. They'll be upping their professional hours in maths,
> science and English because we have to, we're reducing the content
> of their subsidiary course, so in terms of subject knowledge, despite
> school-based assignments, I can only see our students being worse
> off . . . significantly worse off. In terms of practical skills, we hope they
> will be become better but this is a hope – we can't actually guarantee
> that the new model will prove that.

Sheer pressure of time and the demands of working with increased numbers also meant that there was less opportunity than in the past to influence students' development. From our observations of teaching sessions it seemed that many lecturers had not fundamentally changed their way of working with students during their time in college or university. Their sessions were still highly practically oriented, they still made significant use of their own pedagogy as a way of modelling good practice in school. What was different, however, was that in most cases the amount of time they had in which to cover their curriculum had been significantly reduced.

As a result of these changes, lecturers reported feeling out of touch with their students – particularly in the final stages of courses where in the past there had been scope to work on students' more advanced professional skills. Pressure of time also meant that in many courses we noted reduced opportunities for lecturers to teach their specialisms; as well as overall time being reduced, optional courses had been cut to the minimum, and educational and professional studies programmes dramatically reduced in scope.

The special needs teaching in one secondary course illustrates the changes well. Under the old scheme, the lecturer responsible for special needs had led a 'permeation model'; time was assigned for her to work with each secondary curriculum group exploring the implications of special needs in each subject area. In addition, students were given the opportunity to visit special schools and to share their experiences in follow-up discussions at the university. Students therefore had substantial specialist input on this topic – both from the lecturer and from their programme of visits which were carefully chosen to illustrate different models of good practice. Under the partnership arrangements, the course only offered two formal lectures and students were expected to follow up special needs during their existing school placement. As the lecturer herself pointed out, 'Sometimes they see good practice, sometimes they don't.'

Perhaps unsurprisingly therefore, while a minority of lecturers felt that the new regulations were an important opportunity to realize the ideals of 'collaborative partnership', the majority did not. Many expressed strong and principled reservations about what they saw as the challenge to higher education's role in teacher education in the new regulations. For these respondents, the new regulations were seen as having a number of weaknesses. The sorts of concerns most frequently expressed were as follows:

• the narrowness of the experience students were receiving in schools:

> It's because there are so many versions of English. I mean, the English curriculum is not fixed at all and that's precisely what I want the students to understand – that there is this possibility, whereas a lot of them are being closed off into what I see as being rather restrictive practices in English.
>
> (secondary PGCE tutor)

• the variability of student experience:

> Some students come back to us who have had little or no support from their subject mentor and almost non-existent general mentor tutorship and a get a very poor deal.
>
> (secondary PGCE course leader)

> One of the things that we are looking at is ... trying to ensure students get an equal opportunity of access to their teacher – in other words supply coverage being used effectively. Maybe not for an afternoon necessarily but certainly an afternoon's worth of time, but that's one of the things we are looking at the moment, we are looking to develop the way in which one can sensibly monitor the use of the transferred money.
>
> (four-year BEd course leader)

- the loss of opportunities for mutual support by students:

> One of the advantages of coming back to university after being alone is that we learn a huge amount from our peers by coming back and discussing our placements, reflecting on things that we have done that have worked and haven't worked.
>
> (primary PGCE student)

- the loss of opportunities for advanced professional development:

> Having the opportunity to boot them along at the end.
>
> (secondary PGCE tutor)

- the loss of opportunities for specialist work – sixth form experiences, optional courses etc.:

> It would be improper if I were to suggest to you that every single student has a complete range of opportunities in that phase ... we cannot provide because not enough schools offer every single student the chance to do really detailed A-level work.
>
> (secondary two-year BEd course leader)

In addition, as we noted above, it was also apparent that many tutors felt the loss of having a sustained relationship with 'their' students.

As a result of these perceived weaknesses, the vast majority of the course leaders and lecturers we spoke to believed that a continuing and strong role for higher education was essential. Means had to be found of 'managing' school partnerships so that as far as possible under the new arrangements, they continued to achieve what they in higher education considered to be effective training.

Managing partnerships

A concern to see their own principles of teacher education maintained was not the only reason that partnerships had to be 'managed', however. In Chapter 6 we suggested that although generally schools were willing to take on more responsibility for the support of students in developing practical classroom competence, the majority did not wish to take on more than this. They did not want to take the leading role that was envisaged for them either in the SCITT experiment or in the circulars (DfE 1992; 1993a). This was particularly the case in primary courses where many schools were seen as being content with their existing, limited, responsibilities. As one primary course leader explained:

> We tried to get schools to take on the delivery of courses but they did not want to get involved.

As a consequence, in the vast majority of courses, those in higher education remained firmly in charge. Indeed, as the circulars left schools' involvement to be entirely voluntary, those in higher education had little option but to take the lead where schools were unwilling to do so. As the same course leader went on to explain:

> Our new course will [therefore] still be led by us and we will say what percentage of time they ought to be teaching for example; what percentage of time should be split between the whole class and groups; we will also be providing tasks for them to do in the school.

A further pressure was the growing demand for external accountability. The extension of the remit of Her Majesty's Inspectorate to students' work in schools was of considerable concern to those in higher education. As we noted in Chapter 6, many courses had experienced difficulty in establishing their partnerships; they were working with large numbers of schools; they had little choice in who they accepted; and the training that it was possible to make available was extremely limited. Formally, Circular 9/92 stated that 'ensuring the overall quality of a course is a *joint* responsibility of the schools and the HEI' (DfE 1992: part 1, para. 3.3, our emphasis). Yet schools' lack of statutory responsibilities in relation to teacher education meant that, if they were found to be failing to deliver adequate quality, they could withdraw from training; it was in the end a voluntary commitment. In contrast, those in higher education were held responsible for training wherever it took place. If it was found to be inadequate, even in a partner school, then there was the threat of withdrawal of accreditation from the whole course. Not surprisingly, in virtually all courses we studied, it was those in higher education who were most concerned about quality control.

As a result of these pressures, as well as the continuing commitment to seeing their own ideals in teacher education achieved, the 'management' of partnerships became of growing importance for those in higher education during the period of our research. The opportunities for direct contact with students might have been reduced, but the need to manage the course as a whole through forms of quality control became ever more pressing. In developing that management, a number of strategies were of significance:

Contracts – At the most fundamental level, relationships within partnerships were increasingly managed through contracts. As one primary lecturer explained:

> There's a contract. There's a partnership contract where they formally enter partnership with us and further to that there is a letter which they sign saying they will take trainees to a particular phase.

This was a dramatic change from the way in which relationships between schools and higher education had been conducted. In the past, what those in higher education could expect for their students while in school was highly variable – dependent on the goodwill of teachers giving their time freely. With the development of contracts, theoretically at least, those in higher education had the right to insist that students had certain training opportunities made available to them.

In our national survey, 57 per cent of higher education-based courses reported that they had established some kind of contract with all of the schools in their partnership. In secondary courses, the figure was nearly 70 per cent.

Quality control – In our national survey, course leaders were asked what mechanisms were in place to ensure that all contributors to the course helped to realize its key aims and, more specifically, about mechanisms to ensure consistency and quality in school-based work. Most courses reported multiple strategies. For example, the course leader of a primary postgraduate course reported the following procedures for ensuring the delivery of the aims of the course:

1 clear school-based work task books;
2 preparation days for teachers before the main teaching practices;
3 formal evaluations by students of every placement;
4 a university link-tutor in every school to moderate across clusters;
5 external examiners' specific role.

A secondary undergraduate course respondent described quality assurance as 'a difficult issue to grapple with'. The main approaches used on this course were:

1 faculty based mentor training;
2 regular visits by faculty (university tutors) to ensure that school mentors have a shared understanding of responsibilities;
3 gaining feedback from students regarding school experience;
4 external examiners.

In our national survey the most frequently mentioned mechanisms were:

Increased documentation – Course leaders placed growing emphasis on clear documentation, particularly course handbooks, to ensure an understanding of the aims of the course for all involved. This comment from a secondary PGCE course leader was typical:

> The course handbook translates our aims into three termly themes, each with a set of objectives . . . built into the structure and content of the course via a planning matrix and assessment scheme.

Proliferation of meetings – Both higher education tutors and teachers reported attending a large number of meetings: steering groups, partnership committees, consultation committees, management committees, working parties, cluster meetings, moderation and evaluation meetings, termly and annual review meetings. Quality assurance was an important part of the remit of many of these meetings. As the leader of one four-year BEd course commented:

> I mean we have a regular dialogue with schools formally and informally – about quality – it's all about quality. It's not about resources – it's not about structure – it's about quality.

Student feedback – Student feedback became much more formalized and took on greater significance. Typical mechanisms included: staff–student committees, questionnaires, journals, assignments and formal review meetings.

Tutor visits – At the heart of the new quality control system were tutor visits. Virtually every respondent to our national survey reported that quality control was now an important part of the tutor's role in visiting schools. As the leader of a primary PGCE course explained:

> The tutorial role is beginning to change from the direct supervision of the student's practice to one involving them in 'monitoring the mentoring'.

A secondary two-year BEd course leader put it more directly:

> And we are going to make sure that the trainees are getting appropriate experience from one school to another . . . we look at the kinds of programme that the school are [sic] offering students in terms of subject and in terms of whole school issues . . . I mean we literally have to go in and troubleshoot as it were.

However, as this secondary PGCE lecturer commented, this new role as troubleshooter was not without its difficulties:

> It puts us in a very difficult position because we're in some cases going in and having to tell senior members of staff that they are not doing the job that we've actually paid them to do.

Other mechanisms – Other mechanisms included staff development and training (mentor training was seen as a key means to ensure the consistency of the course, though as we saw in Chapter 6, this was often quite limited); external examiners' visits and reports; using university-wide teaching quality assessment procedures; and Ofsted inspections. In addition, two courses mentioned 'external agencies or external assessors'.

On SCITT courses, respondents indicated that their courses used a similar range of quality assurance mechanisms to partnership schemes and that they sometimes involved those in higher education and other external agencies in their procedures. However, institutionally they had little prior experience of such matters and course leaders commented on the heavy burden that quality assurance meetings and procedures placed upon participating schools, which they felt was inadequately reflected in the current level of SCITT funding.

Overall, the growing demand to 'manage' partnerships had a significant impact on the work of university and college-based tutors. Accountability was a source of added pressure on tutors. As one four-year BEd course leader explained:

> The inspections, the monitoring, all these little bits to go with it which I have a general feeling of unease about – increasing accountability actually reduces the quality of what you can deliver because you spend too much time looking over your shoulder and not enough getting on and doing it.

In addition, lecturers seemed to spend substantially increased amounts of time in 'generalist' roles – liaising with senior school staff, teaching generalized 'professional' programmes, and overseeing mixed groups of students. While these tasks had to be undertaken by somebody if the devolved structures of school-based programmes were to be managed effectively, they resulted in fewer opportunities for lecturers to utilize their specialist skills. As a result they can be seen as part of a move within higher education from individual to collective responsibility. In the past, those in higher education had been granted considerable autonomy in their teaching. Increasingly, individual lecturers were no longer able to act as autonomous experts. Rather they were part of a larger scheme in which their personal expertise had to be deployed within a clearly defined and publicly accountable framework.

A new model of partnership

The nature of higher education tutors' work in initial teacher education therefore changed substantially during the middle 1990s. Since 1984 we have seen the progressive undermining of the notion of lecturers as independent academic specialists. Interestingly, our evidence would suggest that the most significant factor to challenge the autonomy of lecturers was not the government prescription of the curriculum in the form of competences. Far more significant were the financial pressures, particularly those induced by the transfer of funds to schools, and the increasing demand for public accountability.

What are the implications of our findings on the changing role of higher education for models of partnership that were actually being developed in the mid-1990s? In the last chapter we presented two ideal typical models – 'complementary' and 'collaborative' partnership – each of which had different implications for the professionalism of students training within them. However, we also suggested that, despite the growing role for schools, these models only seemed relevant to a small minority of courses. The evidence on the changing role of the higher education set out in this chapter would imply a rather different model – one we would call 'HEI-led'. Below we set out what some of its idealized features seemed to be. Although it is idealized, we would suggest that the model does serve to illuminate the reality we witnessed more closely than the other ideal typical models we presented in Chapter 6.

The HEI-led model of partnerships

An HEI-led model is fundamentally different from the collaborative or the complementary model in that it is indeed led by those in the higher education, though sometimes with the help of a small group of teachers acting as consultants. The aim, as far as course leadership is concerned, is to utilize schools as a resource in setting up learning opportunities for students. Course leaders have a set of aims (often set out as a set of competences) that they want to achieve and this demands that schools act in similar ways and make available comparable opportunities for all students. Within this idealized model, quality control – making sure students all receive comparable training opportunities – is a high priority.

The motivation for the higher education-led model may either be pragmatic or principled. Course leaders may in principle be committed to the idea of collaboration but find insufficient schools willing to take on this degree of responsibility or they may have insufficient resources to support the degree of liaison necessary to develop a collaborative approach. They may also feel extremely challenged by the demand to be accountable for the quality of training delivered through a highly devolved system. Alternatively, course leaders may be committed to a model of training that is antithetical to the demands of partnership. They may, for example, maintain a strong commitment to introducing students to 'the best' in educational practice within their subject area; they may maintain a strong commitment to the role of educational theory within initial teacher education. In courses that approach this ideal, course leaders' aims may not have changed significantly from the past, though the means of achieving them certainly has. If a higher education-led vision of training is to be achieved in the new context, then the challenge is how to achieve it within a highly devolved system; schools and teachers have to be drawn into the process of training in a systematic and structured manner. It may well be that it was the challenge of working in such a devolved context that encouraged course leaders to embrace the notion of competences so readily despite their early opposition to the idea.

Whether the motivation was principled or pragmatic, or some combination of the two, we would suggest that the vast majority of the courses we examined had some or all of the features shown in Table 7.1 within them.

These then are the principal findings from both of our MOTE studies on the impact of policy change on course design and course management. In the next chapter we turn our attention to the student teachers on these courses, exploring whether the changes introduced during the early and mid-1990s did indeed impact on their experience.

Table 7.1 The idealized features of the HEI-led model

Planning	HEI-led with at most some consultation of small group of teachers
HE visits to school	strong emphasis on quality control; monitoring that school is delivering agreed learning opportunities
Documentation	strongly emphasized, defining tasks for schools
Content	HEI defines what students should learn in school, often utilizing an explicit competency framework
Mentoring	mentors trained to deliver the competences the course defines as necessary
Assessment	HEI-led and defined
Contractual relationship	directive with lists of tasks and relationship responsibilities
Legitimation	acceptance of HEI-defined principles of ITE

Note

1 Top-slicing refers to the central university tax on student fees to cover university overheads – libraries, buildings, administration, etc.

8 Researching student experience

Introduction

In previous chapters, following Ball's framework (Bowe and Ball 1992), we have considered teacher education in three interlinked contexts of the policy process in two successive periods – the early and mid-1990s. In each period, we have looked at the contexts of influence, text production and practice. However, as we indicated in Chapter 1, if we are to understand the impact of the changes to teacher education that we have documented, then there is one further dimension of the policy process that needs to be considered and that is the context of student experience itself. How have the changes we have documented influenced what students actually do during their training, their confidence in their own professional preparation and their views on the training process? These are important questions, for just as there is a complex and at times unpredictable relationship between the other contexts, the same is true in relation to student experience. Simply because new forms of training are argued for by politicians or devised by course leaders, it does not necessarily mean that students' experience itself is changed. Trying to capture the implications for students of the policy changes we documented was therefore an important element of the two MOTE studies.

There are, however, numerous difficulties in researching students' views on their training. For example, as they only have their own very specific experience to draw on, they are unlikely to have any detailed historical sense of the changing nature of provision. In addition, if the research instruments used include some self-assessment of their own strengths and weaknesses in teaching (as ours did) then they might be highly partial or simply wrong in their judgements.[1] Finally, given their stage of development, students may have only limited insight into the implications of their training for their long-term, as opposed to their immediate, professional develop-ment needs. For all of these reasons, students' views on the quality of their training need to be treated with caution. Nevertheless, when placed along-side other forms of evidence, they do provide an important additional dimension in understanding the process of change.

In undertaking our research on students' experience, we were fortunate in being able to build on three earlier studies that had been conducted by HMI. The three surveys, each called *The New Teacher in School*, were under-taken in 1981 (HMI 1982), 1987 (HMI 1988a) and 1991 (Ofsted 1992). In each case, the strategy was similar. Approximately 300 newly qualified primary and secondary teachers were observed teaching for two lessons by HMI during their routine visits to schools. In addition, each newly qualified teacher completed a questionnaire which included a self-assessment of their own strengths and weaknesses on a series of key teaching skills (the teaching of reading, classroom management and control etc.), and their views about the quality and relevance of their initial training. Finally, HMI interviewed the newly qualified teachers and their headteachers in order to gain further information on their teaching skills and the quality of their preparation.

These three HMI studies were invaluable to us in providing a baseline of evidence with which to compare our findings and we refer to them through-out this chapter. They were also useful as a source of ideas for a research strategy. In comparison with HMI, our resources were severely limited. For example, in their 1987 survey, HMI report that they were able to draw on a team of 67 to visit schools over half a term. In contrast, for much of the MOTE project, we were able to employ only one half-time research officer! Classroom observation was therefore not possible and we chose instead to use a questionnaire based on that devised by HMI. Like their questionnaire, ours included self-assessment on teaching skills (e.g. for primary trainees, their ability to teach reading) as well as a section exploring trainees' views of the training they had received. Given our interest in the changing nature of training provision, and particularly the reduction of the amount of time for higher education-based studies, it also included a section on trainees' *understanding* of key professional issues as well as their skills (e.g. their understanding of the principles behind different approaches to the teaching of reading). In relation to both skills and understandings, we also asked trainees to evaluate the contribution of both schools and higher education to their professional development.[2]

During our study, we developed and distributed three different but com-plementary questionnaires. The first (the Exit questionnaire) was given to a sample of students as they completed their training, the sample being drawn from the 44 higher education-provided courses used in the first MOTE study.[3] These students were then contacted as they completed their courses. We distributed 1418 questionnaires and 574 were returned, a response rate of 41 per cent. In this chapter we refer to this questionnaire as the 'main Exit survey'. These 574 respondents provided home addresses and were then contacted at the end of their first year of teaching to complete a parallel, Newly Qualified Teacher (NQT) questionnaire, asking them to reflect on their first year of teaching and how their training had prepared them for it. Here the response rate was 215 (37 per cent). Finally, the headteachers of these 215 NQTs were contacted and asked to complete a comparable questionnaire assessing the trainees' competence and training; 118 (54 per cent) of these questionnaires were returned. In order to update our evidence, and take into account the impact of the most recent policy changes, a further sample of students were asked to complete the Exit questionnaire in the summer of 1997. Here the sample was taken from the subsample of 12 case study courses utilized for more detailed research in the second MOTE study. Unfortunately, on this occasion the response rate of 23 per cent (377 responses) was particularly low and we have therefore treated the findings from this 1997 survey separately from the main Exit survey.

In addition to this questionnaire data, we also held focus group discussions with six to 10 students during our visits to case study courses during both MOTE studies (55 discussion groups in all each lasting 30 to 45 minutes) and sat in on a number of teaching sessions. The semi-structured discussions focused on the students' evaluation of their training and particularly the differential contribution of the school and higher education-based parts of it; the observations acting as a limited form of triangulation.

Inevitably our findings must be treated with some caution. Our survey response rates, even for the main Exit survey, were at best satisfactory and our 'snowballing' sampling strategy meant that, given the attrition of respondents, the sample of headteachers in particular could not be considered representative. In addition, during our case study visits to courses, we were dependent on course leaders drawing together a group of students to act as a focus group. Though each group of students we met assured us that their views were representative, we had no means of verifying this claim. However, taken together, our data do constitute a very substantial body of evidence and through it we can gain some insight into students' experience of initial teacher education during the 1990s. As we will see, the views we recorded were in marked contrast to those documented by HMI a decade earlier.

In reporting our findings here, we have concentrated on two main issues: the outcomes of training and the differential contribution of schools and higher education to professional development.

The outcomes of training

Overall quality and value

Despite some inevitable specific criticisms, our respondents' satisfaction with their training overall was remarkably high. In our 1997 Exit survey, 97 per cent of students graded the overall quality of their training as at least satisfactory and 78 per cent of them thought it was good or very good. This is a considerable improvement on the findings from the HMI 1991 (Ofsted 1992) survey where the figures were 89 per cent and 65 per cent respectively and is a dramatic improvement on the situation in the early 1980s. The 1981 HMI survey did not report an overall level of satisfaction, but the more detailed comments revealed considerable criticism. For example, nearly half of all the respondents were critical of their courses for devoting too much time to educational studies and nearly 70 per cent thought that too little time had been spent on teaching methods and on teaching practice. By contrast, in our main Exit survey, 70 per cent of students thought that the balance of time between school and the HEI had been 'good' or 'very good' with only 3 per cent thinking it was 'poor'. The overwhelming majority of written comments on the questionnaires supported these positive views:

> There was a good balance of college/school. College gave the basics and the school experience gave the opportunity to put it into practice and experiment.

> The whole ethos and attitude towards teaching has enabled me to begin teaching in a positive and enthusiastic manner. I thoroughly enjoyed the PGCE and can honestly say it was the most valuable qualification I have gained.

> It prepared me well – gave me confidence and ability to teach effectively. Very encouraging, realistic and valuable.

In our main Exit survey, nearly 99 per cent of students reported that their course had maintained or even increased their initial enthusiasm for teaching. The following written comments were typical of many:

> Despite a very hard teaching practice I am still enthusiastic about teaching. It has highlighted the use of various teaching methods and approaches which work in varying situations. I am eager to have my own class and try out many of the things I have been taught in college but unable to do in other people's classes.

> It has increased my enthusiasm and set out a picture of teaching for me which is much more complex than I realized before I set out on training. It has widened my interest in teaching and proved to me my increasing liking for children as I experience working with them more.

Similarly positive views emerged from group discussions during our visits to courses. As a student on a two-year secondary conversion degree said:

> I think teaching practice and being in school, you realize that they all felt the same on their first job; they didn't feel they had sufficient grasp of their own subject and you realize that you don't know it all but at least you know how to sit down and apply yourself to study and pull out what you need to teach and how to read the syllabus . . . I feel that

the course has given me a tremendous ability to go out and research for myself. This is really what you need for life, dig it out for yourself.

However, there was a small minority (about 2 per cent) who reported that they had been put off by their training. In almost every case this was because of their experience in school. One postgraduate wrote:

It made me realize that as the education system stands at the moment, I'm not prepared to enter the profession. I don't agree with the current National Curriculum and I feel that too much time is spent doing paper-work and not enough time is spent really helping children learn and develop socially and mentally. The profession is full of people advising you not to go into teaching – which to me is a very bad sign of the current state of the education profession.

The vast majority of respondents did not take such an extreme view, though a great many commented on the negative views of the profession to which they were exposed. As one respondent wrote:

The teacher training course provided the enthusiasm to do the job but press, news and general attitudes towards teaching is a real off-put.

Many implied that they were saddened by the low morale of the teachers themselves:

I loved working with children but hated the negative attitudes and ethos of many who have been in the profession for years.

The increased time in schools, though appreciated, had, it seems, given trainees a clearer understanding of the hard work and dedication which the teaching profession demands as well as the time and energy required. As one primary student aptly put it, 'It is no easy life', while a secondary trainee told us:

Most teachers I see at this school don't even have time to go to the loo, let alone reflect on what they're doing!

Teaching skills and understandings

A core element in our questionnaires involved respondents making a self-assessment in relation to a series of key professional competences and under-standings. In this aspect of our work we explicitly built on and extended the HMI research and it is instructive to begin by looking at their findings.

In 1981, in HMI's own judgement, 25 per cent of their sample were 'markedly deficient in a number of the teaching skills which they might have been expected to acquire' (HMI 1982: 31); 10 per cent of the sample were judged to be entirely unsuited for teaching. The commonest weakness appeared to be the failure to assess pupils' work and to match teaching methods and materials to their needs, particularly where there was a wide range of ability, aptitude or cultural background present. The newly qualified teachers' own self-assessments were on the whole equally negative. One in five felt that they had not been well prepared to plan work, to manage classrooms, or to teach mixed ability groups; around a third felt they had been inadequately prepared to assess pupils, to teach maths, reading, and to teach less able pupils; and around a half felt they had been inadequately prepared to teach difficult and less able pupils or to undertake pastoral care duties. HMI felt that, in half of the cases, the newly qualified teachers' judgements were well founded and in a third they were over-generous. They concluded that 'it is difficult to resist the conclusion that more attention should be given to these areas of professional preparation in the course of training' (1982: 31).

By 1991 the situation had improved considerably. Eighty per cent of the new teachers were judged to be satisfactory or better and HMI considered that they were teaching a higher proportion of very good lessons than the majority of fully experienced teachers. Eighty-five per cent of secondary teachers felt adequately or well prepared to teach their subject specialism, though amongst the primary teachers the picture was more variable. Well over 80 per cent felt well prepared to teach mathematics and science but only 54 per cent felt even adequately prepared to teach reading.[4] Beyond these core subjects, confidence was considerably lower: in technology, geography, history, music and RE, between a third and a half of primary teachers felt underprepared. In relation to specific skills in 1991, the overwhelming majority of new primary and secondary teachers felt well prepared in general classroom management, cross-curricular issues, use of resources and the ability to evaluate one's own teaching. Among the aspects where new teachers felt least well prepared were assessment, recording and reporting on pupils' work and the meeting of pupils' special educational needs. In all of these areas, PGCE-trained teachers felt significantly less confident than their BEd counterparts.

How do these figures compare with our own findings in the middle and late 1990s? One important finding was that by the mid-1990s, primary teachers' confidence in relation to the teaching of reading had improved substantially. In our main Exit survey, 82 per cent felt well prepared to teach reading and at the end of their first year of teaching this figure had risen to 88 per cent. The same was true in relation to the teaching of mathematics. At the end of their course, 80 per cent thought they had been well or at least adequately prepared in this regard. Looking back at the end of their first year of teaching, 94 per cent rated their initial training in this positive way. In science, the figures stayed the same, at 88 per cent in each survey.

Overall, headteachers were even more positive about newly qualified teachers' levels of competence than the new teachers themselves. This was perhaps of greatest significance for the teaching of the core National Curriculum subjects (82 per cent thought their new colleagues had been well or adequately prepared to teach reading, 93.5 per cent maths and 98 per cent science). There were just two exceptions to this pattern: concern was expressed by a higher proportion of headteachers than by new teachers with regard to preparation for maintaining discipline and understanding the role of language in reading (but then only by 15 per cent and 12 per cent of respondents respectively). These apart, there was a remarkable consensus between newly qualified teachers and headteachers in their judgements.

With regard to training by different routes, there was some evidence that primary headteachers felt that newly qualified teachers who had been trained through the BEd were better prepared than those who came through the PGCE. A greater number of PGCE-trained primary teachers were seen as having difficulties with classroom management, discipline, differentiation and curriculum development. As one headteacher wrote, 'PGCE students would benefit from more opportunity for whole class management'. Interestingly, although numbers were small, headteachers made particularly positive judgements on those who trained through the Articled Teacher route. Articled teachers were not reported as having some of the same deficiencies as other trainees; none was seen as having difficulties with discipline and none with teaching children with special educational needs. As one headteacher wrote:

I have been very impressed by the depth of her training which has enabled her to complete a very successful first year in our school. She has been an asset to the school.

In our 1997 Exit survey, these high levels of confidence in the core subjects were maintained and confidence in non-core material had increased. Both primary and secondary trainees were also very confident in all of their basic teaching skills: selecting appropriate teaching materials, utilizing a range of teaching strategies etc. Where there were perceived weaknesses it was in relation to issues that had perhaps received less explicit attention during their training in school. This was either in areas where schools are known to be reluctant to give sufficient practical experience – for example, taking exam classes (one-quarter of secondary trainees felt inadequately prepared to teach GCSE and nearly 60 per cent to teach A-level classes) or meeting parents (nearly two-thirds of all trainees felt inadequately prepared here) – or in areas where there are known weaknesses amongst many established teachers. So, for example, over half of primary trainees and two-thirds of secondary trainees felt inadequately prepared to teach children with English as a second language; a third felt inadequately prepared to use ICT in the classroom; and a quarter felt inadequately prepared to teach children with special educational needs. In nearly all of these areas, PGCE trained teachers felt significantly less confident than their BEd counterparts.

Significantly, our NQT study demonstrated that similar proportions of respondents still lacked confidence in these specific skill areas at the end of their first year of teaching. So, after a year's teaching, two-thirds felt inadequately prepared to teach children with English as a second language and one-third felt inadequately prepared to teach personal and social education and to use ICT. Amongst primary teachers there were still significant worries about competence in the areas of RE, PE and art and amongst secondary teachers a third still felt poorly prepared to teach A-level classes, though this worry was not endorsed by their headteachers. Given that these concerns remained a year after the completion of their training, it would seem that teaching experience alone is not capable of making up for specific skill weaknesses in initial training – at least not in the short term.

However, as we indicated above, we were not only interested in skills; we also wanted to assess trainees' *understanding* of key professional issues. In our main Exit survey, our newly qualified teachers reported very high levels of confidence in their understandings of issues surrounding both the curriculum and assessment, for example, the arguments in favour of a broad and balanced curriculum, and the impact of the National Curriculum and assessment on teaching and learning. They were also very confident in their understanding of the role of critical reflection in professional development. In other areas – for example their understanding of differing views of the aims of education, different theories of child development and their relevance for education, and the reasons for different levels of pupil attainment – the vast majority reported at least adequate levels of understanding. However, despite their reported confidence in *teaching* reading, nearly one-fifth were less confident that they understood the principles behind different approaches to the teaching of reading. Other weaknesses were reported in relation to understanding contemporary political debates about education, the effect of inequalities on educational achievement and the relationship between the educational system and the economy.

Again there was some evidence that different modes of training led to different levels of confidence in understanding these key professional issues. In the primary area in particular, levels of confidence were frequently higher among those trained through the BEd route in comparison with those trained through the PGCE. In addition we found that students on school-based Articled Teacher Schemes reported less understanding of child development than those on conventional courses, but felt better prepared for talking with parents. Overall, the findings from our 1997 Exit survey did not show any significant change in trainees' confidence in their understanding of key professional issues compared with the main Exit data.

Taken together, our findings and those of HMI suggest that trainees' levels of confidence in their core skills and understandings progressively increased throughout the 1980s and 1990s. As each wave of reform started to have an impact on provision, levels of confidence seemed to grow, so that by the late 1990s, newly qualified teachers were at least as confident in most areas of their work as the experienced teachers they were working alongside. Where there were areas of weakness, in most cases these were closely matched by known weaknesses in the teaching population at large. By and large, headteachers seemed to substantiate this very positive picture.

Of course, how external judges, such as HMI would have evaluated their practical competence is unknown.[5] We also do not know whether trainees' confidence in their understanding of key professional issues, such as child development, was justified. What our evidence does show, however, is that, by the mid-1990s, trainees were largely satisfied with their preparation. In the past, newly qualified teachers had evaluated their training against the realities of what they were expected to do in their first posts and found it wanting. The growing emphasis on practical school-based work meant that by the mid- and late 1990s, newly qualified teachers and their headteachers felt that there was a close match between the training that was provided and the levels of skill and understanding currently demanded by schools.

Were these high levels of confidence entirely a product of the growing role for schools in the training process, however? As far as the students were concerned, had schools in reality become the main providers of initial teacher training? In the next section, we will explore these questions by reporting on what trainees themselves saw as the differential contribution of higher education and schools to their professional development.

The contribution of schools and higher education to professional development

Quantitative findings

As we have already seen, during the 1980s, HMI's evidence suggested that the majority of students were critical of their professional preparation for two important reasons. First, they considered that the balance between time in school and higher education had been inappropriate with insufficient time being devoted to school-based activities such as classroom observation and teaching practice. Second, many were critical of what they saw as the overemphasis on 'theory' within higher education-based work. As HMI wrote in their (1982: 4) report:

> There was widespread criticism of the lack of application of much of the work in both PGCE and BEd courses to the task of teaching. The statement that the courses 'seemed to be preoccupied with the theory of education without any attempt to consider the practical problems that would be faced in the classroom' was typical of many.

At that stage then, higher education was largely seen to be synonymous with 'theory' and school-based work with 'practice' and it was against this background that the drive to a more practically based form of training took place during the 1980s. In 1987, students were still being critical of too much emphasis on 'theory', but by 1992, HMI reported a very different picture. They said:

> New teachers were generally well satisfied with the college-based elements of their course. Two aspects were particularly highlighted: the sound preparation in specialist subject teaching and the general introduction to teaching. Two thirds of new teachers considered that education courses had been useful. Only a small minority considered that their course had been too theoretical.

> (Ofsted 1992: 27)

Table 8.1 Students' assessment of most significant contributor to development of their key professional competences (main Exit survey, n=574)

Prepared:	Significant contributors	
	HEIs (%)	Schools (%)
to use a range of strategies appropriate to different learning purposes	75	67
to plan lessons to ensure continuity and progression	69	57
to select and use appropriate teaching materials	69	66
to use information and communication technology	65	38
to differentiate the curriculum in order to meet the needs of individual pupils	60	56
to respond to pupils with special educational needs	54	45
to team-teach with your colleagues	54	56
to teach mixed ability groups	52	71
to undertake the pastoral responsibilities of a teacher	52	68
to use the appropriate discipline strategies to maintain an orderly classroom environment	45	82

As we have seen in earlier chapters, despite this dramatic change, the New Right drive towards practice continued; so much so that, in 1993, the then Secretary of State for Education, John Patten was able to declare, 'We are ensuring that teacher training is precisely that, training – undertaken as much as possible in school – and not wasted studying dated and irrelevant texts on theory' (Patten 1993).

What then did our respondents say in the mid- and late 1990s? What did they see school and higher education as contributing to their professional preparation? As we have already indicated, one group of questions within our Exit questionnaire asked students to rate their confidence on a range of key professional competences and understandings. Within the same questionnaire, we also asked them to indicate whether it was school, higher education or both institutions that had contributed most to their training in each of these key areas of professional learning.

Quantitative results from this question are set out in Tables 8.1 and 8.2. What the tables reveal is that despite the increased time spent in schools, both school and higher education were seen as making important contributions to students' development. However, it would seem that from the trainees' point of view, each institution contributed somewhat different things.

It is clear from Table 8.1 that in contrast to HMI data a decade earlier, our respondents saw higher education as contributing significantly to their preparation for a number of important practical teaching competences. In particular, respondents reported that higher education had made a significant contribution to their ability to use a range of teaching strategies (75 per cent), to plan lessons in order to ensure continuity and progression (69 per

Table 8.2 Students' assessment of most significant contributor to development of their key professional understandings (main Exit survey, n=574)

Understanding of:	Significant contributors	
	HEIs (%)	Schools (%)
the impact of the Education Reform Act (1988) on education	86	19
the role of critical reflection in evaluating your teaching	84	52
the impact of the National Curriculum on teaching	83	66
the arguments in favour of a broad and balanced curriculum	83	43
the main changes in the education system since 1944	80	3
the role of language in learning	78	38
the impact of assessment on teaching and learning	76	61
contemporary political debates about education	73	28
differing views about the aims of education	73	36
the effect of inequalities on education	69	37
the way children learn	69	37
the reasons for children's different levels of attainment	62	59
the relationship between schools and the economy	49	34
the relationship between schools and the community	44	78

cent), to select and use appropriate teaching materials (69 per cent) and to use information and communications technology (ICT) (65 per cent). In each of these areas, fewer students saw schools as major contributors. On the other hand, over 80 per cent of respondents reported that school had made a significant contribution to their ability to use appropriate disciplinary strategies in the classroom (less than half saw higher education making a significant contribution here). Over 70 per cent felt that the school had contributed significantly to their ability to teach mixed ability groups, while only just over half felt that higher education had made a significant contribution to the development of this competence.

Turning now to the issue of professional understandings, our questionnaires revealed that once again, both school and higher education were considered important. Nevertheless, Table 8.2 shows that the overwhelming majority of students saw higher education as a major contributor – even *the* major contributor – to the development of their professional understandings. So, for example, around 80 per cent of them saw higher education as contributing significantly to their understandings of such issues as the arguments in favour of a broad and balanced curriculum and the role of language in learning. Schools were seen by most students as the leading contributors in one main area of understanding – the relationship between school and community; and both institutions were seen by significant numbers of students as contributing to an understanding of the impact of the National Curriculum and the impact of assessment on teaching and learning. In relation to key professional understandings therefore, both higher education and schools were seen as making an important contribution but again in somewhat different areas. Higher education was seen as contributing to a broader range of topics.[6]

What these quantitative findings suggest overall is that, by the mid-1990s, the simplistic association of higher education with 'theory' and schools with 'practice' had started to break down. Schools were certainly seen as having a very strong practical role but this was not exclusively so, and higher education was now seen as an important contributor to the development of both 'understandings' and 'competences'. But what did our more qualitative data suggest that students actually valued about their time in school and in higher education?

Qualitative findings

School experience – 'Real kids, real life, real teachers'
In group discussions and in written comments, most students made it clear that they saw both schools and higher education as important. As one student explained:

> Both institutions should have a role in every aspect of training. You can't just take it from one or the other. Every aspect of training needs to be done by both school and college but with improved communication and organization.

Another respondent saw this as knitting in well with the higher education-based aspect of the course:

> Practical experience in teaching complemented the institution-based theory.

However, despite valuing both institutions, for the majority, it was work in school that was seen as the heart of the course. So, for example, when respondents to both of our Exit surveys were asked what aspects of school-based work contributed most to their professional development, many simply wrote 'all' or 'everything'. It was the 'real' aspects of school that were valued most: 'real kids', 'real life context', 'real teachers'. As one secondary PGCE student wrote:

> Being in the classroom and gaining hands-on experience . . . all the theory in the world will never prepare you for actually being there.

Another wrote:

> Real hands-on experience with children that cannot be produced in a college environment and understanding of what it is really like in school.

Interestingly, trainees did not just appreciate school experience as an opportunity to develop new skills and understandings; they also valued it as an opportunity to find out things about themselves. Comments such as, 'Being able to experiment with different teaching strategies to find the most appropriate for me' and, 'The enjoyment of teaching proved that I had chosen the correct job for me' were common.

On the process of learning, a number of students talked about the challenge of being 'thrown in the deep end', and of having the opportunity to make mistakes, using words like 'trial and error' and 'the opportunity to experiment':

> How to be in the classroom, what to say and do. Teaching practice is a process of trial and error; in other words if it doesn't work, don't do it again and find something else. You can only learn to teach by actually doing it.

> Making mistakes and being advised how to avoid them in the future.

As we have already seen, in the 1980s, HMI studies had indicated that students were frequently critical of their school experience. Not only was it not long enough but when they were in school they complained of insufficient opportunities to observe and work alongside experienced teachers. Our respondents presented a very different picture. Being observed by teachers who then provided feedback and having the opportunity to observe was frequently mentioned as a valuable part of school experience. Sometimes, observation had the effect of 'watching how teaching should not be done':

> I discovered how I did not want to teach, i.e. I saw very unmotivated pupils being taught in the completely wrong style with no encouragement.

Mostly, however, the teacher input – from headteachers, from other colleagues and particularly from mentors – was positively assessed as having contributed greatly to students' professional development. Students wrote and talked positively about the importance of a range of different opportunities: to see experienced teachers in action and have access to a 'variety of teaching experience'; to talk with teachers of 'difficult classes after I had taught them'; to discuss lessons before and after observing and teaching; and to have the opportunity of working alongside a variety of different professionals. In all of this, having explicit support from mentors was seen as critical:

> Subject mentor support and feedback was essential and worked best on a daily basis to start with – it built confidence in your abilities and helped set targets to work towards.

> Discussion of lessons with the mentor for the week ahead was helpful – about what will and will not work.

If there was a downside to school experience, it was that, through it, a significant minority of students was exposed to negative and cynical attitudes:

> It's depressing when on TP [teaching practice] to see that all the staff ever talk about is early retirement, lowering standards and personal stress-related crises.

I feel the need to guard against becoming as cynical as many teachers that I met in my TP school.

Even so, the fact that, as we have already noted, the vast majority of students felt that their enthusiasm for teaching had been maintained or even enhanced by their course implies that most of them were able to rise above these negative comments.

From a review of all of our qualitative evidence it is hard to avoid the conclusion that, for the overwhelming majority of our students, work in school was the most important aspect of their professional preparation. It was here that they learned how to manage classes, how to discipline pupils, how to plan lessons and how to carry out assessment. As so many of them said and wrote, there is no substitute for actually doing the job. Yet despite this recognition, there remained a sense in which most students did not see work in school as sufficient in itself. Some skills, such as discipline and classroom management, were seen as being learned primarily in the classroom. For many other skills and understandings, however, the classroom was the context where, with appropriate support from mentors and others, they were able to *put into practice* what they had learned elsewhere. Practical experience, although vital, was not seen as sufficient in itself.

Higher education – learning from 'theory'

'Theory'
Despite having more time in school and despite the growing professionalism of the work of mentors, learning in higher education (what many students still referred to as 'theory') was seen by the overwhelming majority of our respondents to have a vital role to play. Comments such as the following were common:

> Having studied and discussed 'theory' before being sent to schools gave great confidence.

> Teaching practice was the most helpful but I definitely needed the theory first.

What did our respondents mean by 'theory', however? What they were *not* referring to was the sort of explicit theoretical knowledge directly taken from the foundation disciplines of sociology, psychology, philosophy and history that had dominated the teacher education curriculum in the 1970s and early 1980s. In the vast majority of cases, the students we spoke to were describing something that they saw as much more professionally focused and practical.[7] Primary students, for example, commented favourably on their 'theoretical' coverage of the core and foundation subjects, subject knowledge, and the importance of learning how to 'operationalize' the National Curriculum and cross-curricular themes. These were things that were not necessarily well covered in school. One primary PGCE student spoke for many when she commented that she gained most from:

> Training to deliver and interpret the content of the National Curriculum, the core aspects particularly. These curriculum studies plus educational studies combined to contribute significantly to my professional training and equipped me to teach all areas, but with more confidence in the core subjects.

Another spoke of working in the area of primary mathematics:

> Our maths has been incredible – really full . . . some of it has been particularly useful in explaining where the children would have difficulty with the steps. So theory of what the subject is about, children's problems, the sorts of things you can do to cope with the subject . . . It's been very supportive as well. They didn't pretend that we were all brilliant mathematicians and really confident – that has helped build our confidence.

The following comment from a student on the same course illustrates an approach that was commonly adopted in primary courses in particular. Given the limited amount of time available and the potentially huge range of the curriculum to be covered, the emphasis in curriculum studies such as history or geography had to be on teaching the students how to find things out for themselves rather than teaching them content directly. In this particular course, the time available for covering history, and the remainder of the non-core subjects in the curriculum, was 10 hours.

> So how do you make up for your lack of subject knowledge in history?

> Most of it has been linked to the National Curriculum but from the history point of view it was looking at sources. It told you a lot about where to find the sources and what you needed. When we did a project we were told to be resourceful. Go to the museum and get somebody in with some artefacts, or you could have a day when you'd bring in all sorts of other things, maps and this is how you could use them.

Both primary and secondary students also commented favourably on what they had learned about the 'theory' of planning. Interestingly, planning was something that was also mentioned when considering the contribution of school-based work. As such, it throws further light on what the students actually meant by 'theory' and the differences in what was learned in the two contexts. School experience was appreciated because it gave practice at planning for 'real' teaching; the need to plan was immediate and pressing. Higher education, on the other hand, focused on planning sustained schemes of work. As one four-year BEd student explained:

> They give us so many ideas for lesson plans. We could have a whole scheme of work for five weeks just from what we've done.

None of our respondents mentioned this aspect of planning when describing what they had learned about the issue in school. Perhaps because longer term planning was not part of students' day-to-day work in schools, it remained 'theory' – valuable, but detached, no matter how practically oriented the sessions that were run.

Despite the largely practical and professional orientation, there were some negative comments on theory in our two Exit surveys, but, in line with our quantitative findings, very few indeed. Comments like the following were rare:

> The institution-based side of the course confirmed my previous views that there is a lot of talking in such places but little action or practical help!

Interestingly, our group discussions with students revealed slightly more dissatisfaction. However such criticisms were usually because of the way 'theory' was taught rather than its existence in principle. For example, one student said:

> It's vital that we get the theory but is the delivery of it in the university the best way to do this?

> We had bad lecturers on gender and discipline. Equal opportunities we only touched on. This left you to deal with these things if they occur.

During our fieldwork it became apparent that the perceived value of theory changed over time. Students in years one and two on undergraduate courses or in year one of a two-year programme often felt the need for more practical experience and less theoretical input. However, the students we spoke to who were entering the final stages of their training, like those who completed the Exit questionnaires, were frequently appreciative of the theoretical input they had received. Some students explicitly referred to the fact that their view of theory had changed during the course. As a part-time PGCE student commented:

> I find myself constantly going back to the OU [Open University] frame-works – I really need that. But we needed the school experience to make them relevant. In year one, a lot of stuff didn't mean much to me. And a lot of the seminars didn't seem relevant.

For many students then, the key issue was the way in which theoretical inputs were integrated with the more practical elements of the course. In the early stages of training, the lack of practical experience sometimes made the theoretical inputs appear irrelevant. However, as one primary under-graduate student noted

> When you observe the children doing it you can fit the theory and make the links.

A secondary licensed teacher on a Licensed Teacher Scheme, which pro-vided some higher education-based training, described a similar experience:

It was more on classroom management than on how to teach science. At the time I could not see the point of it all but then it started to click, particularly after we had started going into school – not during the visits but during the two terms' job. Now, looking back on it, it was brilliant. It provided you with everything you needed.

Range

Also appreciated was the fact that through higher education, students were exposed to a broad range of practice – more so than was available in any one school:

You've got a huge range – the lecturers have all got different ideas and therefore you get to learn different ideas, different philosophies – you don't necessarily agree with them but you are exposed to them – you are not just channelled in one direction.

Or as other students put it, the higher education course provided:

Individual modules that dealt with each curriculum area, providing opportunities for gathering ideas, resources, planning and assessing a particular area of the curriculum.

While many students were strongly appreciative of the support they had received in schools, there was lots of evidence that school experience was still extremely variable and higher education was expected to 'plug the gaps'.

In my subject area the school department was a bit outdated. It was really at a parochial level.

One danger of putting us in school more is that we would be too dependent on them. Their input is restricted. We need college. They haven't got time or expertise to cover assessment with us for example.

Vision

As we indicated above, nearly 98 per cent of the respondents to our main Exit survey indicated that their course had maintained or enhanced their enthusiasm for teaching. For many students, higher education played an important part in this process by providing a vision of what good teaching actually was. For example one student said:

It gave me a very idealistic way of teaching in the institution-based part of the course, giving me very high expectations of what to expect in a school. The school experience gave me a realistic attitude but I am still maintaining my high expectations and lots of enthusiasm for the subject I teach.

Another commented:

The best examples of teaching came from my main subject tutors. Their enthusiasm for the subject was infectious and it made me realize how much the attitude of the teacher can affect the attitude of the learner.

They encouraged us to experiment, to look at things differently, try different approaches and in the end enabled me to achieve very highly, higher than I thought was possible. It was an awesome example of the power of successful teaching.

This last student, who was on a four-year BA/QTS programme, was particularly eloquent, but many others wrote and spoke positively too:

My own enthusiasm has been kindled by the infectious enthusiasm of my subject tutors at school and at university.

The detailed information provided by my subject tutor – including different approaches to teaching English – has made me more enthusiastic about entering the teaching profession.

Despite the increased time and contribution of schools, higher education was, for significant numbers of our students, still seen as an important source of ideals and models for teaching. Sometimes these ideals were matched by what they found in school and sometimes they were not:

I think it's been successful because a lot of us have gone into school and been reflectively critical of the maths in school. We may have reserved judgement but what we have been told in college goes on in schools which is wrong practice, i.e. book work. This is one way that the course has helped us to see that it's not just a case of putting a book in front of a child. This is useful up to a point. I think the course as a whole has been like this – it's been an enabling course, to say 'Good practice is . . . see what goes on in school'.

How students experienced the differences between school and higher education varied considerably. Some felt that they received similar messages from school and higher education. As one secondary BEd student aptly put it:

Everybody plays the same tune but in a slightly different way.

Others, such as this two-year secondary BEd student, experienced tensions:

I felt there was still a very traditional approach in school – they didn't have time for the new approaches. I found that it was difficult because you were encouraged in college to try new things, try experiential learning and more varied and interesting ways, which gives you a totally different relationship with the pupils, whereas in school a lot of the time – not all of the time because there were some members of staff who did that – but I did find there was a certain area of conflict. I decided to do what suited me.

Other students persevered with the visions they had been given. As a secondary PGCE student commented:

They give us ideas to try out in schools, such as new approaches. We didn't use them at first and I thought, 'Why are we doing this?' but now, at the end of the course, we are able to apply them.

Reflection

As we have indicated in earlier chapters, in both of our national surveys, the overwhelming majority of course leaders stated that their courses were based on the principle of 'reflection'. As many others have commented (Alexander 1984), the dominant model of professional learning advanced by teacher educators has changed from the receiving of theory to 'theoriz*ing*' through reflection. We have seen that our students had little or no exposure to the traditional theory of education – at least as it was conceived in an earlier generation – but did they recognize and value 'reflection' as a key part of their professional development instead and, if so, what did they mean by it?

Certainly many (though not all) students recognized the importance of reflection within their course. Some complained that tutors had pushed the idea too hard:

> Critical reflective, space to reflect, reflective teacher . . . we are battered to bits by it. The tutors feel very flattered when we start reflecting! Reflective practice – we got punch drunk with the term!

Despite such reservations, the overwhelming majority of the respondents to our two Exit surveys considered themselves well prepared in this area with higher education seen as the main contributor. For example 84 per cent of our main Exit survey reported that higher education had made a significant contribution to their understanding of the role of critical reflection in evaluating their own teaching and nearly three-quarters reported that higher education had contributed significantly to their ability to appraise the effectiveness of their own teaching. The contribution of schools in each of these areas was significantly less.

In our questionnaires, it was we who provided students with the term 'reflection'; as a result we may have made the concept appear more concrete and real than it actually was for them. Some support for this interpretation comes from the fact that, in group discussions, we found that not all of our respondents recognized the term despite its significance for tutors. However, what nearly all of our respondents did recognize and value was the opportunity provided by higher education to think about what they were learning in school. As one secondary PGCE student put it:

> There's no time to think when you're in the classroom.

Another said:

> It is difficult to be genuinely reflective in school. We need the period of college-based work and we need to know what good practice is. We need the theory because otherwise it is difficult to stand back.

This last student implied that, for him, theory was an important resource for reflection. However, for the majority of our respondents, reflection was rather more pragmatic – it was a collective sharing of experience. It involved:

Discussion with other students about successes and problems. Exchanging experiences with other members of the group, exchanging material and ideas. The opportunity to discuss experiences and teaching strategies and to share reading materials with fellow students.

For many students it was this aspect of higher education that was one of its most valuable contributions to their professional learning. Formal and informal discussion with fellow students provided emotional support – and an opportunity for sharing ideas.

The main value was pouring my heart out with the PGCE students.

As two students explained:

I think from day one we've been very much encouraged to draw on our colleagues. If you can't do it then find somebody who can . . . Everybody has got a great big pool of information, everybody can contribute their knowledge and experience, and we pass it on to our colleagues.

For some students, therefore, reflection had the characteristics that writers such as McIntyre (1993b), Hirst (1996) and others have urged. It implied a critical process, reviewing personal experience in the light of other forms of professional knowledge (descriptions of practice; principles derived from practice; the findings of research; theoretical insights derived from the 'foundation' disciplines etc.). For the majority, however, it seems that reflection was much more of a 'lay' activity where trainees struggled to come to terms with their own experiences by articulating them and sharing them with others. As a model of reflection, this approach has much more in common with Schön's (1983, 1987) ideas of 'reflection-on-action'. It is certainly a very valuable part of professional learning. It is through capturing practical experience in language that we come to 'know' it in a different way; we re-interpret and thereby better understand what we have learned through our practice (Furlong 2000). This is why it was appreciated by so many of our respondents. However, if reflection remains only this, rooted in particular practical experiences, then its implications for professionalism are significantly different from when trainees are systematically provided with opportunities to engage with other forms of professional knowledge (Zeichner 1994; Hill 1996).

Conclusion

If we compare our findings with those of the HMI *New Teacher in School* surveys, particularly the two conducted in the 1980s (HMI 1982; HMI 1988a), then it is hard to avoid the conclusion that, from the students' point of view at least, the reforms to teacher education carried out during the 1980s and the first part of the 1990s were a success. In the course of 10 years or so, the response of students to what is one of the UK's largest sectors of higher education had been turned from a significantly negative one to an over-whelmingly positive one. Certainly there remained some criticisms and identified weaknesses but the criticisms were from a very small minority of students and the identified weaknesses were in relation to specific issues rather than the training overall. By and large the students we met and surveyed felt well prepared for teaching and their employing headteachers confirmed this view.

Of course our central research question concerns not so much how well prepared students felt but the model of professionalism that was being engendered by the training they received. What insights have our student data given into this issue? Certainly our evidence confirms the view that, by the middle and late 1990s, initial teacher education had become an overwhelmingly practical affair. The fact that students felt well prepared to teach and the fact that their headteachers confirmed this view, implies that the training they received was very closely related to the world of school. The development of school-based teacher education meant that the curriculum students studied was now closely defined by the world of schools.

In one sense, given that students were spending substantially more time in schools, this growing practical orientation is unsurprising. However, our student evidence confirmed our own observation that, by the mid-1990s, work undertaken in higher education as well as school-based work was overwhelmingly practical. Higher education tutors not only took their agenda of issues to address from school, they also saw it as their responsibility to provide practical preparation for their students. Despite the growing role for school-based support provided by mentors, our evidence demonstrates that the formal responsibility for providing key elements of this practical preparation remained firmly with those in higher education.

Does the fact that the training had become fundamentally practically oriented mean that there was now no difference between the forms of professionalism sponsored by tutors and those currently found in schools? Here our evidence was equivocal. Certainly significant numbers of students looked to their higher education tutors for a sense of vision in their teaching. That vision came through the forms of practical preparation in which students engaged while in higher education. Of course curriculum studies and methods tutors have always seen it as their responsibility to provide their trainees with a sense of what constitutes good practice in their subject area. However, in the past such tutors were often accused of being out of touch with reality. Our respondents certainly recognized that what they witnessed in schools often failed to live up to the ideals they had been given, but only a small minority complained that the vision was inappropriate.

However, traditionally, teacher education has not only sought to provide students with a practical vision of good teaching, it has also sought to develop their ability to take a critical perspective on educational practice. In the past this was intended to be achieved through the study of educational theory. The 'disciplines of education' – sociology, psychology, philosophy and history – were justified within the teacher education curriculum because they were seen to provide a source of critical questions with which to interrogate current practice. As we have seen in earlier chapters, our course leaders saw their courses achieving similar objectives through the development of students as 'reflective practitioners'. Certainly some students we met did interpret the notion of reflection in this critical way. However, as we have also seen, the majority did not. For most students, reflection was a pragmatic strategy for thinking through and sharing the practical experiences they were having in school. The opportunity for the concept to take on a role in critical education was therefore unfulfilled for many students.

Throughout the 1970s and 1980s student teachers were frequently critical of their initial teacher education and that criticism, documented and publicized through HMI's three *New Teacher in School* surveys, was politically extremely significant in the reform of teacher education, especially in the 1980s and early 1990s. Negative findings reporting student dissatisfaction, especially from the 1981 and 1987 surveys, easily translated into inflammatory headlines which helped pave the way for the reforms that were introduced. However, one has to ask why it was that the new teacher surveys came to an end in 1991. Given the centrality of teacher education reform within government policy, such a decision seems remarkable. Presumably there were many reasons, but it strikes us as significant that the surveys were dropped once they started to tell a positive story. As we have seen, the 1991 HMI survey was largely positive and our own findings from the mid- and late 1990s were even more so. We therefore cannot avoid the conclusion that once students had stopped being critical, their voice became less politically significant in justifying the reforms that the government and their advisers wished to introduce. In the middle and late 1990s, it was the development of a new National Curriculum for initial teacher education and a different form of evidence, derived from a newly devised inspection regime, that were used to drive the change process forward; the student voice was silenced. It is to consideration of these more contemporary changes that we turn in the next chapter.

Notes

1 HMI, in their 1981 survey of new qualified teachers (HMI 1982), suggest that when teachers' self-assessments were compared with HMI judgements on teaching performance, the self-assessments were more or less accurate in 50 per cent of cases. In one-third of cases, HMI judged the teachers to be overgenerous in their self-assessments.
2 See Appendix for details of the self-assessment items used in the MOTE questionnaires.
3 These covered all different types of course – conventional BEd and PGCE courses as well as non-conventional ones – conversion courses, shortened BEd courses, and Articled and Licensed Teacher Schemes.
4 Significantly this was a time when the debate over the teaching of reading first started to reach the popular consciousness. It could well be that this factor had to

some degree undermined these new teachers' confidence in their abilities. This interpretation would certainly help explain the very dramatic improvement in confidence that we recorded in our own research.

5 As we will report in the next chapter, the findings of Ofsted inspection at the time were themselves deeply contested and an Ofsted report which would have largely supported trainees' positive views of their training was suppressed (see Kane and Furlong 1996).

6 The difference in range is illustrated by the fact that respondents entered 6292 positive responses in the higher education column compared with only 3717 in the school column.

7 It is however interesting to speculate on how much the 'professional wisdom' they gained from their tutors was perhaps, at one stage removed, influenced by more conventional theoretical knowledge. Our own interpretation would be that the influence of disciplinary theory was still in evidence but that it was much less explicit than in the past.

9 Policy and practice in the late 1990s

Introduction

Throughout this book we have suggested that much government policy since the mid-1980s has been framed with the explicit aspiration of changing the nature of teacher professionalism. We have argued that successive Conservative governments through the 1980s and 1990s aspired to challenge the existing model of teacher professionalism advanced by those in higher education. That model was based on a traditional conception of professionalism; prospective teachers needed to be educated in a way that would allow them to work as autonomous professionals. In order to achieve this aim, those in higher education based their courses on a number of principles. For example, that student teachers needed to develop particular educational values; that they needed to be knowledgeable about current educational practice and theoretically informed so that they could recognize the principles underlying current practice; and that they were capable of combining their values and their knowledge in order to make their own independent judgements as to what was and what was not effective practice. By contrast, we would suggest that the aspiration of successive Conservative governments during this time was to establish a different conception of professionalism where teachers were highly competent practitioners, proficient in working in ways that they considered appropriate to schools facing the demands of a changing national and global economic context. In Chapters 2 and 5 we described how government policy in two different periods (the early and mid-1990s) sought to challenge the autonomy of higher education and establish a more uniform and practically relevant form of preparation.

The empirical aim of the two MOTE studies was to assess how far these aspirations had been achieved in practice. When we came to look at how courses were in fact organized, we saw that, in the early 1990s, there was still considerable latitude available to those in higher education and as a result many of their traditional values were still seen to underpin course design, if in a somewhat different form. Certainly there was a far greater focus on the practical dimension of teaching than in the past, but by and large, what 'the practical' meant and how it was delivered was left to 'the experts' in higher education to decide. As we saw in Chapters 3 and 4, for the most part they chose to deliver it themselves, employing the notion of the reflective practitioner as a means of maintaining traditional commitments to theoretical knowledge and to values while responding to the government's demands for practical relevance.

In the mid-1990s, the focus of our second MOTE study, we saw that the degrees of freedom available to those in higher education had been substantially curtailed. The demand that students should spend far greater amounts of time in school, and that higher education institutions should pay for the school contribution, meant that, if the reflective practitioner model was to be achieved, then the teachers working with students in school had to be drawn more fully into the educative process. After all, school was where students now were for a substantial part of their course. In Chapters 6 and 7 we saw that, while many teacher educators aspired to maintain the ideal of the reflective practitioner by working in collaborative partnership with those in schools, in reality that was increasingly difficult. Relationships in many courses became increasingly bureaucratic and opportunities for influencing the detail of what went on in school were more limited than many of those in higher education would have wanted.

In the previous chapter, drawing on data from across both MOTE studies, we reported on the views of students. We found that the overwhelming majority valued their professional preparation; they appreciated the substantial amount of time they had in school and welcomed the fact that their curriculum – what they were expected to learn – was so closely related to current practice in school. However, as we also saw, higher education tutors remained important both for the practical preparation they gave and for pedagogical vision they provided. Indeed we suggested that 'pedagogy', what Millett (1999), chief executive of the TTA, has described as 'the last corner of the secret garden', remained the only medium through which higher education tutors were able significantly to influence their students. Nevertheless, for many students that influence remained important.

Overall, therefore, we cannot avoid the conclusion that, during the early and mid-1990s, successive governments did make considerable progress towards achieving their aspirations. The cumulative effect of a range of different policies – the invention of new routes into teaching that specifically excluded higher education, the definition of competences, the prescription of how partnerships were to be formed, the undermining of the financial stability of schools of education in universities and college – all of these factors contributed progressively to curtail the influence of those in higher education on the professional development of new teachers. Instead, what students increasingly received was a form of preparation that was in its own way highly professional: it was demanding, relevant, practical and closely mirrored current work in schools. However, it was, we would suggest, significantly less concerned to develop students' ability to work as autonomous professionals than in the past.

The aim of this chapter is to bring our study up to date by examining policy in the late 1990s. Inevitably, the story that we tell will be more limited than our earlier work. By the late 1990s, our empirical research had come to an end and therefore all we can present here is an analysis of the first two contexts of the policy process – the context of influence and the context of text production. How the policy texts of the late 1990s actually changed course design and how students experienced them must remain the focus of further research. However, despite this limitation, we believe that an analysis of policy in the late 1990s is essential to our thesis in that it was a period of important transition in teacher education policy; there was continuity, but there was real change too.

The continuity was in the continued attempt by an increasingly assertive Ofsted and TTA to develop ever tighter forms of control – to insist even more than before that initial teacher education conform to the patterns of provision defined centrally. In order to achieve this aim, new and more effective 'technologies of control' were developed. What was different was the aspiration on the part of government for the first time to define a *content* to the new professionalism. Once control had been taken, it was no longer necessary for those in power to accept that 'the market' should determine the content of professionalism; that students should learn what it is to be a teacher of English or science or mathematics simply through enculturation in *current* practice in schools. Instead, through the development of the National Curriculum for initial teacher education, there was now a concerted attempt to use initial teacher education to define the nature of teaching in those subjects – to set out the content of professional knowledge and even to define the pedagogy that trainee teachers must use. As we will see, the new Labour government of 1997 was quick to recognize the importance of maintaining tight control of the system to achieve its own policy aspirations.

Tightening the grip – Ofsted inspections

As we saw in Chapter 5, one of the early strategies proposed by the TTA to increase their control of the system was through the development of a summative, competency-based career entry profile. In 1995 they began piloting a competency profile which, it was proposed, should be completed for all trainees at the end of their course. If it had been successful, there is little doubt that the competences defined in the profile would have, in effect, become a National Curriculum of initial teacher education; that is how course success would have been measured. However, extensive trials demonstrated to the TTA what many in initial teacher education already knew – the impossibility of ensuring consistency in competency assessment across tens of thousands of school mentors working with up to 30,000 graduating students each year. As a result, the competency element in the career entry profile was quietly dropped. In the event, though, a far more effective strategy for increasing control of the system was achieved through the development of Ofsted inspections and the subsequent use of the results of those inspections by the TTA in its management of the system.

Ofsted was first established under the leadership of Her Majesty's Chief Inspector by the Education (Schools) Act of 1992 and took over and in many ways transformed the traditional work of HMI. Its core principle for much of its work was and is 'improvement through inspection'. In the past, HMI had used a largely qualitative methodology, seeing the main purpose of its inspections as providing a basis for advising government on policy. Some changes, such as the publication of inspection reports, predated Ofsted, but the new body was explicitly intended to make 'independent judgements about schools, teaching and learning based on objective inspection and analysis of performance measures' (Cabinet Office 1991: 41). Through inspection, there was to be 'pressure to emulate the best' (Cabinet Office 1991: 5). Or, as Lawlor put it, Ofsted would be collecting 'objective evidence about schools and reporting on their failings' (1993: 7). Inspection evidence was a key part in the development of a competitive quasi-market in education through which, it was assumed, standards would rise. Critics, however, characterized it as a 'name and shame' approach that would merely demoralize teachers in disadvantaged schools and exacerbate a spiral of decline (Mortimore and Whitty 1997).

Throughout the 1990s, Ofsted pursued its highly controversial inspection strategy in relation to schools; many considered it hostile and invasive. To begin with, under the leadership of Stewart Sutherland, Vice-Chancellor of London University, its work in initial teacher education was less confrontational, perhaps reflecting the more tentative role HMI had had in the past in relation to higher education institutions and particularly to the older universities. However, with the appointment of Chris Woodhead as Chief Inspector in 1994 things began to change.

The move to more quantitative forms of measurement in inspection necessitated the development of a publicly available inspection framework. For the first time, HMI began to work with explicit and publicly available criteria and the inspection framework documents for initial teacher training quickly became key policy texts for course leaders to interrogate; they constituted the criteria on which they were to be publicly judged. In its first format (Ofsted 1993c) the inspection framework was broadly based. Its aim, as in earlier inspections, was to provide a holistic assessment of the quality of a particular training course. However, a revised framework issued in 1996 (Ofsted/TTA 1996) and then later refined in 1998 (Ofsted/TTA 1998) was much more tightly focused and detailed. The movement to this more detailed approach was itself significant and illustrates the increasing politicization of the inspection process. It also illustrates the key role played in those politics by Chris Woodhead.

Until Woodhead's appointment, inspection had been an intermittent process with institutions visited every four or five years, although there had been a previous flurry of activity in the mid-1980s in preparation for the accreditation of courses by CATE. However, in just one year, 1995/6, Woodhead oversaw an inspection of all primary initial teacher education courses in England, with HMI surveying 67 institutions in all. The inspections reported on the quality of training and of students' teaching in four key areas: English, mathematics, assessment, recording and reporting, and quality assurance. Because of the comprehensiveness and speed of this inspection, it became known as the 'primary sweep'. Following such a substantial programme of inspections, it is normal practice for Ofsted to produce a summary report, commenting on the strengths and weaknesses of provision. In this case, an interim report based on findings from two-thirds of the survey was informally in circulation. However, that report was never published. What was announced instead was a controversial 're-inspection' of 20 institutions including a number which had been assessed as being of the highest quality during the primary sweep.

Interestingly, the interim (unpublished) report gave a largely positive view of provision. Each area was judged on a four-point scale: 'Very good', 'good', 'sound' (significantly changed from 'satisfactory') and 'unsatisfactory'. The interim report concluded:

> Across the four areas inspected, standards are generally sound or good. These findings indicate the extent to which HEIs are responding, often very quickly, to the changing training demands . . . These developments have all helped to drive up standards.
>
> (Ofsted 1996a)

Such a view of the health of the system was considered profoundly flawed by the chief inspector and he ordered the 're-inspection'. As the leader article in the *Daily Telegraph* put it:

> The courageous decision by Chris Woodhead, Her Majesty's Chief Inspector, to order a mass re-inspection of teacher training is dramatic recognition of how thoroughly the education system has been corrupted by the debilitating ideology of the liberal establishment . . . In all but three cases, the inspectors judged everything was going swimmingly. How could it be otherwise? Did they not share with those they were inspecting a view of education that discounts academic rigour, glorifies child-centredness, rejects phonics – the only sure way to teach reading – and scorns repetition and drill for example in the teaching of arithmetic?
>
> (*Daily Telegraph* 1996)

Woodhead, it seems, was particularly hostile to the finding that 'almost without exception, courses are training students to teach phonics as well as other approaches to teaching reading' (Ofsted 1996a: 3). The issue of how reading is taught, and the importance of using phonics, has for many years been a rallying point for those on the political right. Indeed the promotion of other strategies, for example 'real' books, has been seen as symbolic of all that is wrong with 'progressivism' in primary education.

The debate about the use of phonics, and whether student teachers are adequately prepared to utilize it as a teaching strategy, was one with which Woodhead had become personally and publicly involved. In 1996 he commissioned and backed a highly critical Ofsted enquiry into the teaching of reading in three inner London boroughs. In that report it was suggested that many of the teachers were strongly critical of their initial training to teach reading. Inadequacies in the teaching of reading, which the report claimed to demonstrate, were laid firmly and publicly at the door of initial teacher education. The report was subsequently shown to be significantly flawed (Mortimore and Goldstein 1996; Richards *et al.* 1997) and the three boroughs involved (Tower Hamlets, Islington and Southwark) complained that the report had been drastically rewritten to highlight the most negative findings. However, the fact that the interim report of the primary sweep presented such a different view of the quality of initial teacher education probably explains why it was never published. In the event, UCET published its own summary of the 67 inspections (Kane and Furlong 1996), confirming their overwhelmingly positive nature.

In later 1996, the proposed 're-inspection' became a *cause célèbre*. A number of institutions that had received the highest grade, most notably the London Institute of Education, declined to take part, thereby precipitating a crisis. The outcome of the dispute was that Ofsted announced its intention to inspect (not 're-inspect') all primary and secondary courses again over the course of the next two years. It would also develop a more detailed and specific inspection framework.

By the late 1990s, therefore, the inspection process of initial teacher education had become as controversial and perhaps even more politicized than inspection in schools. It had also become a major undertaking. Over the next two and a half years the Ofsted teacher education team inspected some 80, mostly postgraduate, primary courses and over 500 secondary subject specialisms and, in 1998, a further cycle was announced. Given that each inspection was conducted over the course of a year, for many institutions, Ofsted inspections became a continuous affair.

In the revised and more detailed inspection framework of the late 1990s (Ofsted/TTA 1996, 1998), the focus was on three key issues: *intake* (the appropriateness of the admission policy and selection process, and trainees' qualification and suitability for teacher education); *training and assessment processes* (the quality of the training, the accuracy and consistency of the assessment of trainees against the standards for QTS); and *outcomes* (trainees' subject knowledge and understanding; their planning, teaching and class management; their monitoring assessment, recording reporting and accountability; their knowledge and understanding of other professional requirements).

Generally, the response to the inspection process from teacher educators was negative (Graham 1997; Sutherland 1997); they were seen as heavy handed and invasive. In the secondary area in particular, the fact that inspectors took each subject area as a separate course meant that the approach was highly atomistic. Inspectors were prohibited from looking at courses as a whole (educational and professional studies were, for example, explicitly excluded) and the fact that different teams inspected different subject areas led to significant variations in gradings within the same course even when they were structured identically. Even more problematic was the fact that, in relation to 'training and assessment', the inspection ran equally across school and higher education provision. Inspectors could and did visit any school of their choosing in the partnership in order to assess the quality and consistency of the training being provided and assessment judgements being made. Only one grade was given to the school and higher education parts of the training overall; and only one significantly flawed judgement of the quality of one trainee teacher was sufficient for a 'failing' grade to be recorded. Given the fact that those in schools were and are voluntarily involved in initial teacher education, this superficial evenhandedness meant that those in higher education found themselves being held accountable for training quality in schools over which they had very little control. It was after all they, not schools, who were threatened with reduced numbers or withdrawal of accreditation if standards were inadequate.

Nevertheless, as a means of increasing conformity to the spirit and the letter of government regulations, the inspections were effective. The fact that a revised circular (DfEE 1997b) was reflected immediately in a revised inspection framework meant conformity to the new regulations was extremely rapid. Despite the voluntary nature of their involvement, there was also increasing pressure on schools to provide more effective and consistent forms of training. Higher education simply could not afford to take the risk of underperforming schools.

How was this pressure applied? As in school inspections, individual reports were published and became important public documents within universities and colleges; achieving a good Ofsted result became institutionally extremely important for departments of education. In addition, the TTA used Ofsted data to produce its own four-point 'quality ratings'; and, despite considerable lobbying, in 1997 the new Labour government confirmed that these quality ratings were to be published as 'league tables' (TTA 1998b). In a small minority of cases, quality ratings led directly and indirectly to the disciplining of higher education institutions – re-inspections, then the withdrawal of accreditation and the closure of courses. More frequently, quality ratings have been used to 'reinforce quality' through the distribution of student numbers. Those courses rated in the highest quality categories have been prioritized for any new numbers available; they have also been protected when there have been number reductions.[1]

By the end of the 1990s, therefore, government, through the work of the TTA and Ofsted, had developed a system of initial teacher education that was highly responsive to policy changes. In the course of just 15 years, the system had been moved from one of diversity and autonomy to one of homogeneity and central control. What the government, and particularly the TTA, had wanted was a common system with common standards and procedures no matter who was providing the training or where; this was how the TTA defined quality. By the end of the 1990s this had been largely achieved.

Inventing a content

It is important to recognize that, in relation to the control of the system, the aspirations of governments of both parties in the 1990s were virtually identical. As Furlong had predicted prior to the commencement of the MOTE studies:

> Future governments will have different political priorities and the list of competences to be acquired will change. However, in the foreseeable future, it seems unlikely that governments of any political persuasion will retreat from the attempt to take a tighter control of initial teacher education.
>
> (Furlong 1992: 181)

Once that aspiration was achieved, once there was a centrally controlled and highly responsive national system with explicit and tight accountability, a different policy agenda became possible. That was the aim of intervening in the content of training itself.

Up until 1996, the content of training had only been lightly prescribed. Certainly, in the 1992 and 1993 Circulars (DfE 1992; DfE 1993a), there was some concern to emphasize the importance of primary teachers' subject knowledge by specifying the numbers of hours to be spent by trainees on English, mathematics and science; there was a list of competences which all teachers had to address. The competences were broadly based, however – little more than a series of headings ensuring breadth and balance within training courses – and the primary circular said nothing about what should be studied during the prescribed hours that had to be spent on core subjects.

During the middle 1990s in particular, the most important influence on the content of training was 'the market' to which students were increasingly exposed, that is, practice in schools. Because of their substantially increased time in schools and because of the growing role for school-based mentors, what students inevitably came to learn was significantly influenced by current practice in the limited numbers of schools to which they were attached. It was, potentially at least, a very localized market.

In sharp contrast, policies in the late 1990s increasingly sought to exploit the new control of the system to begin specifying the content of professional education in much more detail. Two strategies were involved: first the transformation of competences into more elaborate 'standards'; second the development of a national curriculum for initial teacher education in English, mathematics, science and information and communication technology (ICT).

From competences to 'standards'

> The standards [for the award of QTS] set out in more detail than ever before the core knowledge, understandings and skills on which effective teaching rests. These standards replace the more general 'competences' which have been in force previously and apply to all those assessed for QTS, no matter what initial teacher training course or route into teaching they may be on.
>
> (Millett 1997)

The TTA first produced its draft standards for initial teacher education in early 1997 and, after a period of consultation (which covered the 1997 general election), they were then incorporated into a revised government circular – Circular 10/97 (DfEE 1997b) – which was published soon after the election in May. It was the first policy document in this field by the new Labour government, but despite this, the document changed little as a result of the consultation with perhaps one notable exception – the confirmation that teaching was to be a graduate career. After the equivocation on graduate status of the early 1990s (the first licensed teacher regulations; the failed proposal for a Mums' Army of early years teachers (DfE 1993c)), this was an important concession to the teaching profession. However, in virtually all other respects, the priorities established under the previous government remained the same. There was, for example, a reassertion of the need for subject specialist teachers at the upper primary phase, and the regulations for SCITT schemes remained unchanged. In addition, readers were left in little doubt that, through the standards, it was government that was controlling entry into the teaching profession. Trainees had to be 'rigorously and regularly assessed':

> Successful completion of a course or programme of initial teacher training including employment based provision, must require the trainee to achieve *all* these standards. *All* courses must involve the assessment of *all* trainees to make sure that they meet *all* the standards specified'.
>
> (DfEE 1997b: 7; original emphasis)

The structure of the standards document was broadly similar to the list of competences set out in Circular 9/92 (DfE 1992), which it replaced. As we saw in Chapter 5, in Circular 9/92 the main headings for secondary teachers had been: subject knowledge, subject application, class management, assessment and recording of pupils' progress, and further professional development. In the new standards document the headings for both primary and secondary teachers were: knowledge and understanding; planning, teaching and class management; monitoring assessment, recording, reporting and accountability; and other professional requirements. However, the content under each of these headings was now set out in considerably more detail amounting to many hundreds of different standards. In 1992, there were simply four or five short statements under each heading; by 1997 the numbers had increased to 15 to 20, each using more precise and prescriptive language than in the past.

For example in relation to assessment, instead of simply stating that 'newly qualified teachers should be able to assess and record systematically the progress of individual pupils' (DfE 1992: 8), the new standards documents (DfEE 1998a: 15) stated that:

> Those to be awarded Qualified Teacher Status must, when assessed, demonstrate that they:
> assess and record each pupil's progress systematically, including through focused observation, questioning, testing and marking and use these records to:
>
> (i) check that pupils have understood and completed the work set;
> (ii) monitor strengths and weaknesses and use the information gained as a basis for purposeful intervention in pupils' learning;
> (iii) inform planning;
> (iv) check that pupils continue to make demonstrable progress in their acquisition of the knowledge, skills and understandings of the subject.

Other standards were set out in similar detail.

Clearly the main aim of the move from 'competences' to 'standards' was to define the content of training in more explicit detail than before. As the circular stated, 'the standards have been written to be specific, explicit and assessable and are designed to provide a clear basis for the reliable and consistent award of Qualified Teacher Status' (DfEE 1997b: 6). Of course, in the field of education, the change of language from 'competences' to 'standards' had added advantages. Rather than the notion of a minimum ability as is implied by the word 'competency', the idea of 'standards' of professional training crossed easily into government concerns to raise educational standards more generally. As such the change in term had political advantages, making enforcement even more difficult to resist. Who, after all, could be opposed to raising standards? Fortuitously, perhaps, this change proved to be particularly resonant with the wider educational rhetoric of New Labour.

It is also important to recognize that the concept of standards did not simply emerge in the field of initial teacher training. At the same time as the TTA was developing standards for new teachers, it was employing a similar approach to setting out the training requirements for other parts of the teaching profession – for subject leaders, special educational needs coordinators and headteachers. It clearly had aspirations to develop a coherent framework for progression through all stages of teacher development, although the government has subsequently restricted the TTA's remit to ensure that it focuses largely on the initial phases. Meanwhile, the concept of standards was being utilized within other areas of the public sector management too. It was, for example, central to the Management Charter Initiative (1997) (a factor that influenced the TTA in developing its standards for headteacher training) and in nurse education.

Despite the change in terminology, the move to standards in reality overcame none of the difficulties associated with the earlier competency model. In theory at least (MCI 1997), professional standards of this sort, like competences before them (Jessup 1991), need to be derived from a functional analysis of the task to be performed. In addition, a key difference claimed for the notion of standards as opposed to competences (MCI 1997) is that they are intended to be more broadly based, including the values, attitudes and personal qualities that are contributory to effective perform-ance. However, as in the past, no functional analysis has been performed in the field of teaching and, in the teaching standards, explicit references to values, attitudes and personal qualities are largely avoided. Instead what we are given is a list of tightly prescribed topics, expressed in behavioural lan-guage, the form and language of the document being driven more by the need to establish ever higher levels of accountability by 'providers', who are to be held to account for their students' performance on these new standards.

As we have already seen, the list of standards itself was not new, it was simply a development of earlier lists – an amalgam of historical precedent moderated by current political demands.[2] The form of presentation gave little insight into the nature of quality teaching – how it is fundamentally related to aims and goals; how skills, knowledge and understandings are interrelated and in part intuitive (Atkinson and Claxton 1999); and how teaching performance is inseparable from teaching context. It also gave little insight into how effective performance might be judged. As Daugherty (1997) commented, 'It neatly side steps [the formidable problems of assessment] by not having an assessment model at all.'

A national curriculum for teachers

The second and more explicit strategy for establishing greater control of the content of initial teacher education courses was the development of a national curriculum in four subject areas – English, mathematics, science and information and communications technology (ICT) for both primary and secondary school teachers. The idea of a national curriculum for initial teacher education was first put forward on the advice of the TTA by the Conservative government in 1996, though it was not formally put in place until 1997, after the general election in May.

Woodhead, as Chief Inspector of Schools and head of Ofsted, was clearly part of the 'context of influence' in the development of the National Cur-riculum outlined below; his views were particularly influential in the area of the teaching of reading. However, the curriculum itself was drawn up by the

TTA working in collaboration with teams of 'subject experts', many of whom were themselves involved in initial teacher education. The curriculum was eventually published in two documents. The first, covering primary English and mathematics, was developed and published alongside the standards document in June 1997 (DfEE 1997b). The remaining parts (primary and secondary science, secondary English and mathematics and ICT) were published in 1998 (DfEE 1998a).

All seven elements of the National Curriculum are based on the same structure, organized in three sections. They are: knowledge and understanding ('to secure pupils' progress' in the subject); effective teaching and assessment methods; and trainees' own knowledge and understanding of the subject. In this third area, an extensive checklist is provided against which trainees' personal subject knowledge has to be 'audited'. Where there are identified gaps, institutions have to devise strategies (including self-study) for trainees to complete their knowledge before the end of the course. In the other two areas, the curriculum defines what trainees 'must be taught' in considerable detail. For example, the primary English curriculum specifies that all courses must include time dedicated to the explicit and systematic teaching of reading, writing (including grammar, spelling, punctuation and handwriting), speaking and listening, for example through a dedicated literacy hour. Grammar has to be taught 'systematically through direct instruction on grammatical rules and conventions'.

In an elaboration on the teaching of reading, the primary English curriculum insists that trainees:

> **must be taught:**
> how to teach **the essential core of phonic and graphic knowledge** explicitly and systematically, first teaching the alphabet and how the letters of the alphabet are used singly and in different combinations to make graphic representations of the sounds of English, *e.g. digraphs – sh ch, th, and trigraphs*:
> **then**
> how to identify initial and dominant sounds in words and how to identify and write the graphemes that represent them;
> **then**
> how to identify and blend the sounds into words starting with consonant–vowel–consonant words *e.g. c–a–t* and moving on to words requiring more complex blending; how to read such words automatically; and how to split them into their constituent sounds, identifying each sound in order to spell the word;
> **then**
> how sounds can be represented by different graphemes, including common ways to read and spell each of the long vowel sounds, *e.g. ay, a–e, ea; y, igh, i–e; ow, oa, o–e; oo, ew, u–e,* and ways to represent other common vowel sounds, *e.g. ur, er, ir, ou, or, a, aw.*
> [DfEE 1998a: 37; original emphasis]

In the words of the first chair of the TTA, such specifications are intended to 'ensure that trainees are taught how to teach reading, writing and number effectively, *using methods that are known to work*' (Parker 1997; emphasis added). Although the curriculum is designed to constrain teacher educators rather than trainees, it might also be argued that the 'hidden curriculum' of this approach provides appropriate socialization into a profession in which official prescription of teaching approaches is beginning to encroach on autonomous professional judgements, as in the case of the literacy and numeracy strategies.

Each of the other primary and secondary subject areas is set out in similar detail. Perhaps unsurprisingly, the TTA (1998a) made it clear that given the detail of prescription, they expected most courses would need to be fundamentally redesigned rather than simply adapted if they were to cover the ground specified in each element of the curriculum.

How did course leaders respond to this major intervention in the detail of what is to be taught to prospective teachers? In an apparent attempt to ensure a consensus on the new curriculum, the TTA consulted extensively on draft versions. In each case, between seven and ten thousand copies were distributed and a series of national meetings were held. As a result of the consultation the TTA made changes to ensure that teaching was presented as an 'intellectually and managerially challenging profession' (presumably reflecting the fact that a number of commentators felt that the draft version undermined this view). They also emphasized that neither the TTA, DfEE nor Ofsted intended a 'tick-list' approach to assessment. Rather,

> To reflect the complexity of the teaching process being assessed, providers are likely to make overarching judgements, taking account of evidence from the wide range of sources available to them across the partnership.
>
> (TTA 1998a: 6)

However, it would seem that most criticism of the draft documents was concerning their authoritarian tone and particularly the pedagogical implications of the recurring phrase 'trainees must be taught'. Here the TTA were uncompromising, arguing that:

> Since the verb 'to teach' covers methods and strategies which providers include in their courses in order that trainees should learn . . . the use of 'trainees must be taught' has been retained. *This further reflects the fact that the curriculum is a requirement on providers to secure entitlement for trainees rather than a requirement on trainees themselves.*
>
> (1998a: 7; emphasis added)

One teachers' union, the Association of Teachers and Lecturers, commissioned its own report on each curriculum document as it emerged (Richards *et al.* 1997; Maguire *et al.* 1998). In these reports, the general principle of government intervention in the detail of teacher education was considered to be highly retrogressive, a further undermining of the autonomy of the teaching profession. Nevertheless, the actual content of the maths and science curricula was considered largely uncontroversial. Indeed, in relation to mathematics, Richards *et al.* comment that they wanted to include more rather than fewer topics. The ICT and English curricula however were seen as very different; much more explicitly political and therefore much more controversial, though for different reasons.

In relation to English, Richards *et al.* note that the whole history of central government intervention in the field of English is fraught with debate. Both the Cox Report (DES 1988b) and the Kingman Report (DES 1988c) were set up against a background of concerns that there was insufficient focus on the uses of standard English in contemporary schools. More recent controversy, as we have already noted, has focused on the teaching of reading by phonics. The new national curriculum for English in initial teacher education is controversial in relation to both of these.

We have already seen the detailed prescription of the curriculum in relation to the use of phonics in the teaching of reading; other methods got much shorter shrift. As Richards *et al.* say,

> In the document's treatment of reading, the extensive and detailed exemplification of the terminology of phonic teaching with only cursory treatment of other aspects of reading inevitably suggest that joy in reading – the complex critical and discriminatory skills and insights which mature reading can require – and the capacity to enter in imagination into the world of a book and empathise with its characters, are not much valued. This amounts to a tragic disregard of the uses of literacy . . .
>
> What ever happened to those references, which got prominence in the earlier National Curriculum English documents for schools, to 'enthusiastic, independent and reflective readers' to 'opportunities to read a wide variety of literature', to extending pupils' ideas and their moral and emotional understanding, to 'imagination', to 'poetry', and to 'enjoyment'?
>
> (1997: 20)

Equally controversial was the emphasis on standard English and grammar. Once again, Richards *et al.* emphasize that there is no longer any opposition to either the teaching of standard English or grammar but for social, not linguistic reasons. The national curriculum document is seen as championing very traditional views by implying that there is a 'simple, right answer in English that is always and everywhere correct and that it has to be learnt by heart' (Richards *et al.* 1997: 23). Indeed, Richards *et al.* claim that the English national curriculum is a thinly veiled political attempt to reassert a very different and largely traditional conception of English and English teaching.

The development of the national curriculum for ICT is equally political but in a very different way in that its aim seems to be to harness initial teacher education to help achieve policies that are close to the government's heart at this time. As Circular 4/98 explicitly says:

> With the introduction of the National Grid for Learning it becomes even more important for newly qualified teachers to be confident and competent in using ICT effectively in their teaching. The ITT curriculum will also form the basis of the Lottery-funded training for serving teachers in the use of ICT.
>
> (DfEE 1998a: 17)

The weakness of the approach lies in the fact that many schools, and indeed universities and colleges, are insufficiently developed in their practice in ICT to provide the form of training that is now defined in the document as an 'essential core'. For example item 4.a insists that trainees must be taught to introduce and review material to whole classes through the use of a single screen or display. However, as Atkinson and Lewis (1998: 8) comment, 'Few schools have facilities for this and we (in a university department of education) have just one, one portable video projector for use in nine subject courses working on three sites'. As Maguire *et al.* (1998: 33) say 'As a document which signposts the way forward . . . it could be described as radical and imaginative. As a document to be implemented later this year for all trainees . . . the contents and specifications are less helpful'.

New Labour, new professionalism?

Clearly the politics behind the development of the English and the ICT national curriculum documents are very different. The first arguably reflects a strong neo-conservative cultural influence; the second the new interventionism that, particularly under New Labour, has begun to temper neo-liberalism as the preferred economic strategy. Nevertheless, that the machinery of a national curriculum is a vehicle for direct political intervention in the detail of what teachers 'know' and how they are trained to teach is now evident. The benefits of being able to intervene at such a detailed level have not been lost on either the TTA or the new Labour government.

For the TTA, the National Curriculum was seen as representing an important marker of the type of intervention they hoped to establish at *all* levels of professional development. As Anthea Millett (1997), chief executive of the TTA wrote in her covering letter introducing the new curriculum:

> The benefits of the standards and curricula extend far beyond initial teacher training. I have no doubt that the new standards for the award of QTS will come to be seen as a landmark for serving teachers in making clear the expectations of them in this most demanding yet rewarding of professions. I believe that the standards will contribute significantly to improving the public perceptions of teaching as a profession. They represent the basis for the first National Professional Qualification for teachers.[3]

At the same time, the new government saw that the National Curriculum could be harnessed as a key means of achieving its broader political ends in education and particularly their public commitment substantially to improve national levels of literacy and numeracy. As Estelle Morris, the Under-Secretary of State responsible for initial teacher education, wrote of the primary English and mathematics curricula after only six weeks in office:

> Raising the standards we expect of new teachers in this way is clearly essential to delivering the government's commitment to raising pupil performance across the education system and in particular, to delivering the major new literacy and numeracy targets.
>
> (Morris 1997)

Where does this leave teacher professionalism in the new millennium? Certainly many in the teaching profession remain deeply hostile to the massively increased central control. As the Association of Teachers and Lecturers has said:

> ATL accepted that the teaching profession has the collective responsibility for maintaining the competence and integrity of the profession but it did not accept that this would be achievable if teachers themselves were unable to question current orthodoxies or scrutinise established practices or ideas . . . what kind of teaching profession is being presented to potential recruits when the emphasis suggests low trust, tight control and a centrally and even ideologically defined environment for teaching when other employers are valuing autonomy, creativity, intrinsic motivations towards quality and improvement and high employee self esteem?
>
> (Richards *et al.* 1997: 30)

The contrasts between such views of teacher professionalism and those advanced by the TTA remain stark. For example in 1999 Anthea Millett reiterated her vision of the future. It was a vision in which the individual teacher is almost wholly silenced and passive:

> I believe that teachers need to be: better regarded; better qualified to enter initial training; better trained initially; better inducted; better developed, after entering teaching; better deployed; better assisted; better led; better managed, appraised and rewarded; and better represented.
>
> (Millett 1999)

After 18 months in office, the new Labour government set out its own vision of the future of the profession in the form of a Green Paper (DfEE 1998b). It was an up-beat, future-oriented document with talk of creating a 'world-class education service for all our children . . . Pupils will need education for a world of rapid chance in which both flexible attitudes and enduring values have a part to play' (DfEE 1998b: para. 1). Schools, it argued, will need to be outward looking, constantly striving to change to meet the challenges of the future. More controversially, employment practices will need to change, with greater flexibility and a need for all teachers to keep their skills and subject knowledge up to date. All this, the Green Paper argued, demands a new professionalism among teachers.

The time has long gone when isolated unaccountable professionals made curriculum and pedagogical decisions alone without reference to the outside world. Teachers in a modern teaching profession need:

- to have high expectations of themselves and of all pupils;
- to accept accountability;
- to take personal and collective responsibility for improving their skills and subject knowledge;
- to seek to base decisions on evidence of what works in schools in this country and internationally;
- to work in partnership with other staff in schools;
- to welcome the contribution that parents, business and others outside a school can make to its success; and
- to anticipate change and promote innovation.

(DfEE 1998b: para. 13)

We would suggest that the reforms to initial teacher education over the last 15 years mean that this vision of professionalism is now significantly in place at least for new teachers coming into the profession. Yet, as the Association of Teachers and Lecturers (ATL) has commented, 'The greatest political mistake of recent years has been the failure to connect the idealism, commitment and hard work of the vast majority of teachers to a sense of a national educational mission' (Maguire *et al.* 1998). While the Green Paper clearly has a sense of national educational mission and where initial teacher training fits into it, it is highly debatable whether its view of professionalism will connect with and mobilize the majority of teachers any more than did the TTA's. Indeed, from the hostile response to the consultation process of the Green Paper's managerialist proposals on performance-related pay, the opposite seems to be the case. However, at the time of writing the government seems set to drive its reforms through even if it is prepared to modify its timetable.

Furthermore, as Pring (1999: 18) points out, 'There is hardly a whisper in "Teachers: Meeting the Challenge of Change" about the role of higher education.' Indeed, he suggests that 'it can no longer be assumed that the main route [into teaching] should be through university courses'. All funding for teacher training may now be channelled through partnerships rather than HEIs and the effect of this may lead some universities to withdraw from teacher training on financial grounds. On this interpretation, New Labour's approach to teacher professionalism could effectively bring to fruition Maclure's nightmare mentioned in Chapter 5. He feared that the 'subtext' of one of the proposed Conservative reforms might be to deprofessionalize teaching by dismantling 'the traditional defences of teaching as a profession' through taking teacher training out of the universities and colleges and ultimately severing 'the connection between the study of education in higher education and its practice in schools' (Maclure 1993). While New Labour's approach is presented as reprofessionalizing teaching, it would certainly bring about a further modification of the model of autonomous teacher professionalism sponsored by higher education and replace it with one firmly driven by a combination of government defined priorities and the character of specific schools. Pring (1999: 18) himself suggests that such a development could ultimately pose a threat to 'that freedom of enquiry, that justification based on evidence, that are at the core of education'.

Conclusion

Talking about education reform more generally, Bernstein (1997) argues that the increasing deregulation of the economic field and the increasing regulation of what he terms the symbolic field are generating new forms of pedagogic identity, in contrast to both the 'retrospective' identity of old conservatism and the 'therapeutic' identity associated with the child-centred progressivism that was evident in England and the USA in the 1960s and 1970s. An emergent 'decentred market' identity embodies the principles of neo-liberalism. It has no intrinsic properties, and its form is dependent only upon the exchange value determined by the market and is therefore infinitely variable and unstable. A 'prospective' pedagogic identity, on the other hand, attempts to 'recentre' through selectively incorporating elements of old conservatism. As we suggested in Chapter 1, Conservative policy for teacher education reflected both neo-liberal and neo-conservative influences. New Labour, it appears, has decided that a more concerted effort is needed within teacher education to create a new 'prospective' pedagogic identity, not merely for the purposes of recreating 'imagined pasts' but rather to serve an 'imagined future' in which Britain has a modern world-class education system capable of competing in a globalized world. Hence the strong national emphasis on literacy, numeracy, ICT and strong and thorough subject knowledge, alongside the capacity to adapt to the local practicalities of the schools in which trainees are placed.

In the final chapter, we explore how far these developments are a peculiarly English phenomenon or whether they reflect broader global trends. We also consider whether a different conception of teacher professionalism, appropriate to the nature of democracies in the twenty-first century, now needs to be developed as an alternative to that inscribed in current policies.

Notes

1 Somewhat strangely, in 1999, in the face of a severe recruitment crisis, the DfEE chose significantly to reduce its target numbers in the shortage subjects of mathematics and science. These reduced numbers fell exclusively on those courses ranked C or D in the rating scheme.

2 See, for example, the demand that early years teachers must be familar with SCAA's *Desirable Outcomes for Children's Learning on Entering Compulsory Education* (Schools' Curriculum and Assessment Authority 1997).

3 The decision announced in May 1999 to remove all but initial teacher education and recruitment from the remit of the TTA means that these aspirations for a unified and coherent system may well remain unrealized.

10 Teacher education in new times

> The past decade has seen far-reaching changes in the education
> systems of most Western countries. There is broad agreement at a
> rather general level about the causes and nature of these changes.
> They are seen as part of the wider decline of the post-war welfare-
> state settlement, and that in turn is increasingly linked to changes
> in the global economy . . . [But] far from being weakened, the state's
> role in the control of education has actually been strengthened, if
> transformed.
>
> (Dale 1997: 273)

Introduction

It might be thought that the story we have told in this book is merely that
of the working out of the Thatcherite project in the field of teacher education, with some fine tuning by New Labour. There is indeed a sense in which
it is a footnote in the broader history of the decline of welfarism in Britain.
Le Grand (1997) suggests that, in England, during the so-called 'golden age
of teacher control' from 1944 to the mid-1970s, parents of children in state
schools were expected to trust the professionals and accept that teachers
knew what was best for their children. He claims that the assumptions
underlying the 'democratic socialist welfare state' have now been questioned
and the belief that professionals are concerned only with the welfare of their
clients has increasingly been challenged. Meanwhile, public choice theorists
have argued that the behaviour of public servants and professionals could be
better understood if they were assumed to be largely self-interested.

From this point of view, the teachers of the 'swollen state' that was
postwar British social democracy are regarded as ill-adapted to be either agents
of the reformed state or entrepreneurial service providers in a marketized
civil society. In the light of this there has been a move away from the notion
that the teaching profession should have a professional mandate to act on
behalf of the state in the best interests of its citizens to a view that teachers
(and indeed other professions) need to be subjected to the rigours of the
market and/or greater control and surveillance on the part of the re-formed
state. At the very least, this is, as we saw in Chapter 1, what Dale (1989)
characterizes as a shift from licensed to regulated autonomy.

The attempt to reform initial teacher education can be seen in similar terms. One of the arguments used by proponents of education reform in England to explain their relative lack of impact on achievement and equity to date, apart from the fact that they have not gone far enough, is that they have been stymied by an unreconstructed teaching force. Attempts to reconstruct teacher professionalism and make the teaching force more responsive to the demands of the state and the market are therefore particularly evident in the attempts to reform teacher education. As we saw in Chapter 1, the preferred strategy of the neo-liberal marketeers was deregulation of the profession to allow schools to go into the market and recruit graduates (or even non-graduates) without irrelevant or even damaging professional training and prepare them on an apprenticeship basis in school. The introduction of new routes into teaching and the strategy of locating more and more elements of training in schools have been partly (though not wholly) influenced by such views.

Such policies also had some appeal to neo-conservative critics who detected a collectivist (and even crypto-Marxist) ideological bias among teacher educators in higher education in England. However, neo-conservatives were also concerned with 'enemies within' the teaching profession as a whole as well as within teacher education. Such views, combined with vocationalist concerns about international competitiveness (Hickox 1995), meant that even the Conservative government did not actually pursue a policy of total deregulation or a wholesale devolution of teacher training to the schools. Instead, it showed a growing concern to shape the content of teachers' professional knowledge, initially through the introduction of a common list of competences to be required of beginning teachers, regardless of the nature of the route by which they have achieved them, and subsequently through standards and the National Curriculum. As we have seen, its New Labour successor has taken these aspects of reform considerably further.

This has, of course, given rise to the suspicion that governments want to deprofessionalize teaching by reducing the scope for professional judgement and ensuring that, wherever they are trained, teachers focus on the development of craft skills rather than professional understanding. Thus Jones and Moore (1993) argue that an emphasis on competences will serve to undermine the dominant discourse of liberal humanism within the teaching profession and replace it with one of technical rationality. Adams and Tulasiewicz (1995) complain that teachers are being turned into technicians rather than 'reflective professionals'. Such commentators feel that basing training in particular schools limits the development of broader perspectives on education, and that specifying a limited range of competences, or specifying the content of training through a national curriculum, will encourage restricted rather than extended notions of professionalism or, more precisely, what is sometimes termed professionality (Hoyle 1974). More charitable observers argue that the government is trying to reform teacher education in order to 'reprofessionalize' teaching more in line with the needs of the twenty-first century.

Just as in education reform more generally, there seems to have been a dual strategy in England involving devolution of some responsibilities to schools at the same time as prescribing more things from the centre. Schools and teachers may be 'empowered' to develop their own ways of training teachers and compete with one another in the process but only within a very narrow frame. To this extent, the purpose of the erosion of university domination of initial teacher education may not have been to devolve real responsibility to schools, as D. Hargreaves (1994) or Berrill (1994) might hope, but to impose an alternative and more restricted state mandated approach. In this, the role of the TTA and Ofsted has been particularly significant (Mahony and Hextall 1996). Other potential stakeholders who might foster an alternative collective definition of teacher professionalism, whether HEIs, LEAs, teacher unions, have been marginalized in the process, even if New Labour has recently made some attempt to reincorporate them into its project through its proposed General Teaching Council. This combined use of state control and deregulation to get rid of so-called vested interests is entirely consistent with the Thatcherite project of creating a strong state and a 'free' economy (Gamble 1988).

Exception – or global phenomenon?

Some commentators have suggested that this approach to the reform of teacher education is an example of English 'exceptionality' (Moon 1998). There are certainly aspects of the case that can only really be understood in terms of the particular political conjuncture in England in the 1980s and 1990s. Yet, as a 1996 OECD paper has demonstrated, many countries in the developed world are now engaged in a process of 'systemic reform' of their education service, based on a growing awareness around the world 'that changing one element of an education system has (often unexpected) knock-on effects on the rest of the system and that it is more effective to aim at changing the system as a whole' (Townsend 1996). In many countries that 'whole' is now taken to include the reform of initial teacher education.

The centrality of teacher education to broader educational reform is well expressed in an Irish White Paper on Education issued in 1995:

> The capacity of the education system to cope with and lead change is critically dependent on developing the necessary attitudinal and professional competences of the teaching profession.
>
> (Irish White Paper on Education 1995: 125)

As a consequence, in Ireland, as in many other countries, proposed changes to the education system are being closely integrated with proposed changes in both initial and in-service teacher education.

Systemic change in education, including teacher education, is therefore a transnational phenomenon and not just a peculiarity of the English. But the question we want to pose in this final chapter is, is there an underlying commonality in the direction of those changes or are they pulling in contrary directions? Do recent changes in teacher education constitute a coherent global trend or are they nothing more than a series of local responses to local conditions?

Fortunately, we have some comparative evidence with which to explore these questions, albeit from other largely Anglophone countries. At the same time as we were carrying out the MOTE study, studies of teacher education were also being carried out in Australia and the USA under the acronyms SITE and RATE respectively.[1] A comparison of these three studies demonstrated to us the common complexity of researching in a rapidly changing policy context. In Australia and the USA, as well as England and Wales, change is endemic in teacher education and researching it is therefore like trying to hit a moving target. Each of these studies was large-scale, attempting to capture something of the national picture in the respective countries. Given the time involved in mounting such research, each study has inevitably provided no more than a snapshot of practice at a particular point in time. Moreover, in such a fast moving field, that snapshot quickly becomes out of date. The empirical findings in each of the three countries, therefore, have to be interpreted in the context of dynamic policy change.

Substantively, what the studies have in common is a description of an ongoing struggle in each of the three countries over the nature and form of initial teacher education and, behind that, a struggle over the governance of education and the character of professionalism appropriate for the next generation of teachers. Government-proposed reforms have in many instances met with resistance from those in higher education and schools. At the same time, initiatives from within the profession itself have often articulated a different conception of training and teacher professionalism. Indeed, broader political and ideological conflict over education is often being mediated through a discourse concerning the structure and content of initial teacher education.

So for example, as we have seen, the MOTE study demonstrated how, in England and Wales, the structure and content of initial teacher education has been significantly altered by central government reforms in the 1990s. As a result:

- students have to spend more time in schools during their training;
- schools' involvement in training has been substantially increased;
- higher education institutions have to pay schools for their contribution to the training process;
- the content of training has to a significant degree been externally defined through a series of government-prescribed competences or standards and more recently a national curriculum for beginning teachers;
- within this government-defined content there is a growing emphasis on subject-based knowledge and the 'basics' of literacy and numeracy and ICT.

In addition, the TTA, in conjunction with Ofsted, has established ever more rigorous forms of quality control, linking assessed quality with funding and threatening closure of courses found to be inadequate.

Empirically what the MOTE studies also demonstrate is how, at the level of *rhetoric*, course leaders, lecturers and teachers have attempted to resist the spirit of these national changes through the championing of 'collaborative' forms of partnership, through the overwhelming concern with forms of reflective practice, and through the 'incorporation' of competences into more conventional training agenda. However, they also show how, despite this, successive waves of reform have had a significant effect on many universities and colleges, narrowing and weakening their contribution to the training process. As a result, in many institutions, training has developed an increasingly practical orientation with relationships between those in schools and higher education narrowed to bureaucratic rather than collaborative relationships.

Similar struggles are revealed by the RATE study in the USA. For example, in 1990 the Holmes Group report advocated the development of closer relationships between schools and HEIs through the establishment of Professional Development Schools. Such a strategy, it was suggested, would serve to transform both the quality of teacher education, making it more practical and relevant, and the wider school system.

However, findings from one RATE survey (RATE 1995) suggest that there has been substantial resistance to this vision as well. As the study shows, although lecturers are now more often in schools, they are working there in very traditional ways – supervising students, doing their own research. Relationships between schools and HEIs remain largely personal and ad hoc and teachers have not become involved in the process of training in anything more than conventional areas. RATE VIII therefore concludes that the system as a whole has not, as yet, experienced fundamental change:

> While there is considerable ferment relative to collaboration and the simultaneous reform of teacher education and K–12, the degree to which this activity focuses squarely on changing the nature of teaching and learning, especially teaching and learning for prospective teachers, is suspect.
>
> (RATE 1995: 39)

More recent policy initiatives indicate a rather different reform agenda, however. Individual states have increasingly attempted to influence the curriculum of initial teacher education by defining the numbers of courses to be taken in different subjects, while at a national level other initiatives include the National Commission on Teaching and America's Future and the NCATE (National Council for the Accreditation of Teacher Education) framework for assuring quality in the practice of teaching.

The National Commission on Teaching and America's Future (1996), for example, argued for:

- establishing professional standards boards in every state;
- insisting on professional accreditation for all schools of education;
- closing inadequate schools of education;
- licensing teachers based on demonstrated performance, including tests of subject matter knowledge, teaching knowledge and teaching skills;
- using national board standards as the bench-mark for accomplished teaching.

The National Commission proposals incorporate the NCATE approach to teacher education, which includes an elaborate quality control framework running from student recruitment through to licence renewal and continuous professional development. Significantly, however, despite a plethora of such initiatives, most national codes of practice, including those of NCATE, remain voluntary and a number of institutions – including some of the most prestigious – have not signed up to them.

In Australia, as the SITE study reveals, the form and content of initial teacher education has also been deeply contested in recent years. On the one hand, the profession itself (universities often acting in collaboration with representatives of teacher unions) has been involved in a range of initiatives to reform training. As a result, in many institutions:

- courses have been lengthened;
- there has been a growing emphasis on graduate entry;
- collaborative relationships between HEIs and schools have been developed both for initial training and for school development as part of the National Schools Network.

In addition, a federal initiative to introduce a behaviourist competency framework for training was successfully transformed by university and union leaders into a model that was rather more educationally progressive and consistent with community and social needs (Walker 1996).

At the same time, however, individual states and the federal government have sponsored a number of other initiatives reflecting rather different agendas. Some states have utilized their control of teacher registration to influence the curriculum of courses, insisting on increased time being devoted to preparation in science and mathematics and thereby squeezing the time available for more theoretically based education studies. Nevertheless, although Australia is faced with some similar issues to those in the UK, there has been less evidence of a direct challenge to conventional modes of professionalism and no attempt to 'follow the UK track' in its entirety (Sachs and Groundwater-Smith 1999). Even the rightist Liberal government returned in federal elections in 1996, and re-elected in 1998, has continued to involve existing professional networks and partnerships in developing its agenda for teacher education. Even so, there is no doubt that teacher educators in Australian universities are having to respond to what, for us, is a rather familiar set of challenges:

> pressure of external accountability from a variety of education stakeholders, increased political pressure to direct the processes, structures

and qualifications of teacher preparation, demands for school based teacher education programs, the provision of more economical and efficient teacher education programs, and the preparation of competent practitioners.

(Sachs and Groundwater-Smith 1999: 217–8)

The current and future shape of teacher education and of the professional formation of teachers is therefore deeply contested in each of these three countries, but how should we interpret this? Is there a common agenda behind government-led reform initiatives or are the struggles in the three countries about different things?

Globalizing trends

The almost simultaneous emergence of similar reforms across continents has certainly led some to suggest that the current restructuring of education needs to be understood as part of a broader economic, political and cultural process of globalization in which national differences are increasingly eroded. While contemplating such grand theories, however, we shall also need to consider whether contextual specificities are at least as significant as any broader cross-national developments. Indeed, it should already be clear from our three cases that any cross-national comparison needs to acknowledge the differences as well as similarities.

In seeking to understand the similarities between policies, a range of explanations can be invoked. At one end of the continuum are those that highlight the role of policy 'borrowing', and at the other end are theories of economic and social change of global proportions. Thus one form of explanation is that ideas developed in one context have merely been copied in another. To some extent, the work of international agencies, such as OECD, has certainly helped to 'carry' policies from one context to another, but informal modes of transmission are at least as common (Whitty and Edwards 1998). Policymakers as well as teacher education researchers share experiences in international conferences and journals. In a world of instantaneous communication, ideas such as competences, standards and school-based training rapidly become discursive resources in a whole range of contexts of influence.

While policy-carrying and policy-borrowing have clearly been factors, however, this only begs more questions. What has given similar policies appeal across different countries and different political parties? Here theories of post-Fordism and post-modernity are often brought into play. Post-Fordist accounts suggest that the reforms can be understood in terms of the transportation of changing modes of regulation from the sphere of production into other arenas, including education. They point to a correspondence between the establishment of differentiated markets in welfare and a shift in the economy away from Fordism towards a post-Fordist mode of accumulation which 'places a lower value on mass individual and collective consumption and creates pressures for a more differentiated production and distribution of health, education, transport and housing' (Jessop *et al.* 1987: 109). Ball (1990), for example, has claimed to see in new forms of schooling a move away from the Fordist school towards a post-Fordist one – the educational equivalent of flexible specialization driven by the imperatives of differentiated consumption replacing the old assembly-line world of mass production. These 'post-Fordist schools' are designed

> not only to produce the post-Fordist, multi-skilled, innovative worker but to behave in post-Fordist ways themselves; moving away from mass production and mass markets to niche markets and 'flexible specialisation' . . . a post-Fordist mind-set is thus having implications in schools for management styles, curriculum, pedagogy and assessment.
>
> (Kenway 1993: 115)

The sorts of changes in education management to which Kenway refers are those associated with a wider phenomenon known as the 'New Public Management' (NPM). Hood suggests that there are seven distinct elements to NPM:

- hands-on professional management in the public sector;
- the use of explicit standards in the measurement of performance;
- greater emphasis on control via measures of output;
- the development of smaller manageable units;
- a movement to increased sector competition;
- a stress on private-sector styles of management;
- greater discipline and parsimony in the use of resources.

(Hood 1991: 4–5)

Bottery (1996) has shown how, in England, such strategies can now be discerned in the police and health services, as well as in education. As we have seen, the management of teacher education often has the hallmarks of this 'New Public Management', employing market-type mechanisms and management by objectives, which tend to produce narrower, more technicist versions of professional education than we have traditionally pursued.

Kenway (1993: 119) regards the rapid rise of the market form in education as a postmodern phenomenon, accentuating the nexus between the global and the local. In her own pessimistic version of postmodernity, 'transnational corporations and their myriad subsidiaries . . . shape and reshape our individual and collective identities as we plug in . . . to their cultural and economic communications networks'.

The continuing role of the state

Even so, we would suggest that there are a number of problems with these 'new times' modes of analysis. They are not only 'notoriously vague' (Hickox 1995) but also tend to exaggerate the extent to which we have moved to a new regime of accumulation. They can, on occasion, lead to an unhelpful emphasis on the extent to which policy changes are driven by macrosociological transformations rather than local political conditions. The more optimistic versions also exaggerate the benefits of the changes. Neo-Fordism may therefore be a more appropriate term than post-Fordism (Allen 1992), while Giddens' (1991) concept of 'high modernity' probably captures the combination of change and continuity rather better than that of 'postmodernity'. Indeed, new cultural forms and more flexible modes of capital accumulation may be shifts in surface appearance, rather than signs of the emergence of some entirely new postcapitalist or even postindustrial society (Harvey 1989).

Nevertheless, as our own studies show, the discourse and the contexts of political struggles in and around education in general, as well as teacher education in particular, have been significantly altered in many parts of the world (Whitty *et al*. 1998). However, what they also demonstrate is an enhanced emphasis on the role of the nation state rather than its marginalization in a postmodern global–local nexus (Usher and Edwards 1994). In England, for example, the government may have opened up initial training to the market through the development of school-based training, but at the same time, it has massively increased its central powers through quality control and funding mechanisms as well as the new National Curriculum for teacher education. Both the RATE and the SITE studies show similar attempts by state or federal authorities to increase rather than reduce their influence, albeit partly in a response to a heightened awareness of the changing global circumstances in which they now have to operate.

However, the modality of their operation has changed from that of the 'bureau professionalism' of the traditional welfare state. England is far from alone in experiencing the emergence of a marketized civil society in which institutions are 'steered at a distance' by the state. Particularly helpful in understanding how the state remains strong while appearing to devolve power to individuals and autonomous institutions competing in the market is Neave's (1988) account of the shift from the 'bureaucratic state' to the 'evaluative state', which we mentioned in Chapter 1. In the education system, as elsewhere, there has been 'a rationalisation and wholesale redistribution of functions between centre and periphery such that the centre maintains overall strategic control through fewer, but more precise, policy levers [including] the operationalisation of criteria relating to "output quality"' (Neave 1988: 11). Rather than leading to a withering away of the state, the state withdraws 'from the murky plain of overwhelming detail, the better to take refuge in the clear and commanding heights of strategic "profiling"' (p. 12). For teachers, this is likely to bring much clearer specification of what they are expected to achieve rather than leaving it to professional judgement. But it is not entirely true that, as Neave implies, the state thereby abandons any interest in how they achieve these things. The specification of outputs itself shapes what teachers actually do, so the state uses its levers to influence the content of teachers' professionalism, both positively (in the sense of what it should consist of) and negatively (in terms of what should be discouraged if not outlawed). Partly, this is a struggle between what Hoyle (1974) termed 'restricted' and 'extended' professionality, though what might be included under each category has probably changed somewhat since 1974.

A. Hargreaves (1994) suggests that the conventional notion of professionalism is one 'which is grounded in notions of esoteric knowledge, specialist expertise and public status' and that this is being superseded by one which involves 'the exercise of discretionary judgement within conditions of unavoidable and perpetual uncertainty' (p. 19). Eraut (1994) similarly emphasizes a whole range of 'process knowledge' that involves making judgements as the hallmark of the modern day professional. Yet, as we have seen, some people argue that current moves towards competence or standards based training for teachers point in entirely the opposite direction by actually reducing the amount of control and discretion open to teachers, both individually and collectively (Jones and Moore 1993; Adams and Tulasiewicz 1995).

One way of understanding this apparent contradiction might be to see it as part of the inevitable heterodoxy of 'postmodernity'. Perhaps the two approaches reflect the juxtaposition of what Barnett (1994) calls 'two grand readings of our modern age'. On the one hand, there is 'a proliferation of forms of knowledge and experience', on the other a 'tendency . . . to favour forms of knowledge of a particular – instrumental and operational – kind' (Barnett 1994: 17). Barnett himself has suggested that 'operationalism' is a 'super-dominant tendency in higher education, which is reflective of . . . wider social forces' (p. 18).

It may, however, be that different elements of the profession are developing different forms of professionalism. Indeed, the state may even be encouraging this, with some members of the profession being given more autonomy and scope for flexibility than others, but only once they have met what might be termed a 'loyalty test'. Hanlon (1998) suggests that virtually all professions are becoming fragmented, with some members enthusiastically adopting the changing agenda of the state and corporate employers while others are resisting it. He argues that, in the period up to about 1980, most professions (and particularly those serving the welfare state in the post-war period) developed a 'social service' form of professionalism in which professional experts were trusted to work in the best interests of everyone and the resources were made available by the state to help them do so. He shows how this is being challenged by what he calls a 'commercialised professionalism' in the public as well as the private sector, which responds more to the needs of profitability and international competitiveness and therefore privileges the needs of some clients over others. Similar developments have been evident within education as a result of policies of 'marketization'. Gewirtz, Ball and Bowe (1995) identify two traditions on the part of education managers, which they term 'bureau-professional' (or 'welfarist') and 'new managerialist'.

Hanlon (1998) suggests that such clashes between the two traditions will ultimately lead to a split in the professional ranks. In teaching, the state is unlikely to be neutral even if some of the battles are fought out in the professional arena, though there are different elements even within the state and often different views within government itself. One reading of the dominant tendency in England is that the state is preparing the leading cadres of the profession for leadership in the new marketized culture of schooling, while others have to be prevented from perpetuating an out-moded social service version of professionalism even if they cannot be won to the new agenda. In these circumstances, one would expect new teachers to be equipped with a rather restricted version of professionality, but also given opportunities to demonstrate their potential to join the leading cadres. Those continuing teachers who, through lack of competence or will, do not pass through the performance pay threshold could be limited to a restricted and highly regulated mode of professionalism. Those who do progress satis-factorily might be given licensed autonomy and more discretion in defining the nature of their professionality.

Resistance to reform

One of the problems about a lot of writing about state responses to globalization and postmodernity, or about the spread of New Right ideas, is that it tends to be based purely on reading policy texts rather than studying the effects and resistances that constitute the policy in practice. This is why, in the MOTE study, we were concerned to go beyond the policy texts to explore whether the changes in teacher education were actually bringing about changes in the prevailing view of what it meant to become a profes-sional teacher in the 1990s.

The importance of this perspective becomes even clearer when we look at the progress of reform in different countries. In the 1990s England may well be more 'governable' than other countries. Theories that explain the English context cannot therefore be directly transferred to other contexts. Indeed, the complexities of globalization, and the importance of different national and local contexts, are highlighted by recognizing the limitations of what has in fact been achieved even in the United Kingdom. The changes in initial teacher education documented in the MOTE study have in reality had most effect in England. In Wales (Daugherty 1996) the same initiative has been introduced but different funding arrangements for higher education and the residue of old 'corporatist' allegiances between members of different state agencies have resulted in HEIs retaining a somewhat stronger role in the process than in England. School-based forms of training were intro-duced into Scotland in 1994 (Elder and Kwiatkowski 1996) only to be rejected by the combined forces of the teacher unions and the universities after one year. In Northern Ireland, the proposal to introduce school-based training was drastically modified in response to objections from the com-bined forces of the profession and the Catholic and Protestant churches.

Such complexities, even within one nation state, yet again undermine any straightforward notion of global change and reassert the realities of political struggles within particular constitutional frameworks.

An interesting point about the London government's attempt to introduce school-based training throughout the United Kingdom was that, in the light of its substantially increased powers in education, it *thought* it could impose such a policy. What it discovered was that the UK was more federal than it had anticipated. Genuinely federal governments seldom make such mistakes. As experience in Australia and the USA demonstrates, national strategies in teacher education, as in other fields, can only be managed through carefully orchestrated initiatives aimed at influencing opinion as well as voluntary codes – NCATE and the National Schools Network being cases in point.

It is not only constitutional factors that influence the power of national governments to have their way, however. As the findings from the SITE study demonstrate, the unions, at state levels (depending on the political complexion of state governments) and at the federal level (at least up to the general election in 1996) have remained a significant force in shaping policy. In the USA, university systems in many states remain significantly more autonomous than those in either England or Australia. Moreover, the fact that in Australia the federal government pays for higher education but that the states control teacher registration adds to the complexities. All national governments have to recognize the reality that individual states and other interest groups may use what power they have available to them to pursue policies that subvert their initiatives.

We also need to recognize that the motivations behind what on the surface may look like similar strategies for reform, may, in reality, vary. Thus in both Australia and the USA, as in England, there has been a range of initiatives designed to encourage HEIs and schools to work more closely together. However, the balance of forces behind the establishment of Professional Development Schools in the USA or the National Schools Network in Australia was significantly different from that in England. Those of their exponents who were concerned to extend rather than restrict notions of professionality and empower the profession to take some responsibility for its own improvement were more often in the ascendancy.

Similar differences emerge in relation to competences and standards. In England (though less so in Scotland and Northern Ireland), competences were initially seen as designed to restrict forms of professionality – though, as the MOTE studies demonstrate, if that was the intention, it has sometimes been subverted. However, in Australia, according to Walker (1996), a more proactive professional alliance of unions and universities seems to have been able to develop a competency framework that enshrined a much broader and more progressive version of professionalism. The fact that alternative versions of partnership and competences were developed in Australia and the USA and, at least until recently, given official sanction, indicates that there is not a simple or unilinear process of change around the world.

Any cross-national discussion of educational restructuring needs therefore to bear in mind a wide range of variance. Despite globalizing influences, educational reform is being conducted within contexts with different histories, different constitutional and administrative arrangements and different cultural and political complexions. As Featherstone puts it, 'one paradoxical consequence of the process of globalisation, the awareness of the finitude and boundedness of the plane of humanity, is not to produce homogeneity but to familiarise us with greater diversity' (1993: 169).

Does that mean, however, that all global change in initial teacher education can illustrate is the diversity and complexity of local systems? We suspect not. While variance needs to be acknowledged, it should not obscure the common factors. As Fowler (1994) comments, 'important variations among institutions and cultures do not erase deeper similarities' – particularly between advanced industrial democracies. Despite the differences, there does appear to be considerable congruence in the policies in different countries. We cannot ignore the fact that strategies such as partnership school-based training and centrally-defined standards came to prominence in a number of countries at more or less the same time.

It is perhaps significant that, in their latest round of policy initiatives, both the USA and Australia are moving closer towards aspects of the English model, attempting to narrow definitions of professionality and increase central control of the training process. So, for example, in Australia, the prospect of narrower versions of professionality has been raised recently by the new Liberal Government's questioning of the length of academic courses. At the same time, higher education in general is being subject to increased central control through the mechanisms of greater competition for government funds in combination with a move towards output measurement. In the USA, Labaree and Pallas (1996) argue that a more recent Holmes Group report (Holmes Group 1995) presents a very different vision of the future profession from that put forward in the 1990 report (Holmes Group 1990). Significantly, the group, in which on this occasion a greater proportion of members were from outside education, was critical of the value of much of the content of teacher education programmes. It may well be that the universities' 'reform from within' strategy argued for in the previous Holmes Group report has been found wanting by other stakeholders, hence the greater interest in national frameworks and renewed licensing outlined earlier.

Thus what we seem to be witnessing in teacher education reform around the world is an example of a broader contemporary policy process in which 'the international is nationalised and . . . the national is exported' (Hannerz and Löfgren 1994: 199). But, despite this dialectical process, there is nothing inevitable in how policies will be interpreted, translated into policy texts and implemented in practice in different contexts and eras. What on the surface look like the same ideas can be utilized for different ends by governments of different political complexions; policies, as they are put into practice in real political contexts, are transformed in distinctive ways, as indeed would be expected from Bowe and Ball's (1992) account of the policy process.

The search for a democratic professionalism?

It should be clear, then, that what is currently happening around the world in response to globalization and the situation confronting modern nation states needs to be seen as part of a political process that has common features and national specificities. While we should not underestimate the significance of those changes that are evoked – but inadequately characterized – by terms such as post-Fordism and post-modernity, we should not assume that the policy responses that are currently fashionable are the most appropriate ones. The particular combination of policies outlined in this book has been heavily influenced by the interpretations of such changes offered by various pressure groups from the New Right.

In many countries, the political left was rather slow in recognizing the significance of the changes and thus allowed the right to take the initiative. This, in turn, has had serious consequences for the direction in which reforms have gone and consequences for the particular notions of professionalism that they encourage, but the current trend towards a narrowing of professionality that seems to be occurring in some countries should not be considered irreversible. To the extent that it is occurring, it is doing so through distinctive political processes. In principle, it can therefore be challenged by political means.

In England, despite claims that its broader policies embody a Third Way (Giddens 1998), the New Labour government has so far refined rather than abandoned the New Right approach to teacher education. Meanwhile, those still on the left have done little yet to develop a distinctive concept of teacher education. Even if the social democratic era looks better in retrospect, and in comparison with more recent policies, than it did at the time, that does not remove the need to rethink what might be progressive policies for the next century. It is perhaps indicative of the paucity of thinking on this that some left teacher educators who, 25 years ago, were criticizing the élitism of the professions, should now be among those who believe that teachers should adopt the modes of self-regulation traditionally associated with the conservative professions of medicine and law. Whether New Labour's General Teaching Council in England can provide a more progressive and inclusive model remains to be seen.

In Chapter 1, we introduced Bowe and Ball's (1992) policy 'cycle' and much of our book has been looking at teacher education policy in their three 'contexts' of 'influence', 'text production' and 'practice'. Ball (1994) has since identified two other policy contexts with which he feels critical social research should be concerned. One is the context of 'outcomes', which is concerned with what he calls the second order consequences for equality and justice of the first order (or practice) effects. Our own reading of the evidence to date is that neither conventional modes of professionalism, nor the new modes currently being sponsored by state control and market forces – nor indeed the sort of compromise between them that seems to be emerging in the contexts of practice – have paid sufficient attention to the needs of those groups who have consistently been marginalized by modern education systems and their styles of policymaking. We therefore need to concern ourselves with Ball's second new context, which involves 'the identification of a set of political and social activities "which might more effectively tackle inequalities"' (Ball 1994: 26). We conclude this chapter with some observations on what this might involve for teacher education in the years ahead.

In standing back and looking at the findings from our own work – and those of the SITE and RATE enquiries – we are forced to recognize that the ever increasing forms of state surveillance are indicative of a 'low trust' relationship between each society and its teachers. Media characterizations of teachers have often encouraged popular suspicion of the teaching profession. Furthermore, the defence of the education service, especially in England and Wales, has too often been conducted within the assumptions of the 'old' politics of education, which involved consultation between government, employers and unions and universities but excluded whole constituencies, some of whom the New Right has subsequently successfully appealed to (Apple 1996). We therefore need to ask some fundamental questions about who does have a legitimate right to be involved in defining teacher professionalism. Are state control and market forces or professional self-governance really the only models of accountability available to us – or can we develop new approaches to teacher professionalism, based upon more participatory relationships with diverse communities?

In this context, it is worth reflecting that some aspects of recent reforms may potentially resonate with progressive impulses. We have already indicated that, in Australia, teacher educators and teacher unions were able to influence developments to a greater extent than those in England. Perhaps, then, it is time to rethink teachers' 'professional project'. In Australia, Knight *et al.* (1993) have argued that the devolutionary aspects of recent reforms could serve to foster a welcome degree of flexibility, diversity and responsiveness, which they suggest have been largely lacking in teacher education as it has traditionally been conducted. They further point out that there has always been a tension between the teaching profession's claim to autonomy and a requirement that it be open to the needs and concerns of other groups in a democratic society. Like Ginsburg (1997) and Apple (1996) in the USA, they suggest that there is a real conflict between the professional project as conventionally conceived and the democratic project. However, they feel that changes in modern societies may now make it possible to resolve that conflict and avoid both the teaching profession's and the state's forms of closure. Thus, for them, the alternative to state control is not traditional professionalism, but a 'democratic professionalism', which seeks to demystify professional work and build alliances between teachers and excluded constituencies of students, parents and members of the community on whose behalf decisions have traditionally been made either by professions or by the state. Davies (1996: 673) similarly identifies 'new professionalism' or a 'democratic professionalism' as relevant to a 'changed policy context and as a solution to some of the problems of professional power long identified in the academic literature'.

However, in teacher education, the positive consequences of 'new times' envisaged by Knight *et al.* (1993) in Australia seem unlikely to be forth-coming on any significant scale in England, where a strong core definition of teacher professionalism based on a restricted notion of professionality is supported by technologies of control that include the specification of standards, government inspections, and TTA funding decisions, etc. These apparently postmodern 'discursive, legislative, fiscal, organisational and other resources' (Rose and Miller 1992: 189) impact upon organizational subjectivities and professional identities. They may appear to constitute a shift away from conventional techniques of coordination and control on the part of large-scale bureaucratic state forms and thus give more scope for resistance and local discretion. Yet, Landman and Ozga (1995) suggest that 'teacher education and training is vulnerable to the combined effects of financial stringency, devolution of budgetary control to individual schools and enhanced managerialism' in ways that may be more effective than prescription by circular. The reality as evidenced in the MOTE projects is anyway that both forms of control are in evidence. Furthermore, under New Labour, some governmental activity in England harks back to the old-style 'bureaucratic' state, rather than the 'steering at a distance' associated with the evaluative state. Indeed, some of the TTA's functions (for example the funding and management of continuing professional development courses) have recently been taken back under the direct control of the Department for Education and Employment, though others may be handed to the GTC in the future.

As we have seen, the combined effect of the policies to date has been to produce a restricted core definition of professionality by government man-date, alongside increasing variability in other aspects of professional prepara-tion. In these circumstances, the nature of the gains that can be made by individual schools and communities is likely to be both limited and variable. Even in what traditionally has been a relatively autonomous higher educa-tion sector, we have seen how a narrower concept of teacher professional-ism is gradually, if unevenly, being achieved. While most courses still aspire to deliver extended notions of professionality, the new accountability mech-anisms and funding cuts are making it ever more difficult to do so. It is fanciful to think that individual school communities will have any greater freedom than universities without broader political support.

There is also a danger that what local autonomy does exist alongside the core definition of professionality by government mandate will have negative rather than positive equity implications. With increasing time being spent by trainee teachers in schools, some aspects of training that were once offered to all students now depend on the particular concerns of schools or even individual mentors. There is, for example, as a report for the Equal Oppor-tunities Commission found, 'wide variation amongst schools and LEAs . . . in the awareness and application of gender issues' (Arnot *et al.* 1996). The shift of more educational and professional studies into schools, with their own 'local' discourses around education, has meant that treatment of such areas of work in initial teacher education is becoming highly variable even across different partner schools of the same university.[2]

In the light of all this, we believe that any attempt to develop an alternative democratic approach to teacher education reform, even under the condition of postmodernity, will require the mobilization of political support at the national level as well as professional and local partnerships. Like the New Right, we can of course also learn from the experiences of colleagues in other contexts, as indeed we have from the SITE and RATE research in Australia and the USA. But the key lesson for teacher educators who wish to address issues of inequality and social exclusion is that we need to stop being purely defensive or reactive and begin working with others to develop approaches that relate not only to the legitimate aspirations of the profession but also those of the wider society – and that must include (indeed prioritize) those groups within civil society who have hitherto not been well-served either by the profession or by the state. In other words, the next re-formation of teacher professionalism needs to be one in which we consider how to harness teachers' professional expertise to a new democratic project in the state and civil society.

Notes

1 Survey of Initial Teacher Education (SITE) and Research About Teacher Education (RATE).
2 This could be a danger in all forms of partnership, though it seemed less so in what we identified as 'HEI-led' and 'collaborative' forms of partnership than in 'complementary' ones (see Chapter 6), where schools and HEIs had their own distinct spheres of influence.

Appendix
The methodology of the
MOTE studies

Introduction

The MOTE studies had two key aims, each of which raised a number of complex issues; as a result, our research design involved the use of a variety of different research strategies. Our first aim was to map the changing nature of provision of initial teacher education in England and Wales in the early and mid-1990s. In order to achieve this aim, both MOTE studies included a national survey of provision and more detailed case studies of a carefully selected sample of 44 higher education-provided courses and five Licensed Teacher Schemes.* Our second aim was to examine the 'outcomes' of training. Here the strategy involved a questionnaire survey of students' views of the quality and effectiveness of their training. Questionnaires were completed by a sample of students taken from the 49 case study courses at the end of their training and at the end of their first year of teaching; questionnaires were also completed by their employing headteachers. The study of provision, Aim 1, was undertaken twice with a similar strategy being repeated in MOTE 1 and MOTE 2. The study of 'outcomes', Aim 2, involved a single research strategy which ran across both MOTE studies.

* This number was originally 45 but one case study course subsequently withdrew.

Aim 1 – Mapping the changing face of provision

MOTE 1

The first national survey

As we indicated in Chapter 3, one of the first difficulties we faced at the beginning of our research was that at the time there was no reliable data available on the provision of initial teacher education in England and Wales. We had intended to begin the project with a telephone survey of all course leaders as a preliminary to selecting a more detailed sample for more intensive study. However, after consulting with a number of bodies (DES, HMI, UCET, SCOP) we came to the conclusion that no reliable list of courses was available. We would have to begin by developing our own topography of provision; only then could we go on to select a sample of courses for our case study work.

In 1991, an initial questionnaire was sent to all higher education institutions (HEIs) in England and Wales which offered initial teacher education courses, asking what courses they were offering in 1990–91. Eighty-six HEIs (98 per cent) returned the survey questionnaire and 317 individual courses in England and Wales were then identified from the survey returns and from official statistics. In order to identify separate routes to qualified teacher status (QTS), the following criteria were applied to these courses: age phase, course award and mode of attendance.

- *Age phase*   Courses were separated into those leading to a secondary qualification and those that led to a primary qualification.
- *Course award*   Courses were first separated into postgraduate (PGCE) and undergraduate course awards. Undergraduate courses were then further classified as BEd degree, BA/BSc (QTS) degree, and degree plus teaching certificate.
- *Mode of attendance*   Within each course award category, courses were separated according to length, as follows: *undergraduate courses*: two-year BEd, three-year BA/BSc (QTS), four-year BEd, BA/BSc (QTS) and degree plus teaching certificate; *postgraduate courses*: one-year PGCE, and two-year PGCE.

Postgraduate courses were further separated into the following distinctive modes of attendance: full-time, part-time, and Articled Teacher Schemes. Courses in different institutions, even if part of the same LEA-coordinated Articled Teacher Scheme, were treated separately.

A more detailed questionnaire was then sent to the course leaders identified by their institutions. This questionnaire collected data on the following issues:

- course characteristics;
- student characteristics;
- course philosophy;
- course structure;
- school involvement;
- assessment.

Table A.1 MOTE 1 survey data: by phase, sector and course award

	Secondary courses			Primary courses			Total
	Univ.	*Poly.*	*CHE*	*Univ.*	*Poly.*	*CHE*	
Total PGCE	49	18	25	19	15	33	159
1 year full-time	29	11	18	16	11	27	112
2 year full-time	7	2	3	–	–	–	12
2 year part-time	6	3	1	1	1	–	12
ATS	7	2	3	2	3	6	23
Total undergraduate	15	21	21	6	19	30	112
2 year	2	12	5	1	4	2	26
3 year	2	–	–	–	–	–	2
4 year	11	9	16	5	15	28	84
Total Courses	64	39	46	25	34	63	271

Note: One course led to the award of either BEd or PGCE and total number of courses therefore equals 271 in this table. Actual MOTE N of courses was 270.

The survey attracted a response from course leaders on 270 (85 per cent) courses of which 108 were run by colleges or institutes of higher education (CHEs), 89 were run by universities, and 73 were run by polytechnics. A breakdown of these course returns, by age phase and course award, is given in Table A.1.

Case studies

The surveys conducted in the first part of our research provided an invaluable and original database on the state of initial teacher education in England and Wales at the time. They also provided a basis for selecting an appropriate sample for an in-depth study of provision with different types of course. The subsample of 44 courses was drawn from the 270 HEI courses that had responded to the surveys using the following procedure.

First, courses were divided up into two main categories – conventional courses and non-conventional courses. Non-conventional courses were defined as conversion, articled and part-time PGCE courses and shortened BEd courses.

Within categories, courses were then sorted according to the following criteria:

• percentage of students aged 31–40;
• targeted student recruitment policies;
• percentage of school-based work;
• course size.

In selecting particular courses for study, a balance was sought in terms of institution type, course type, age phase, geographical location and the national distribution of student numbers. The final sample of 44 courses included 24 PGCE courses (including five Articled Teacher Schemes) and 20 BEd/BA(QTS) courses.

Fieldwork in the 44 courses was conducted in two phases. In phase one during November and December 1991, semi-structured interviews were carried out with course leaders. The purpose of these interviews was to validate the questionnaire returns and to explore a number of issues arising from that questionnaire in more detail. Topics covered in these interviews included recruitment to the course, course philosophy and partnership with schools. In phase two, from February to May 1992, members of the project team conducted individual and group interviews with HEI staff and students and observed teaching sessions in HEIs. On each course, a sample of students completed a questionnaire and took part in a focus group discussion about the HEI and school-based aspects of their courses. The interviews with course tutors addressed the issue of course structure and ways in which the HEI-based course was integrated with school experience. In heavily school-based courses (including the five Articled Teacher Schemes) interviews were also conducted with school-based mentors. These focused on the role and responsibilities they had assumed and the support they were receiving from the HEI.

The licensed teacher study

As we indicated in Chapter 4, at the time of the first MOTE study, 99 per cent of initial teacher education provision was conducted through higher education institutions. However at the time, a new form of provision was being established, coordinated and provided by teachers' employers (local education authorities and grant maintained schools) – this was the Licensed Teacher Scheme. As we explained in Chapter 4, because of its political rather than its numerical significance, we were keen to include the Licensed Teacher Scheme within our research.

In the spring of 1991, the MOTE project conducted a telephone survey of all LEAs in England and Wales in order to identify which planned to offer licensed teacher training in 1990–91 and/or 1991–92. Sixty-three LEAs reported that they were planning to offer a scheme and of these 59 went ahead with their plans. A total of 619 licensed teachers (LTs) were recruited to these schemes; 144 of these had been awarded QTS by the end of 1991 and 46 had dropped out.

In May 1991, survey questionnaires were sent to these LEAs asking for information on the following aspects of their Licensed Teacher Scheme:

- distinctive characteristics of the scheme;
- rationale for the scheme;
- recruitment policy;
- training policy;
- assessment policy;
- profile of licensed teachers.

Thirty-two LEAs of the 63 (51 per cent) returned completed questionnaires. These returns included all the LEAs operating large schemes (four LEAs) and most of the LEAs operating medium sized schemes (14 LEAs) during 1990–91. Thus, although the response rate for the MOTE survey of Licensed Teacher Schemes was just over half, they represented 70 per cent (402) of all trainees on schemes in the first year of the initiative's operation (1990–91).

In the summer of 1992, a sample of five schemes was drawn from the survey respondents in order to conduct a more in-depth qualitative survey. The sample design was based on the following criteria: size, geographical location, extent of LEA involvement, place of training and recruitment policy. The selected LEAs included two London schemes (with an inner and outer London borough) and schemes in the north, southwest and southeast of England. At the time there were no licensed teachers in Wales.

Visits were made to the case study LEAs and associated schools in order to interview LEA personnel, headteachers, mentors, licensed teachers and others directly involved in running the schemes. A total of five LEA staff, 10 headteachers, 10 mentors and 10 licensed teachers (five primary and five secondary) were interviewed. The main aim of these interviews was to understand in more detail the issues set out in the initial questionnaire, that is, philosophy, recruitment strategy, training provision in and out of school, the nature of mentoring and support for mentors, assessment procedures and the licensed teachers' experience.

MOTE 2

The second project commenced in 1993 and included a follow up to our earlier work with further case studies of many of the original higher education-provided courses and a second national survey. Because of the plethora of changes being introduced in the field of initial teacher education at the time, we chose, on this occasion, to reverse the order of our research strategy. We conducted a further round of fieldwork with our case study courses in 1994 and 1995 and, in the hope of picking up the impact of the most recent changes, a second national survey in 1996.

Case study sampling and fieldwork

As we have described above, the 44 HEI-led courses used for case studies in 1992 were chosen as a stratified random sample of criteria derived from our first national survey. By spring 1995, when we returned to these courses for our second round of fieldwork, nine of the original sample courses had closed, while some new ones had been established. In addition, we chose not to continue with our work on the Licensed Teacher Scheme. It therefore became necessary to 'repair' the original sample to bring the total back up to the full number of 49. The most significant changes were that all Articled Teacher Schemes were in their final year (and had not therefore recruited new students) while two quite new routes had been added to provision

– The Open University (OU) PGCE course and School-Centred Initial Teacher Training (SCITT) schemes. In order to maintain comparable sampling of geographical location and institutional type, Articled Teacher Schemes and other 'closed' courses within the original sample were replaced by comparable courses within the same institution (for example Primary Articled Teacher Schemes were replaced by Primary PGCE courses). In addition, a sample of three Open University regions and three SCITT providers was added to the sample to replace the Licensed Teacher Schemes.

Within the 'repaired sample' there were now 46 higher education-based courses and three SCITT schemes. From the higher education-based courses, 12 were chosen for detailed analysis. Members of the research team visited these 12 courses on two occasions in autumn 1994 and spring 1995. During their visits, they conducted semi-structured interviews with the course leader, at least one other lecturer, a teacher 'mentor' and a group of students. In addition they sat in on one or more taught sessions in the university or college and at least one in a partner school. These observed sessions then became the focus of further discussion and interviews with the participants. For the remaining 34 courses and the three additional SCITT courses, data were collected through semi-structured interviews with course leaders.

The second national survey

In the autumn of 1995, a pro forma was sent to the Dean of Education, or equivalent, of the 93 HEIs offering initial teacher education in England and Wales. This pro forma asked for a list of all the discrete courses in initial teacher education offered by that institution, and for a course contact for each. All but one institution returned the information requested and, except in the case of this one institution (offering three courses), a detailed course questionnaire was later sent to the named contact for each course.

For the school-centred courses (SCITTs), a list of schemes and contacts was obtained from the Teacher Training Agency (TTA) and a specially designed but comparable course questionnaire was sent to each of the named contacts.

Two hundred and eleven completed course questionnaires were received out of the 280 identified courses, representing a response rate of 75 per cent. Only nine of the 19 SCITT courses provided returns, a response rate of 47 per cent. The overall questionnaire response rate was thus 73.6 per cent, compared with a rate of 85 per cent for the 1990–91 MOTE survey. However, the Teacher Training Agency projected targets for the 1995–6 intake suggest that 77.3 per cent of teacher training students (77.7 per cent secondary and 76.7 per cent primary) were represented in our returns. Details of the respondent courses were as follows:

Conventional courses
- one-year postgraduate (112);
- four-year undergraduate (included one course that gave an additional PGCE, and two intercalated courses which led to a separate Certificate of Education award) (63).

Non-conventional courses
- distance learning PGCE courses (3, two of which were 18 months, and the other two years);
- other part-time PGCE courses (2, of which one was 18 months, the other two years);
- other two-year courses (20): two-year postgraduate *or* undergraduate (1); two-year undergraduate (19, including one with a part-time attendance option);
- three-year undergraduate (10, including one course which offered a part-time option for the equivalent of the first year);
- SCITT courses (9).

Response rates varied considerably between modes of provision. High rates of response were achieved from primary one-year postgraduate courses (89 per cent), primary three-year undergraduate courses (90 per cent), secondary four-year undergraduate courses (96 per cent), and distance learning courses (all three). Low response rates came from conversion courses (8.3 per cent), primary two-year undergraduate courses (25 per cent), two-year part-time courses (25 per cent) and secondary SCITT courses (40 per cent).

The questionnaire itself covered similar issues to those used in our first national survey, that is:

- course characteristics;
- student characteristics;
- course philosophy;
- course structure;
- school involvement;
- assessment.

In addition it included a range of questions on the management and implementation of 'partnership' and on competences.

Aim 2 – Examining the outcomes of training

Developing research instruments

Given that initial teacher education was changing so rapidly in the early and mid-1990s, a second aim of our research was to examine the outcomes of different programmes. As we discussed in Chapter 8, during the 1980s and early 1990s, HMI made three major studies of the outcomes of training. Each was called *The New Teacher in School* (HMI 1982; HMI 1988a; Ofsted 1992). In these studies, HMI utilized a range of methods: self-assessment questionnaires for the newly qualified teachers (NQTs) to complete, interviews and, most important of all, classroom observation to inform their judgements. Their substantial workforce as well as their extensive experience of conducting classroom-based assessments made them well placed to undertake such evaluations on a large scale. Unfortunately we were not in that position, having neither the experience nor the staffing to undertake classroom observation on any significant scale. In order to assess the 'outputs' of training we therefore had to develop our own instruments; we were, however, able to build on those self-assessment instruments developed by HMI.

Three research instruments, to be administered as postal questionnaires, were developed. They were:

- an 'Exit' questionnaire to be administered to students on completion of their teacher training course;
- a 'Newly Qualified Teacher' (NQT) questionnaire to be administered at the end of the trainees' first year of teaching;
- a 'Headteacher' questionnaire to be administered to the NQT's headteacher/ senior colleague at the end of the trainee's first year of teaching.

Each questionnaire contained three distinct elements:

Self-assessment on practical teaching competences
This part of the questionnaire focused on a list of practical skills that students were expected to be able to undertake at the end of their course. In developing these self-assessment statements we were able to draw extensively on those developed for the HMI *New Teacher in School* surveys. Our list included items such as: 'able to use a range of strategies appropriate to different learning purposes'; 'able to use the appropriate discipline strategies to maintain an orderly classroom environment'.

Other professional abilities
While we recognized that the list of practical competences drawn from HMI were relevant and important in measuring the outcomes of courses, we also felt that something more was required if we were to be able to examine the forms of professionalism being engendered by current courses. In designing the questionnaires therefore we were concerned to produce instruments that would give students the space to represent relevant areas of their training experience. We were aware that, although many courses did focus on competences, there were likely to be many other dimensions of professional preparation that were not tapped by a narrow competency list. It was therefore necessary to design an additional range of self-assessment items.

The research instruments we developed therefore included a list of 'professional understandings' as well as a list of 'professional competences'. Thus the practical competence 'able to teach pupils of all abilities' was supplemented with the professional understanding of 'understand the reasons for differences in children's attainment'. Similarly, the practical competence 'to assess pupils according to National Curriculum requirements' was supplemented with the professional understanding of 'understand the impact of assessment on teaching and learning'.

On both the Exit and NQT questionnaires, trainees were asked to look back on their training and complete these self-evaluation statements in relation to themselves. On the Headteachers questionnaire, heads or senior teachers were asked to rate the trainee on a comparable set of statements.

The contribution of different partners
The final dimension of the Exit and NQT questionnaires was a series of questions designed to probe the contribution of different partners in training (school and higher education, etc.) to the development of students' practical competences and other professional abilities. Extracts from a sample Exit questionnaire are reproduced at the end of this Appendix.

Timetable

As we indicated in Chapters 2 and 5, the courses we studied in both of our MOTE projects were in a constant process of change as they responded to successive government initiatives. Most of the courses we visited in 1992 for MOTE 1 were working under 1989 regulations (DES 1989a) though a few of the four-year BEd courses still had students at the end of their courses working under 1984 regulations. In MOTE 2 we visited courses in 1994–95. Secondary courses were at that stage in the first year of implementing the 1992 regulations (DfE 1992) for their new intake; primary courses did not have to conform to their 1993 (DfE 1993a) regulations for their new intake until the following year. Given the variety of different regulations different cohorts of students were working under, during our visits to institutions we chose to focus on the second year of any courses that ran for longer than a year. (For one-year PGCE courses we necessarily chose to focus on the year in hand). In our discussions with lecturers and teachers it was this course on which we focused; when we met students or followed them into school, it was this cohort with whom we worked.

The fact that different cohorts of students were operating under different regulations had a significant impact on our research design when we came to study course outcomes. If our questionnaire findings were to relate to our study of courses, we had to follow through to graduation and beyond the same group of students, that is, those who were on the course at the time that we visited. The administration of the Exit, NQT and Headteacher questionnaires therefore had to be undertaken as this particular cohort moved through the system. Given the time-scale involved, it was only possible to undertake this process once with a sample selected from MOTE 1 case study courses. In order to capture something of the impact of the most recent changes, a more restricted 'supplementary' study was undertaken with a sample of one-year PGCE students selected from MOTE 2 case study courses. For this group, only the Exit questionnaire was completed.

Table A.2   Timetable for 'outcomes' study

Course type	Exit questionnaire completed	NQT and Headteacher questionnaires completed
1 year courses	June 1992	June 1993
2 year courses	June 1992	June 1993
3 year courses	June 1993	June 1994
4 year courses	June 1994	June 1995
1 year PGCE supplementary study	June 1997	n/a

The timetable for the administration of the questionnaires is shown in Table A.2.

Sampling and responses

The aim of the survey of course outcomes was to compare and contrast competences and understandings of a sample of students drawn from a variety of courses. As some conventional courses recruited very large numbers (up to 400 per year) while some non-conventional courses recruited only small numbers (sometimes as few as six) different sampling strategies had to be adopted for different course types. With smaller courses (conversion courses, part-time PGCEs, Articled and Licensed Teacher Schemes) we took the whole cohort; with medium-sized courses (one-year PGCE courses, two and three-year BEds) we took a 50 per cent sample and with the four-year BEd (normally large courses) we took 25 respondents from each course. A total of 1418 questionnaires were distributed in all. For the supplementary (1997) study, the sample was 100 per cent of all graduates from the 10 one-year case study PGCE courses used in MOTE 2 (n=1639).

Given the size of the research task, the administration strategy for the Exit questionnaire involved us in recruiting the support of course leaders. Course leaders agreed to distribute questionnaires, and where necessary, to select the sample we defined. A pre-paid envelope was included for the return of the questionnaire. As a strategy this was only partially successful. From some courses there was 100 per cent return, indicating that perhaps the questionnaire was completed during teaching time; from eight courses there was no response whatsoever, possibly indicating that the course leader had not distributed the questionnaire as promised.

Respondents to the Exit questionnaire were asked to provide a contact address. The NQT questionnaire was posted to this address a year after they had graduated with a pre-paid return envelope. This questionnaire asked for details of their school and current headteacher. These headteachers were then

Table A.3 Questionnaire response rates

Instrument	n distributed	n returned	Response (%)
Main Exit questionnaire	1418	574	41
NQT questionnaire	574	215	37
Headteacher questionnaire	215	118	54
Supplementary Exit questionnaire	1639	377	23

contacted with the last of our three research instruments, the Headteachers questionnaire.

As indicated in Chapter 8, the response rates to our three questionnaires were as shown in Table A.3. Data from these questionnaires were then analysed with the Statistical Package for Social Sciences (SPSS).

Questionnaire extracts

Below we have reproduced extracts from the secondary Exit questionnaire. Other questionnaires, (the primary Exit questionnaire, the NQT and Headteacher questionnaires) included almost identical questions though where necessary, they were adapted for their particular target audience.

Professional understanding and professional competences: extract from secondary Exit questionnaire*

---

4 (a) In column A, rate on a scale 1 to 3 the extent to which your initial teacher training course has helped you to understand the key professional issues listed below.
Please use the following coding scheme:

1 Good understanding
2 Adequate understanding
3 Poor understanding

(b) Tick the appropriate box(es) in column B to indicate whether your training institution and/or your school experience contributed *significantly* to your understanding of these issues.

	A *Select 1–3*	B *Please tick*	
Understanding of:		*Training institution*	*School*
the main changes in the education system since 1944			
the impact of the Education Reform Act (1988) on education			
the arguments in favour of a broad and balanced curriculum			
differing views about the aims of education			
the relationship between schools and the economy			
contemporary political debates about education			
the relationship between schools and the community			
the impact of the National Curriculum on secondary teaching			
the impact of assessment on teaching and learning			
the effect of inequalities on education			
the reasons for differences in children's attainment			
the way children learn			
the role of language in learning			
the role of critical reflection in evaluating your own teaching			

---

* 'Primary' questionnaires were appropriately modified, as were NQT and Headteacher questionnaires.

B. Professional competences

5 (a) In column A, rate on a scale 1 to 3 the extent to which your initial teacher training prepared you for the competences listed below.
Please use the following coding scheme:

1 Well prepared
2 Adequately prepared
3 Poorly prepared

(b) Tick the appropriate box(es) in column B to indicate whether your training institution and/or your school experience contributed *significantly* to your professional preparation for these competences.

	A *Select 1–3*	*B* *Please tick*	
Prepared:		*Training institution*	*School*
to undertake the contractual, legal and administrative responsibilities of a teacher			
to undertake the pastoral responsibilities of a teacher			
to teach your main subject in accordance with National Curriculum requirements			
to teach your subsidiary subject in accordance with NC requirements			
to teach the cross-curricular themes, skills and dimensions			
to prepare pupils for GCSE examinations			
to prepare pupils for A-level examinations			
to use a range of teaching strategies (e.g. group or pair work) appropriate to different learning purposes			
to select and use appropriate teaching materials			
to use information technology			
to use appropriate discipline strategies to maintain an orderly classroom environment			
to teach mixed ability groups			
to plan lessons in order to ensure continuity and progression			
to differentiate the curriculum in order to meet the needs of individual pupils			

	A Select 1–3	B Please tick	
Prepared:		Training institution	School
to respond to pupils with special educational needs			
to teach pupils for whom English is a second language			
to plan your teaching in order to maintain interest and motivation			
to diagnose and evaluate pupil learning			
to assess pupils according to National Curriculum requirements			
to record pupils' progress			
to discuss pupils' performance with parents			
to use results of assessment in teaching			
to take responsibility for personal and social education			
to act as a form tutor			
to take responsibility for curriculum development			
to team teach with your colleagues			
to appraise the effectiveness of your own teaching			

6 Please identify any professional competences which you have gained from your initial teacher training course, in addition to those listed in question 5 above.

_____

_____

_____

_____

_____

_____

_____

References

Adams, A. and Tulasiewicz, W. (1995) *The Crisis in Teacher Education: A European Concern?* London: Falmer Press.

Alexander, R. (1984) *Primary Teaching.* Eastbourne: Holt, Rinehart and Winston.

Allen, J. (1992) Post-industrialism and post-Fordism, in S. Hall, D. Held and T. McGrew (eds) *Modernity and its Futures.* Cambridge: Polity Press.

Ambrose, P. (1996) Modest proposals?: Teacher education and the Education Act 1994, in J. Furlong and R. Smith (eds) *The Role of Higher Education in Initial Teacher Training.* London: Kogan Page.

Anderson, L. (1994) School-centred initial teacher training: a difference of emphasis rather than degree? *Mentoring and Tutoring,* 2(2): 19–24.

Apple, M. (1996) *Cultural Politics and Education.* New York: Teachers' College Press.

Apple, M. (1998) Review Essay, *Educational Researcher,* 27(6): 27–8.

Arnot, M., David, M. and Weiner, G. (1996) *Educational Reforms and Gender Equality in Schools.* Manchester: Equal Opportunities Commission.

Atkinson, T. and Claxton, G. (eds) (1999) *The Intuitive Professional.* Buckingham: Open University Press.

Atkinson, T. and Lewis, M. (1998) The National Curriculum for teacher education – ICT. Unpublished discussion paper. Bristol: University of Bristol.

Ball, S. (1990) *Politics and Policy Making: Explorations in Policy Sociology.* London: Routledge.

Ball, S. (1994) *Education Reform: A Critical and Post-structural Approach.* Buckingham: Open University Press.

Barnett, R. (1994) *The Limits of Competence: Knowledge, Higher Education and Society.* Buckingham: Open University Press.

Barrett, E., Barton, L., Furlong, J. *et al.* (1992a) *Initial Teacher Training in England and Wales: A Topography.* Modes of Teacher Education Project. London: Goldsmiths' College.

Barrett, E., Barton, L., Furlong, J. *et al.* (1992b) New routes to qualified teacher status. *Cambridge Journal of Education,* 22(3): 323–6.

Barrett, E. and Galvin, C. (1993) *The Licensed Teacher Scheme: a MOTE Report.* London: Institute of Education.

Bell, A. (1981) Structure, knowledge and relationships in teacher education. *British Journal of Sociology of Education,* 2(1): 3–23.

Benton, P. (ed.) (1990) *The Oxford Internship Scheme: Integration and Partnership in Initial Teacher Education.* London: Calouste Gulbenkian Foundation.

Bernstein, B. (1997) Official knowledge and pedagogic identities: the politics of recontextualising, in I. Nilsson and L. Lundahl (eds) *Teachers, Curriculum and Policy: Critical Perspectives in Educational Research.* Umea, Sweden, Department of Education, Umea University.

Berrill, M. (1994) A view from the crossroads. *Cambridge Journal of Education,* 24(1): 113–16.

Bottery, M. (1996) Educational markets, post-Fordism and professional consciousness. Unpublished paper, University of Hull.

Bottery, M. (1998) *Professionals and Policy: Management Strategy in a Competitive World.* London: Cassell.

Bowe, R. and Ball, S. with Gold. A. (1992) *Reforming Education and Changing Schools: Case Studies in Policy Sociology.* London: Routledge.

Bridges, D. (1996) Initial teacher education and the reconstruction of the university, in J. Furlong and R. Smith (eds) *The Role of Higher Education in Initial Teacher Training.* London: Kogan Page.

Cabinet Office (1991) *Citizen's Charter.* London: HMSO.

Carter, J. (ed.) (1998) *Postmodernity and the Fragmentation of Welfare.* London: Routledge.

Clarke, J. and Newman, J. (1998) The managerial state, in J. Carter (ed.) *Postmodernity and the Fragmentation of Welfare.* London: Routledge.

Clarke, K. (1991) Speech to Conservative Party Conference. September.

Clarke, K. (1992) Speech for North of England Education Conference. 4 January. London: Conservative Party Central Office.

Coopers and Lybrand (1995) *Allocation of Funding in ITT: A Report to the Teacher Training Agency.* London: Coopers and Lybrand.

Council for National Academic Awards (CNAA) (1992) *Competence-based Approaches to Teacher Education: Viewpoints and Issues.* London: CNAA.

Cox, C.B. and Dyson, S.E. (eds) (1969) *Black Papers Two: The Crisis in Education.* London: The Black Papers.

Daily Telegraph (1996) Back to school they go (Leader comment) *Daily Telegraph,* 11 July.

Dale, R. (1989) *The State and Education Policy.* Milton Keynes: Open University Press.

Dale, R. (1997) The state and the governance of education, in A.H. Halsey, H. Lauder, P. Brown and A.S. Wells (eds) *Education: Culture, Economy and Society,* Oxford: Oxford University Press.

Daugherty, R. (1996) ITT Partnerships in Wales. Paper presented at UCET National Conference, Market Bosworth, England, November.

Daugherty, R. (1997) Bright ideas that will lead to a primary shortage. *TES,* 11 April.

Davies, C. (1996) The sociology of professions and the profession of gender. *Sociology,* 30(4): 661–78.

Department of Education and Science (DES) (1972) *Education: A Framework for Expansion* (White Paper). London: HMSO.

Department of Education and Science (DES) (1983) *Teaching Quality* (White Paper). Cmnd 8836, London: HMSO.

Department of Education and Science (DES) (1984) *Initial Teacher Training: Approval of Courses* (Circular 3/84). London: DES.

Department of Education and Science (DES) (1988a) *Qualified Teacher Status: Consultation Document.* London: DES.

Department of Education and Science (DES) (1988b) *English for Ages 5–11: Proposals* (The Cox Report). London: HMSO.

Department of Education and Science (DES) (1988c) *Report of the Committee of Enquiry into the Teaching of the English Language* (The Kingman Report). London: HMSO.

Department of Education and Science (DES) (1989a) *Initial Teacher Training: Approval of Courses* (Circular 24/89). London: DES.

Department of Education and Science (DES) (1989b) *Licensed Teacher Regulations* (Circular 18/89). London: DES.

Department of Education and Science (DES) (1989c) Letter from DES to all CEOs, and institutions offering courses of ITT dated 27 June 1989. London: DES.

Department of Education and Science (DES) (1989d) *Discipline in Schools* (The Elton Report). London: HMSO.

Department of Education and Science (DES) (1991) *Overseas Trained Teachers* (Circular 13/91). London: DES.

Department for Education (DfE) (1992) *Initial Teacher Training (secondary phase)* (Circular 9/92). London: DES.

Department for Education (DfE) (1993a) *The Initial Training of Primary School Teachers; New Criteria for Courses* (Circular 14/93). London: DfE.

Department for Education (DfE) (1993b) *School Centred Initial Teacher Training (SCITT). Letter of Invitation. 5.3.93.* London: DfE.

Department for Education (DfE) (1993c) *The Initial Training of Primary School Teachers; New Criteria for Courses – Consultation Document.* London: DfE.

Department for Education (DfE) (1993d) Blatch announces second round of school-centred teaching programme. *DfE News 29/9/93,* London: DfE.

Department for Education (DfE) (1993e) *The Government's Proposals for the Reform of Initial Teacher Training.* London: DfE.

Department for Education and Employment (DfEE) (1997a) *Teacher supply and demand modelling: an explanatory paper.* London: DfEE.

Department for Education and Employment (DfEE) (1997b) *Teaching: High Status, High Standards* (Circular 10/97). London: DfEE.

Department for Education and Employment (DfEE) (1998a) *Teaching: High Status, High Standards* (Circular 4/98). London: DfEE.

Department for Education and Employment (DfEE) (1998b) *Teachers: Meeting the Challenge of Change* (Green Paper). London: DfEE.

Department for Education and Employment (DfEE) (1998c) *Teacher Supply and Demand Modelling: A Technical Description.* London: HMSO.

Dunleavy, P. and Hood, C. (1994) From old public administration to New Right management. *Public Theory and Management,* July–September: 9–16.

Edwards, T. (1992) Issues and challenges in initial teacher education. *Cambridge Journal of Education,* 22(3): 283–92.

Elder, R. and Kwiatkowski, H. (1996) Partnership in initial teacher education; the Scottish experience. Paper presented at UCET National Conference, Market Bosworth, England, November.

Eraut, M. (1989) 'Initial teacher training and the NVQ model, in J.W. Burke (ed.) *Competency Based Education and Training.* London: Falmer Press.

Eraut, M. (1994) *Developing Professional Knowledge and Competence.* London: Falmer Press.

Everton, T. and Impey, G. (eds) (1989) *IT-INSET: Partnership in Initial Training: The Leicestershire Experience*. London: David Fulton.

Featherstone, M. (1993) Global and local cultures, in J. Bird, B. Curtis, T. Putnam, G. Robertson and L. Tickner (eds) *Mapping the Futures: Local Cultures, Global Change*. London: Routledge.

Fiske, J. (1987) British cultural studies and television, in R.C. Allen (eds) *Channels of Discourse*. London: Routledge.

Fowler, F.C. (1994) The international arena: the global village. *Journal of Education Policy*, 9(5/6): 89–102.

Furlong, J. (1992) Reconstructing professionalism; ideological struggle in initial teacher education, in M. Arnot and L. Barton (eds) *Voicing Concerns: Sociological Perspectives on Contemporary Education Reforms*. Wallingford: Triangle Books.

Furlong, J. (1996) Do student teachers need higher education? in J. Furlong and R. Smith (eds) *The Role of Higher Education in Initial Teacher Training*. London: Kogan Page.

Furlong, J. (2000) Theorising mentoring; lessons from the English experiment. *Theory into Practice*, 39(1): 12–19.

Furlong, J. and Maynard, T. (1995) *Mentoring Student Teachers: The Growth of Professional Knowledge*. London: Routledge.

Furlong, J. and Smith, R. (eds) (1996) *The Role of Higher Education in Initial Teacher Training*. London: Kogan Page.

Furlong, J., Hirst, P., Pocklington, K. and Miles, S. (1988) *Initial Teacher Training and the Role of the School*. Milton Keynes: Open University Press.

Furlong, J., Whitty, G., Whiting, C. *et al.* (1996) Re-defining partnership: revolution or reform in initial teacher education? *Journal of Education for Teaching*, 22(1): 39–57.

Gamble, A. (1983) Thatcherism and Conservative politics, in S. Hall and M. Jaques (eds) *The Politics of Thatcherism*. London: Lawrence and Wishart.

Gamble, A. (1988) *The Free Economy and the Strong State*. London: Macmillan.

Gardner, P. (1993) The early history of school-based teacher training, in D. McIntyre, H. Hagger and M. Wilkin (eds) *Mentoring: Perspectives on School-based Teacher Education*. London: Kogan Page.

Gardner, P. (1996) Higher education and teacher training: a century of progress and promise, in J. Furlong and R. Smith (eds) *The Role of Higher Education in Initial Teacher Training*. London: Kogan Page.

Gerwirtz, S., Ball, S. and Bowe, R. (1995) *Markets, Choice and Equity in Education*. Buckingham: Open University Press.

Giddens, A. (1991) *Modernity and Self-Identity*. Cambridge: Polity Press.

Giddens, A. (1998) *The Third Way: The Renewal of Social Democracy*. Cambridge: Polity Press.

Gitlin, A. and Smyth, J. (1989) *Teacher Evaluation: Educative Alternatives*. London: Falmer Press.

Ginsburg, M.B. (1997) Professionalism or politics as a model for educators' engagement with/in communities. *Journal of Education Policy*, 12(1/2): 5–12.

Grace, G. (1991) Welfare Labourism versus the new Right: the struggle in New Zealand's education policy. *International Studies in Sociology of Education*, 1(1): 25–42.

Graham, J. (1997) Initial teacher education: TTA/Ofsted quality framework, *UCET Occasional paper 9*. London: UCET.

Hanlon, G. (1998) Professionalism as enterprise: service class politics and the redefinition of professionalism. *Sociology*, 32(1): 43–63.

Hannerz, U. and Löfgren, O. (1994) The nation in the global village. *Cultural Studies* 8(2): 198–207.

Hargreaves, A. (1994) *Changing Teachers, Changing Times: Teachers' Work and Culture in the Postmodern Age.* London: Cassell.

Hargreaves, D. (1994) Another radical approach to the reform of initial teacher training. *Westminster Studies in Education,* 13: 5–11.

Harvey, D. (1989) *The Condition of Postmodernity.* Oxford: Basil Blackwell.

Henig, J.R. (1994) *Rethinking School Choice: Limits of the Market Metaphor.* Princeton, NJ: Princeton University Press.

Henke, D. (1977) *Colleges in Crisis.* Harmondsworth: Penguin.

Her Majesty's Inspectorate (HMI) (1982) *The New Teacher in School.* London: HMSO.

Her Majesty's Inspectorate (HMI) (1983) *Teaching in Schools: The Content of Initial Teacher Training.* London: DES.

Her Majesty's Inspectorate (HMI) (1987) *Quality in Schools: The Initial Training of Teachers.* London: DES.

Her Majesty's Inspectorate (HMI) (1988a) *The New Teacher in School.* London: HMSO.

Her Majesty's Inspectorate (HMI) (1988b) *Initial Teacher Training in Universities in England, Northern Ireland and Wales.* London: HMSO.

Her Majesty's Inspectorate (HMI) (1991) *School-based Initial Training in England and Wales: Report by HM Inspectorate.* London: HMSO.

Hextall, I., Lawn, M., Menter, I., Sidgwick, S. and Walker, S. (1991) *Imaginative Projects: Arguments for a New Teacher Education.* London: Goldsmiths' College.

Hickox, M. (1995) Situating vocationalism. *British Journal of Sociology of Education,* 16(2): 153–63.

Hill, D. (1996) Reflection in teacher education, in K. Watson, S. Modgil and C. Modgil (eds) *Educational Dilemmas: Debate and Diversity, Volume 1: Teacher Education and Training.* London: Cassell.

Hillgate Group (1989) *Learning to Teach.* London: The Claridge Press.

Hirst, P. (1996) The demands of professional practice and preparation for teaching, in J. Furlong and R. Smith (eds) *The Role of Higher Education in Initial Teacher Training.* London: Kogan Page.

Holmes Group (1990) *Tomorrow's Schools.* East Lansing, MI: Holmes Group.

Holmes Group (1995) *Tomorrow's Schools of Education.* East Lansing, MI: Holmes Group.

Hood, C. (1991) A public management for all seasons? *Public Administrations,* 69: 3–19.

Hoyle, E. (1974) Professionality, professionalism and control in teaching. *London Education Review,* 3(2): 13–19.

Hoyle, E. and John, P. (1995) *Professional Knowledge and Professional Practice.* London: Cassell.

Irish White Paper (1995) *Charting our Educational Future – A White Paper on Education.* Dublin: Department of Education and Science.

James, Lord (1972) *Teacher Education and Training* (The James Report). London: HMSO.

Jessop, B., Bonnett, K., Bromley, S. and Ling, T. (1987) Popular capitalism, flexible accumulation and left strategy. *New Left Review,* 165: 104–23.

Jessup, G. (1991) *Outcomes: NVQs and the Emerging Model of Education and Training.* London: Falmer Press.

Jones, L. and Moore, R. (1993) Education, competence and the control of expertise. *British Journal of Sociology of Education,* 14: 385–97.

Kane, I. and Furlong, J. (1996) *Recognising quality in primary initial teacher education; findings of the 1995/6 Ofsted Primary Sweep,* UCET Occasional Paper 6. London: UCET.

Kenway, J. (1993) Marketing education in the postmodern age. *Journal of Education Policy*, 8(1): 105–22.

Knight, J., Bartlett, L. and McWilliam, E. (eds) (1993) *Unfinished Business: Reshaping the Teacher Education Industry for the 1990s*. Rockhampton: University of Central Queensland, Australia.

Labaree, D.F. and Pallas, A.M. (1996) Dire straits: the narrow vision of the Holmes Group. *Educational Researcher*, 25(5): 25–8.

Landman, M. and Ozga, J. (1995) Teacher education policy in England, in M. Ginsburg and B. Lindsay (eds) *The Political Dimension in Teacher Education: Comparative Perspectives on Policy Formation, Socialization and Society*. London: Falmer Press.

Lawlor, S. (1990) *Teachers Mistaught: Training Theories or Education in Subjects?* London: Centre for Policy Studies.

Lawlor, S. (1993) *Inspecting the School Inspectors*. London: Centre for Policy Studies.

Le Grand, J. (1997) Knights, knaves and pawns: Human behaviour and social policy. *Journal of Social Policy*, 26: 149–64.

Macdonald, K. (1995) *The Sociology of the Professions*. London: Sage.

Maclure, S. (1993) Fight this tooth and nail, *Times Educational Supplement*, 18 June.

McElvogue, M. and Salters, M. (1992) Models of competence and teacher training. Unpublished paper, Belfast: Queen's University of Belfast.

McIntyre, D. (1991) The Oxford internship scheme and the Cambridge analytical framework: models of partnership in initial teacher education, in M. Booth, J. Furlong and M. Wilkin (eds) *Partnership in Initial Teacher Training*. London: Cassell.

McIntyre, D. (1993a) The partnership between university and schools. Paper delivered at Oxford University/NUT/'Education' conference on: 'Teacher education today and tomorrow', 17 March.

McIntyre, D. (1993b) Theory, theorizing and reflection in initial teacher education, in J. Calderhead and P. Gates (eds) *Conceptualizing Reflection in Teacher Development*. London: Falmer.

McIntyre, D., Hagger, H., and Wilkin, M. (eds) (1993) *Mentoring: perspectives on school-based teacher education*. London: Kogan Page.

Maguire, M., Dillon, J. and Quintrell, M. (1998) *Finding Virtue, Not Finding Fault: Stealing the Wind of Destructive Reforms*. London: Association of Teachers and Lecturers.

Mahony, P. and Hextall, I. (1996) Trailing the TTA. Paper presented at the Annual Meeting of the British Educational Research Association, University of Lancaster, 12–15 September.

Management Charter Initiative (MCI) (1997) *The National Occupational Standards for Management*. London: MCI.

Miles, S., Barrett, E., Barton, L. *et al.* (1993) Initial teacher education in England and Wales: a topography. *Research Papers in Education*, 8(3): 275–305.

Millett, A. (1997) Letter to providers, 26 June, London: TTA.

Millett, A. (1999) *The Implications for Teacher Training of the Government's Green Paper – Teachers: Meeting the Challenge of Change*. London: TTA.

Moon, R. (1998) The English Exception: International Perspectives on the Initial Education and Training of Teachers, *UCET occasional paper 11*. London: UCET.

Morris, E. (1997) Letter to TTA, 26 June, London: DfEE.

Mortimore, P. and Goldstein, H. (1996) *The Teaching of Reading in 45 Inner London Primary Schools: A Critical Examination of Ofsted Research*. London: Institute of Education.

Mortimore, P. and Whitty, G. (1997) *Can School Improvement Overcome the Effects of Disadvantage?* London: Institute of Education.

National Commission on Teaching and America's Future (1996) *Report.* New York: National Commission of Teaching and America's Future.

Neave, G, (1988) On the cultivation of quality, efficiency and enterprise: an overview of recent trends in higher education. *European Journal of Education,* 23(1/2): 7–23.

O'Brien, S. (1998) New Labour, new approach: a critical view of educational theory. Paper presented at BERA Conference, Belfast, 27–30 August.

Office for Standards in Education (Ofsted) (1992) *The New Teacher in School: A Survey by HM Inspectors in England and Wales, 1992.* London: HMSO.

Office for Standards in Education (Ofsted) (1993a) *The Articled Teacher Scheme.* London: HMSO.

Office for Standards in Education (Ofsted) (1993b) *Licensed Teacher Scheme: September 1990–July 1992.* London: HMSO.

Office for Standards in Education (Ofsted) (1993c) *Working Papers for the Inspection of Secondary Initial Teacher Training.* London: Ofsted.

Office for Standards in Education (Ofsted) (1995a) *Partnership; Schools and Higher Education in Partnership in Secondary Initial Teacher Training.* London: Ofsted.

Office for Standards in Education (Ofsted) (1995b) *School-centred Initial Teacher Training 1993–1994.* London: HMSO.

Office for Standards in Education (Ofsted) (1996a) *Draft Primary sweep inspections 1995–6. Interim Report.* Unpublished.

Office for Standards in Education/Teacher Training Agency (Ofsted/TTA) (1996) *Framework for the Assessment of Quality and Standards in Initial Teacher Training 1996/7.* London: Ofsted.

Office for Standards in Education/Teacher Training Agency (Ofsted/TTA) (1998) *Framework for the Assessment of Quality and Standards in Initial Teacher Training.* London: Ofsted.

O'Hear, A. (1988a) *Daily Telegraph,* 12 December: 8.

O'Hear, A. (1988b) *Who Teaches the Teachers?* London: Social Affairs Unit.

Organization for Economic Cooperation and Development (OECD) (1996) *Teachers and their professional development.* Paris: OECD.

Parker, G. (1997) Letter to David Blunkett, June. London: TTA.

Patrick, H. Bernbaum, G. and Reid, K. (1982) *The Structure and Process of Initial Teacher Education within Universities in England and Wales.* Leicester: Leicester School of Education.

Patten, J. (1993) New framework for school based teacher training. *DfE News 26/5/93,* London: DfE.

Pollitt, C. (1994) *Manageralism in the Public Services.* Oxford: Blackwell.

Porter (1996) The James Report and what might have been in English teacher education, in C. Brock (ed.) *Global Perspectives on Teacher Education.* Wallingford: Triangle Books.

Pring, R. (1999) Who should teach how to teach? *Times Higher Education Supplement,* 25 June: 18.

Ranson, S. (1990) From 1944 to 1988: Education, citizenship and democracy, in M. Flude and M. Hammer (eds) *The Education Reform Act 1988: Its Origins and Implications.* London: Falmer Press.

RATE (1995) *RATE VIII: Teaching Teachers – Relationships with the World of Practice.* Washington, DC: AACTE Publications.

Richards, C., Harding, P. and Webb, D. (1997) *A Key Stage 6 Core Curriculum: A Critique of the National Curriculum for Initial Teacher Training.* London: Association of Teachers and Lecturers.

Robbins, Lord (1963) *Higher Education* (The Robbins Report). London: HMSO.

Rose, N. and Miller, P. (1992) Political power beyond the state: problematics of government. *British Journal of Sociology*, 43(2): 173–205.

Sachs, J. and Groundwater-Smith, S. (1999) The changing landscape of teacher education in Australia. *Teaching and Teacher Education*, 15: 215–27.

Salter, B. and Tapper, T. (1981) *Education, Politics and the State*. London: Grant McIntyre.

Schools' Curriculum and Assessment Authority (SCAA) (1997) *Desirable Outcomes for Children's Learning on Entering Compulsory Education*. London: SCAA.

Schön, D. (1983) *The Reflective Practitioner*. London: Temple Smith.

Schön, D. (1987) *Educating the Reflective Practitioner*. New York: Basic Books.

Sutherland, Sir Stewart (1997) *Teacher Education and Training: A Study, Report 10 of the National Committee of Inquiry into Higher Education* (The Dearing Report). London: HMSO.

Townsend, M. (1996) An overview of OECD work on teachers, their pay and conditions, teaching quality and the continuing professional development of teachers. Paper presented at International Conference on Education, Geneva, 20 September–5 October.

Teacher Training Agency (TTA) (1998a) *Initial Teacher Training National Curriculum, Consultation*. London: TTA.

Teacher Training Agency (TTA) (1998b) *Initial Teacher Training; Performance Profiles*. London: TTA.

Times Educational Supplement (TES) (1988) Leader Comment, 25 May.

Times Educational Supplement (TES) (1995) Inspectors cast doubt on in-school training, 10 March.

Times Educational Supplement (TES) (1998) Woodhead's project gets bad marks, 27 February.

Tuxworth, E.N. (1982) *Competency in Teaching: A Review of Competency and Performance-based Staff Development*. London: Further Education Curriculum Review and Development Unit.

Universities Council for the Education of Teachers (UCET) (1997) *The Role of Universities in the Education and Training of Teachers* (Occasional Paper 8), London: UCET.

Usher, R. and Edwards, R. (1994) *Postmodernism and Education*. London: Routledge.

Walker, J. (1996) Professional standards for teachers in Australia, in D. Hustler and D. McIntyre (eds) *Developing Competent Teachers: Approaches to Professional Competence in Teacher Education*. London: David Fulton.

Weber, M. (1948) *From Max Weber: Essays in Sociology* (translated and edited by H.H. Gerth and C. Wright Mills). London: Routledge and Kegan Paul.

Whiting, C., Whitty, G., Furlong, J., Miles, S. and Barton, L. (1996) *Partnership in Initial Teacher Education: A Topography*. London: Institute of Education.

Whitty, G. (1989) New Right and the National Curriculum: state control or market forces? *Journal of Education Policy*, 4: 329–41.

Whitty, G. and Edwards, T. (1998) School choice policies in England and the United States: an exploration of their origins and significance. *Comparative Education*, 34(2): 211–27.

Whitty, G., Barrett, E., Barton, L. *et al.* (1992) Initial teacher training in England and Wales: a survey of current practices and concerns. *Cambridge Journal of Education*, 22(3): 293–306.

Whitty, G., Power, S. and Halpin, D. (1998) *Devolution and Choice in Education: The School, the State and the Market*. Buckingham: Open University Press.

Whitty, G. and Willmott, E. (1991) Competence-based teacher education: approaches and issues. *Cambridge Journal of Education*, 21(3): 309–18.

Wilkin, M. (1991) The development of partnership in the United Kingdom, in M. Booth, J. Furlong and M. Wilkin (eds) *Partnership in Initial Teacher Training*. London: Cassell.

Wilkin, M. (1992) The challenge of diversity. *Cambridge Journal of Education*, 22(3): 307–31.

Wilkin, M. (1996) *Initial Teacher Training; The Dialogue of Ideology and Culture*. London: Falmer Press.

Zeichner, K. (1994) Research on teacher thinking and different views of reflective practice in teaching and teacher education, in I. Carlgren, G. Handal and S. Vaage (eds) *Teachers' Minds and Actions; Research on Teachers' Thinking and Practice*. London: Falmer Press.

Index

Numbers in parenthesis indicate notes.